THE AUTHOR   Richard Stoneman is an editor and writer specialising in classical antiquity and the history of archaeology. His books include *Land of the Lost Gods: The Search for Classical Greece*; *Across the Hellespont: Travellers in Turkey from Herodotus to Freya Stark* and *Tuchia, Guida Culturale* (with Stefano Masi).

SERIES EDITOR   Professor Denis Judd is a graduate of Oxford, a Fellow of the Royal Historical Society and Professor of History at the University of North London. He has published over 20 books, including the biographies of Joseph Chamberlain, Prince Phillip, George VI and Alison Uttley, historical military subjects, stories for children and two novels. His most recent book is the highly praised *Empire: The British Imperial Experience from 1765 to the Present*. He has reviewed and written extensively in the national press and in journals, has written several radio programmes and is a regular contributor to British and overseas radio and television.

The front cover shows a detail from a late sixteenth-century painting of a café in Istanbul, reproduced by kind permission of the Trustees of the Chester Beatty Library, Dublin.

Other titles in this series
A Traveller's History of France
A Traveller's History of Paris
A Traveller's History of Spain
A Traveller's History of Italy
A Traveller's History of Greece
A Traveller's History of Scotland
A Traveller's History of London
A Traveller's History of Ireland
A Traveller's History of England
A Traveller's History of India
A Traveller's History of Japan
A Traveller's History of China
A Traveller's History of North Africa
A Traveller's History of South Africa
A Traveller's History of the Caribbean
A Traveller's History of the USA
A Traveller's History of Southeast Asia
A Traveller's History of Russia
A Traveller's History of Athens
A Traveller's History of Germany
A Traveller's History of Portugal
A Traveller's History of Oxford
A Traveller's History of Canada

A Traveller's History of Turkey

A Traveller's History of Turkey

RICHARD STONEMAN

Series Editor   DENIS JUDD
Line drawings   JOHN HOSTE

Interlink Books

An imprint of Interlink Publishing Group, Inc.
Northampton, Massachusetts

This edition published 2009 by

INTERLINK BOOKS
An imprint of Interlink Publishing Group, Inc.
46 Crosby Street, Northampton, Massachusetts 01060
www.interlinkbooks.com

Text © Richard Stoneman 1993, 1996, 1998, 2006, 2009
Preface © Denis Judd 1993, 1996, 1998, 2006, 2009

Library of Congress Cataloging–in–Publication Data
Stoneman, Richard.
A traveller's history of Turkey/Richard Stoneman ; line drawings,
    John Hoste. —1st American ed.
        p. cm — (A traveller's history series)
    Includes bibliographical references and index.
    ISBN 978-1-56656-620-9
    1. Turkey—History. 2. Historical sites—Turkey—Guidebooks.
    I. Title. II. Series.
    DR416.76 1998
    915.6140'39—dc20   92-42424
                                                              CIP

Printed and bound in Canada by Webcom

Contents

Note on Spelling and Nomenclature

Greek: It is impossible to be absolutely consistent in the spelling of Greek names. In general I have used the accepted Latin forms (Dorylaeum not Dorylaion, Herodotus not Herodotos), or English versions where these are current (Alexander). The same principle has been used for the names of Persians and other peoples encountered by the Greeks and Romans.

Placenames: Where it seemed helpful, I have given both the contemporary and the modern Turkish names for places mentioned in the text (e.g. Kanesh and Kültepe, Nicomedia and Izmit, Adrianople and Edirne).

Turkish spelling and pronunciation: The Turkish alphabet introduced by Kemal Atatürk in 1928 uses the Latin alphabet with some additions. The letters are pronounced as in English except that u is as in 'put' not as in 'cup,' and c is pronounced j. In addition Turkish uses the following letters:

ç	like ch in church
ğ	lengthens the preceding vowel but is not sounded; between front vowels (e, i) it has a y sound
ı	(without a dot) is like i in cousin
ş	like sh in shoe
ö	has no English equivalent; it is the same as the German ö
ü	has no English equivalent; it is the same as the German ü

Modern Turkish spelling has been used in this book for all Turkish names including Ottoman ones (thus Şevket not Shevket, Köprülü not Kiuprili or whatever).

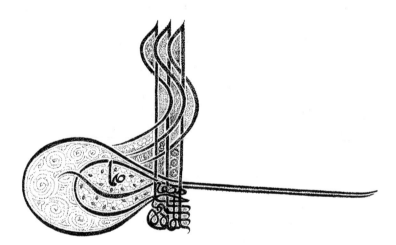

The Inğra of Süleyman the Magnificent

Preface

Turkey stands at the historic meeting place of east and west. Indeed modern Turkey is exceptional, perhaps unique, in that it is both a member of NATO and a Middle Eastern state; a power in the Eastern Mediterranean (witness the swift efficiency of its intervention in Cyprus in 1974) but also one of the strong men of what is, in effect, western Asia. As Richard Stoneman puts in this comprehensive, clear and entirely fascinating book: 'Turkey thus represents a meeting point of eastern and western lands and ways of life, and its inhabitants have always looked in both directions in trade, the exercise of power, and defence.' Looking both ways, rather like Russia with its appropriate Tsarist symbol of the two-headed eagle, can be a painful and exhausting business, but it can also be enriching and stimulating.

I imagine that, to many in the West, the image of Turkey, past and present, is at best a confused, and at worst a threatening one, laced with fantasies of corruption and violence. The sweetmeat, 'Turkish delight', was once advertised as being 'full of eastern promise', but a more enduring western impression of Turkey might be that of an uncomfortably close, yet strangely distant country 'full of eastern menace'.

It is not difficult to see why this might be the case. From the Ottoman conquest of Constantinople in 1453 (a fall which, by comparison, and in portent, makes the recent destruction of the Berlin Wall seem a trivial affair) the Turks were an alien threat to European integrity and self-esteem for nearly five hundred years. Ottoman armies laid siege to Vienna in 1529 and again in 1683. For a while in the early sixteenth century, the great issue of the day was not whether the rise of Protestantism could be checked, but whether the Turks would cross the Rhine and march on Paris.

Turkish dominion over much of Eastern Europe became associated, often unfairly, with arbitrary rule and the barbarous massacres of Christians. The oriental luxury of the Sultan's court was equated with a decadent sensuality, incorporating the harem, eunuchs, and unspeakable sexual practices. In the work of Mozart, Molière and many others, the Turk was used as a metaphor for all that was strange, exotic, and a challenge to western convention. In the nineteenth century, bawdy Victorian novels, designed to titilate and shock, made a good deal of the 'lustful Turk', bent on ravishing Christian maidens. Yet Victorian statesmen spent much time in propping up the Ottoman Empire, especially as a first line of defence against Russian aggression. In the Crimean War, Britain, France and Turkey fought on the same side.

But there was, and is, another Turkey, one brought vividly to life in this accomplished book. It is a nation with deep and unexpected roots, and a past richer and more complex than might superficially be expected. Religious toleration, not ruthless persecution, was more typical of Turkish overlordship. The court of Süleyman the Magnificent was the scene of a great artistic and cultural flowering rather than of debauched and perverse activities. The fabulous city of Troy had been set on the western shores of Anatolia, and great and civilised cities like Ephesus had flourished there. Turkish social convention was marked by kindly and hospitable good manners, not by an insensitive and habitual cruelty. Modern Turkey owes far more of a debt to the enlightened reforms of Kemal Atatürk, than to a blood-stained and warring sultanate. Today's traveller to this still somewhat mysterious country will be amply rewarded by what he or she finds there.

Denis Judd, London

CHAPTER ONE

Prehistoric Anatolia

Modern Turkey is roughly conterminous with the geographical region of Anatolia, which for the most part consists of a high plateau continuous with the steppes of Central Asia, bordered on east and south by two great mountain barriers, the mountain chains of Armenia in the east, reaching their highest point in Mt Ararat, and the almost impassable Taurus range in the south. The former represent a natural border with Iran and the regions of the Caucasus, the latter cut Anatolia sharply off from the flatter regions of modern Syria and Iraq. To the west the geological affinities of the region are with the Aegean. Lower mountain ranges, running east to west, divide broad fertile river valleys and, at their western end, descend into the Aegean to re-emerge at intervals as the Greek islands. Turkey thus represents a meeting point of eastern and western lands and ways of life, and its inhabitants have always looked in both directions in trade, the exercise of power, and defence.

Man begins to leave evidence of his presence in Anatolia in the Palaeolithic period (from about 500,000 BC to about 12,000 BC), with flint hand-axes and scrapers and other tools, as well as paintings on the walls of caves, becoming more prominent during the Upper Palaeolithic (40,000–12,000 BC) and the Mesolithic period (12,000–6500 BC). These periods are divided by the gradual warming of the climate and the retreat of ice to the higher regions of the mountains. It is sometimes thought that this geological change is reflected in the legend, common throughout the Middle East, of a great Flood. The best known of these legends is the Hebrew one of Noah and his Ark, which is traditionally said to have come to rest on the summit of

1

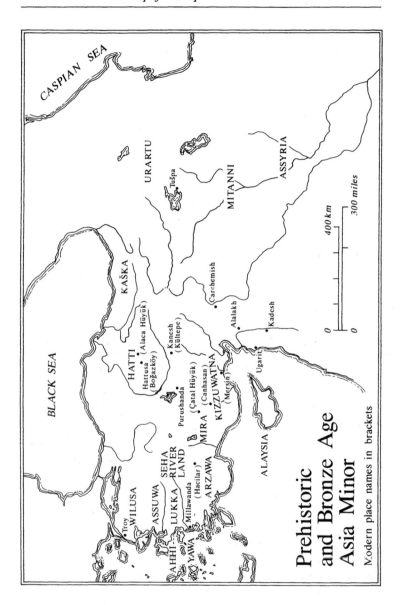

Prehistoric
and Bronze Age
Asia Minor

Modern place names in brackets

CASPIAN SEA

URARTU

Tuşpa

ASSYRIA

MITANNI

300 miles

400 km

0

0

KAŠKA

Carchemish

Alalakh

Kadesh

Alaca Hüyük

Kanesh
(Kültepe)

HATTI

Hattusa
(Boğazköy)

Purushanda

(Çatal Hüyük)

(Canhasan)

Mersin

KIZZUWATNA

MIRA

Ugarit

BLACK SEA

SEHA
RIVER
LAND

ASSUWA

ALAYSIA

WILUSA

LUKKA

Troy

Millawanda
(Hacilar)

ARZAWA

AHHI-
YAWA

Mt Ararat. Some recent expeditions have indeed visited a curious rock-formation resembling a ship on the slopes of Mt Ararat, which may be connected with this legend.

At all events the Mesolithic period represents a significant advance in human culture, with the use of the bow and arrow and the domestication of the dog. But the real change came with what is often called the Neolithic Revolution, the introduction of agriculture and hence of a settled life instead of that of semi-nomadic hunter-gatherers. By 7000 BC evidence of grain cultivation – querns, mortars, and sickle blades – becomes prevalent in Mesopotamia. This development led to the need to construct dwellings in regions where grain would grow, and man ceased to live in caves.

Çatal Hüyük

One of the most remarkable discoveries in Turkey in recent years is the extensive Neolithic settlement of Çatal Hüyük in the Konya Plain. The archaeologist, D.G. Hogarth, in the early years of the twentieth century encountered a local tradition that Konya had been the first city to emerge after the Flood. In about 16,000 BC this plain was a lake; the gradual retreat of the waters left a fertile alluvial plain which apparently supported a population of such numbers that they built what is in effect the first known human city. Its beginnings date from about 7000 BC and it covers an area of 32 acres. Mudbrick single-storey houses are built in terraces up the hillside. Though they look out on to inner courtyards, the houses have no doors and are entered through openings in their flat roofs which are reached by ladders. The arrangement suggests a consciousness of a need for defence as well as shelter. Besides its agricultural prosperity, Çatal Hüyük drew on the reserves of obsidian to be obtained from the nearby volcanoes Hasan Dağı and Karaca Dağı. Obsidian is a hard black stone which can be worked to a finish as smooth and sharp as glass but much harder, and before the discovery of metalworking it was in wide demand for tool-making: it represented one of the first objects of trade among prehistoric man, and this would have been a further stimulus to the prosperity of Çatal Hüyük.

A remarkable feature of Çatal Hüyük is the lavish quantity of wall paintings depicting religious scenes, but also scenes of nature and wildlife, and even the world's first landscape painting, a depiction of the eruption of Hasan Dağı with the city in the foreground. Artistic effort also went into the beginnings of a metallurgical industry, with smelting of copper and lead to make small trinkets.

Copper came from the more eastern region in the mountains around Elaziğ, where the metal was being extracted and used in the Neolithic site of Çayönü as early as 7000 BC. Such developments led from the Early Chalcolithic (Stone-bronze) age to the Chalcolithic age (4000–3200 BC) which ushered in the wealth of the Early Bronze Age.

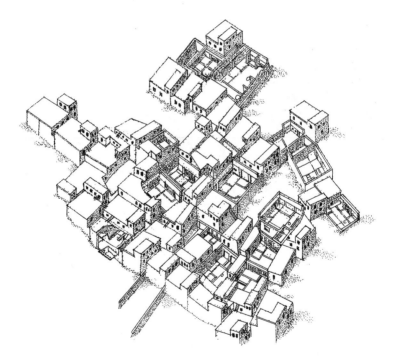

A reconstruction of the dwellings at Çatal Hüyük

Hacılar

By about 5400 BC a further development took place with the emergence of fortified towns, notably at the important site of Hacılar in the Turkish 'Lake District' which was excavated by James Mellaart from 1958. Here for the first time we find houses with front doors, and narrow streets. The mud brick fortification wall enclosed a granary, a shrine and potters' workshops: it is at Hacılar that painted pottery first makes its appearance. Wall paintings however are no longer found, and the religious life now focusses on figurines representing a type which can fairly be called a Mother-Goddess, a female with exaggerated hips representing fecundity. In the course of the next millennium similar sites are also found at Can Hasan in the region of Konya and at Yümüktepe on the outskirts of Mersin in Cilicia. Similar fortified citadels are found also in western Anatolia and even in Greece (e.g. at Dimini, 3000 BC).

The Early Bronze Age, 3200–2200 BC

The Bronze Age opens on a region already populated by numerous small city states with fortified centres. These include Troy, Poliochni on the island of Lemnos, Beycesultan, Boğazköy and Alaca Hüyük. Troy I seems to have been culturally dominant in the northern Aegean and to have had links with the culture of Thrace and Bulgaria. The identity and racial affinities of the inhabitants of these sites is unknown. Prosperity grew with the addition to an expanding agricultural economy of metalworking and trade in metals. Trade with Mesopotamia probably began early, as the latter region lacked metals of its own, and Akkadian merchants were visiting the city of Purushanda (probably to be identified with Acem Hüyük) by 2300 BC.

Early Bronze Age II (from about 2600 BC) is represented by a number of sites at which spectacular treasures, of gold and other metals, have been found: the treasure of Troy II probably belongs to this period, as does that of Alaca Hüyük; both show affinities with a similar treasure from Maikop north of the Caucasus, and it may be that the famous treasures of Ur in Mesopotamia had their origin in Anatolia.

ROYAL TOMBS

Alaca Hüyük seems to have been the dominant city of central northern Anatolia, where thirteen spectacular Royal Tombs were excavated in the 1930s. The tombs contained artefacts in gold, silver, bronze and copper, and even iron, including vessels, weapons, jewellery, figurines of bulls and stags and musical instruments. There were several other settlements of this period nearby, including Boğazköy and Eskiyapan. Alaca was probably a religious centre also, and analogous evidence for religious practice comes from the site of Beycesultan, where shrines

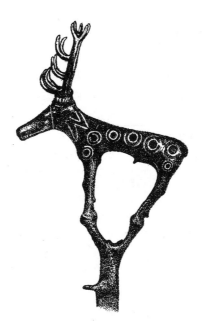

One of the 'standards' from Alaca Hüyük

are dedicated to both male and female deities and contain altars in the form of rams' horns and bulls' heads.

About 2300 BC the entire region was affected by upheavals, probably caused by movements of populations from the north into Anatolia. Troy II was destroyed by fire, though there does not seem to have been a radical break in culture. Similar destructions at other sites, as here, usher in a period of reduced prosperity which continues until the emergence of Hittite domination in Anatolia. At the same time, however, the various peoples of Anatolia and their relations with their neighbours in Mesopotamia begin to come into clearer focus.

Hatti, Mitanni and Assyrians

The Middle Bronze Age brings us into the era of protohistory, for it is from this period that we have for the first time written records to fill out the archaeological record. We owe these writings to the Assyrians who left numerous records on cuneiform tablets at their trading sites in Anatolia. Of these the most important was Kanesh, modern Kültepe. Kanesh was known as a trading centre as early as the twenty-fourth century BC, as can be seen from its frequent mention in the tablets from Mari in Syria. However, it was in the twenty-first century that Assyrian trade became an important feature of the Anatolian economy. The Assyrians purchased metals such as gold, silver and a little iron, which went for a far higher price than gold. In exchange they seem to have brought textiles and clothing, and perhaps tin — though the source of tin for Anatolian bronze-making is a perplexing question, as the local sources that are known seem insufficient, and the Assyrian records do not in fact mention tin.

The wealth of Kanesh, consisting, besides the above mentioned goods, in items of obsidian, rock-crystal, ivory and faience, indicates with some certainty that it was the capital of the region, which included other sites of similar culture such as Alışar and Alaca. Other prosperous sites at this time include Acem Hüyük, Karahüyük near Konya, and Boğazköy, now known by the name of Hattus. This kingdom was that of the Hatti, who may for lack of any identifiable predecessors be regarded as the indigenous people of central Anatolia.

They used no writing, and our information about them — including their name — comes from the Assyrians. Their religion focused on the planets, on figurines of bulls and stags like those known from Alaca and Beycesultan half a millennium earlier, and on the Mother-Goddess called Kubabat (later to be known to the Greeks as Cybele).

Following the end of the Empire of Sumer and Akkad centred on Ur, the Assyrians had risen to prominence in northern Mesopotamia (from about 1900 BC). However, the period of Assyrian prosperity and free intercourse with Anatolia was interrupted by the emergence of another race, the Hurrians, who entered the region from the east around Lake Urmia in modern Iran and founded the kingdom of Mitanni on the upper Tigris and Euphrates, and that of Kizzuwatna, equivalent to the region of Cilicia. Assyria's decline ended when it was incorporated into the empire of Babylon in the course of the eighteenth century, while Anatolia embarked on the slow growth of a period of political unity under the now-emerging Hittites.

CHAPTER TWO

The Hittite Age,
2000–1250 BC

A Powerful Empire

The Hittites dominated Anatolia for the best part of a millennium. They are known to us from a number of spectacular monuments, notably at Boğazköy and neighbouring Yazılıkaya, and reveal themselves to us through the very extensive writings that have been recovered on clay tablets. Nevertheless, there is no certainty as to exactly where they came from.

One of the surprises of the rediscovery of the Hittites (in the 1860s) and of their written records (from 1906) was the fact that this people, hitherto known only from passing references in the Old Testament as a source of trouble in northern Palestine, were in fact a powerful empire, and that their language was Indo-European. The decipherment of the Hittite language by the Czech scholar B. Hrozny in 1915 made this plain; it is however, though close in grammatical structure to Greek and Latin, widely divergent in vocabulary. The most commonly accepted view is that the Hittites arrived in Anatolia about 2000 BC, in the wake of the widespread disturbances of that era, from the Caucasus region. (This dating is that of the 'Middle Chronology' established by O.R. Gurney, which I shall follow; an alternative 'Low Chronology' dates all events some fifty years later.)

They established themselves around Kussara and Hattus and apparently rose to become a dominant caste among the indigenous Hatti, borrowing from them — rather surprisingly — their religion as well as many words for common concepts such as 'father' and 'mother' (though not for 'water', the Hittite word for which is *water*). The rise of the Hittites seems not to have been achieved by violent means, and this gives pause for thought over the real relation between Hatti and Hittites; were they more closely related in race than appears?

This was the position in the mid-eighteenth century when King Anitta of Kussara founded the Hittite kingdom, destroying Hattus and transferring his capital to Kanesh, which now became known as Nesha, the Hittites referring to themselves as Neshites. Anitta overran a number of neighbouring kingdoms. About a century later a ruler called Labarna moved the capital back to Hattus — now to be called Hattusa or Hattusas — and took the name Hattusili; his former name came to be used as a title of all the subsequent kings, and that of his wife Tawannanna came to mean 'queen'.

Hattusili undertook extensive military campaigns, conquering Alalakh on the Orontes, the major port of the Hurrian kingdom of Yamhad centred on Aleppo. He also campaigned for the first time to the west, against a region known as the Arzawa lands. This is certainly somewhere to the west, and is sometimes located by scholars in Lycia. It may alternatively be a general name for a number of peoples of western Anatolia. This campaign was interrupted by a counter-attack from Yamhad, who had enlisted the Hurrians as allies. The war with Yamhad was continued with marked success by Hattusili's son and successor Mursili I (1620–1590) who prosecuted the war as far as Babylon and made the Hittites masters of that city in 1595 BC. Mursili was then assassinated by Hantili, in whose reign many territories were lost, including Kizzuwatna. The slightly later Telipinu I (1525–1500)was a reforming king who reconsolidated Hittite power and was responsible for a decree which regulated the law of succession and the rules of behaviour of the feudal nobility.

The Middle Kingdom

A new dynasty, the Middle Kingdom, emerges in the mid-fifteenth century, possibly with an increased Hurrian component. The first king of the new dynasty was Tudhaliya II, who reconquered the Arzawa lands as well as a region called Assuwa. This last name intriguingly echoes the name Asia, which, in Roman times, became applied to the region as a Roman province. This is perhaps the moment to consider the nature of the inhabitants of western Anatolia at this period.

TROY

The most significant settlement in the west in the second millennium BC is that on the hill at Hisarlık now accepted as the site of Troy. As we have seen, Troy II had been a city of wealth comparable to Alaca Hüyük on its collapse in 2200 BC. Several succeeding settlements on the same site culminated in the major fortifications of Troy VI (*c.* 1800–1375 BC). The new period is marked by the arrival of a new kind of pottery with similarities to the grey Minyan ware brought to Greece by the arrival of the first Greeks. It is possible that the inhabitants of Troy VI were Greek-speakers. This possibility receives intriguing corroboration from the mention, in the Hittite annals of Tudhaliyas, of a ruler named Attarissiyas of a land called Ahhiyawa, names which have been compared to the Greek Atreus and Achaea (the name which the Bronze Age Greeks gave their lands, as shown in the Homeric poems which record their exploits). Records from the reign of Muwatallis (1300 BC) refer also to places named Taruisa and Wilusa, which resemble the Greek names for Troy, Troia and (W)Ilion. The ruler of the latter place is identified as Alaksandus, which sounds like the name of Prince Alexandros whom the Greek also called Paris. The series of coincidences, despite philological difficulties, seems too good to be chance, and it seems highly likely that these are Hittite references to the Bronze Age Greeks and Troy.

What is not clear is where Ahhiyawa is to be located. It may be a name for the whole of Mycenaean Greece, with its islands; it may refer to Rhodes; or it may be the name for the Troad and Hellespont region. A further problem is that the name Attarissiyas, even allowing for Hittite vocalisation, seems more Anatolian than Greek in form. Attarissiyas is mentioned because he drove out of his kingdom a man called Maduwattas, whose name resembles in form that of the early kings of Lydia, Alyattes and Sadyattes: so Attarissiyas might be based on the Anatolian mainland too.

Despite the difficulties, there does seem to be a distinct possibility that western Anatolia was already inhabited by Greeks in the second millennium BC.

But they were not very important to the Hittites. The westerners looked west, while the Hittites were secure on their high central plateau. It has sometimes been suggested that Troy derived its importance from its control of the trade route to the north-west, and through the Hellespont to the Black Sea, but it is doubtful whether the Hittites traded in this direction.

Their problems were more political, focussed on the disturbances caused by the Kaška on the south-east coast of the Black Sea (the wild region later known as Paphlagonia), who succeeded, in alliance with other peoples including the Isuwa located around modern Elazığ, in reaching Hattusa and burning it in the reign of Arnuwanda I (1420–1400). In the wake of this catastrophe the Arzawa thrust eastward to the Cilician Gates and reduced Hittite control of the region.

UPWARD MOBILITY

The situation was redeemed by King Šuppiluliuma I (1380–40) who recovered Isuwa and Kizzuwadna and mounted a major campaign against Mitanni, incorporating this Hurrian kingdom into the new Hittite 'Empire'. So important did Šuppiluliuma become that he even received an invitation from the young widow of Tutankhamun of Egypt to send one of his sons to marry her; no mere Egyptian noble would do, and only the Hittite king was of a dignity fit for the queen. Unfortunately the son was murdered on the way to Egypt and the queen had to make do with her vizier, Ay.

Šuppiluliuma died in 1340 of plague and his son Mursili II (1339–06) reconquered the Arzawa lands and a place called Millawanda, which is probably Miletus. Arzawa, like Carchemish and Aleppo in the previous reign, became vassals of the Hittite Empire. Mursili also succeeded in containing the Kaška by the construction of a series of border fortresses. Piyamaradus the vassal king of Millawanda transferred his allegiance to Ahhiyawa and had to be extradited, after which he was restored to his throne on giving a promise of good conduct.

THE BATTLE OF QADESH

The reign of Muwatalli II (1306–1282) saw continuing warfare, culminating in the major battle of Qadesh (1286) between the Hittites and the Egyptians, in which the Egyptians, despite the grandiose claims made by Ramesses II on the inscriptions and reliefs recording the battle, were certainly defeated. However, one result was the loss of control over Mitanni, which became an Assyrian vassal. Muwatalli's death led to a power struggle between two rivals for the succession, Urhi-Tešub and Mursili. The victory went to the former who became Hattusili III. He rebuilt Hattusa, and one of his daughters married the Pharaoh of Egypt. His wife Pudu-hepa, a Hurrian, has been thought to have been instrumental in the construction of the magnificent rock-shrine at Yazılıkaya, which honours her son as Tudhaliya IV (1250–1220): the gods by whom he is surrounded are Hurrian not Hittite deities, further evidence – like the names of Pudu-hepa and Urhi-Tešub – of the strong Hurrian element in Hittite culture at this time.

By this time the days of the Hittite Empire were numbered. A major battle was fought with the Assyrians. A further influx of peoples into Anatolia from the north-west, notable among them the Phrygians, combined with the obscure movement described in Egyptian records of the Sea Peoples, was about to bring Anatolia into a Dark Age. Hittite power ended with the burning of Hattusa about 1200 or 1180, perhaps by the Kaška. But before the darkness descends we should attempt a summing up of the Hittite achievement, and also cast a final glance to the west.

THE END OF THE EMPIRE

The Hittite Empire, despite its reputation for justice and a lack of cruelty striking in near eastern states at this time, was essentially devoted to warfare, though the use of diplomacy and strategic marriages is notable. The structure of the kingdom was strongly feudal, centred on a priest-king who after 1500 became more absolute in his power (the *pankus*, or assembly of nobles, was abolished). Power was supported by a scribal class or bureaucracy, and slavery seems to have been used. There was a high degree of decentralisation, appropriate to the difficult terrain, with scattered townships ruled by their own councils of Elders. Other kingdoms, such as Kizzuwatna, were administered by vassal rulers.

The Hittite lands were predominantly agricultural, and probably more forested and more fertile than the region is today. Barley and wheat were grown; the vine was indigenous; many kinds of tree fruit were cultivated, such as apples, pears, apricots and medlars, as well as peas and beans and some flax, as today. But the wealth of Anatolia was based on its mineral resources, especially metals, of which gold, iron and silver were all plentiful; silver being the basic medium of exchange. Hittite policies may have been determined, as J.G. McQueen has argued, by an overriding desire to secure the tin routes from the north-west to support bronze manufacture; but this cannot be regarded as certain.

It seems probable that the Hittite kings were guilty of failing to establish proper administrative arrangements in their conquered territories, resulting in constant revolts that needed pacification: whether this failing was so severe as to result, as James Mellaart has stated, in the ruination of Anatolia, must remain debatable.

Law was important in Hittite society; an extensive law code is preserved which covers civil as well as criminal affairs, and in which there are notably few capital offences (perhaps partly because the blood feud still persisted as the basic way of dealing with murder). Most of the laws reflect the overwhelmingly agrarian nature of the economy, and contain such provisions as the penalty for (accidental) arson in a vineyard – a fine of six shekels of silver – and the remedy for the owner of a pig which wanders on to another's land and the owner of the land kills it: the owner of the land has to replace the pig. The law code even contains a table of prices, from which we learn that the cost of a sheep was one shekel, of a horse 14 shekels and of a ploughing ox 15 shekels. Clothing was expensive, with a 'blue woollen garment' costing 20 shekels – more than the price of a horse.

The criminal law is based mainly on restoration rather than revenge. The penalty for breaking a freeman's leg or arm is a fine of 20 shekels, but a similar offence against a slave costs only 10 shekels. Arson is compensated by rebuilding and the restitution of any living creatures destroyed in the fire. Even murder is normally compensated by fines of land or silver. The only capital offences are rape, bestiality and treason. Judgment was probably carried out by courts of elders in the provincial cities.

A large part of the law code was also devoted to the regulation of marriage and land tenure: most land was held in fief by large landowners, who presumably let small parcels to tenant farmers. The law code in its fullness recalls that of Hammurabi of Babylon, but Hittite law seems to represent a real advance in humanitarian terms on the Mesopotamian practices.

RELIGIOUS PRACTICES

The Hittite reliefs and records display a bewildering variety of religious traditions and practices. The Hittite rulers, as has been stated, came to dominate an Anatolian population whose religion was centred on a mother-goddess and in which worship was offered to local natural features such as the sacred spring at Eflatunpınar. The state religion was centred on the holy city of Arinna, whose location is not known, where the Hurrian sun-goddess and weather-god were worshipped as consorts under the names of Tešub and Hebat (Hepa). There were important local festivals in spring and autumn in which the image of the god was carried in procession and a blood sacrifice was performed. The king seems to have had divine status, as demonstrated by the complex palace and temple remains at Boğazköy; a syncretistic approach to religion is apparent in the surrounding of the king by Hurrian deities at Yazılıkaya, where the sun–goddess and the weather–god are surrounded by a numerous progeny. Some of these gods are also players in Hittite creation myths which seem to have a direct influence on early Greek cosmogony as known from Hesiod.

The Hittites, despite their extensive records, and despite this last slight link with the Greeks, remain a shadowy people, and their greatest surviving monument, the gallery of gods at Yazılıkaya, casts little light on their psychology. An atmosphere of single-minded menace hangs around these reliefs. Prayers there are, but of literature

The Hittite Weather God

almost nothing is preserved, and their art is as narrow in its focus as
Achaemenid sculpture.

None of these things is true, it seems, of the western state of Troy
which looms so large in the traditions of the western world. What was
happening, in these last days before the Dark Age, at the city which
Hittite texts refer to so fleetingly and tantalisingly — at Troy?

Troy VIIa and the Trojan War

Troy VIIa represents a direct continuation of Troy VI, which ended
about 1275 BC. If the inhabitants of Troy VI were Greeks, then those
of Troy VIIa must have been also. Troy is of central importance to

the Greek literary tradition, for the earliest of all Greek epics, the *Iliad*, concerns a war of the Greeks of the mainland against Troy. The fame of this war made Troy a place of pilgrimage for tourists from the classical period of Greece up to the present day. For many years the site of ancient Troy was unknown, and from Elizabethan times onwards travellers might pay their respects at Alexandria Troas in error. In the eighteenth century several hills were proposed as sites for Troy, including one close to the pools of Pinarbaşı. But in 1822 the case for the site of Novum Ilium, the Roman city, was revived by Charles MacLaren, and in 1870 the German millionaire Heinrich Schliemann began an excavation at this site, which was now known as Hisarlık.

SCHLIEMANN'S DISCOVERIES

His discoveries were astounding. He excavated a palimpsest of cities of which the main settlements are known as Troy I to Troy IX. He took Troy II to be the city of Priam, though it is now known to be a thousand years older than the traditional date of the Trojan War. He strengthened his case by the discovery in this level of a treasure, including gold and silver jewellery, weapons and vessels of many kinds. He had photographs made of his Greek wife Sophia wearing what he called the Jewels of Helen (the Greek princess about whom the war was supposed to have been fought). These treasures were housed in the Ethnographical Museum in Berlin, from which they disappeared in the last days of the Second World War. It now appears that they have been rediscovered in a secret hiding place in Moscow, raising hopes that they may soon become visible to the public again.

This would be of particular value as the truth of Schliemann's account of the discovery has been impugned by scholarly examination of his diaries. It is highly likely that the treasure was assembled piecemeal and not found in one cache as Schliemann claimed.

Though this claim casts doubt on Schliemann's veracity, few now doubt that Hisarlık is the site of ancient Troy. But from the existence of Troy to the historicity of the Trojan War is a large step, and it is increasingly regarded as doubtful whether the Trojan War ever took place.

Troy VI was a wealthy city, drawing its riches from fishing (the sea came closer to the walls than it does now) as well as from textile production (quantities of spindle whorls have been found), and importing ivory goods, Cypriot pottery and small items of electrum and silver from the east. Homer characterises Troy as a city noted for its horses, and indeed the flat temperate plain of Troy is good horse country. Furthermore, Troy commands the entrance to the Dardanelles, which has suggested a motive for war in its possible interference with Mycenaean trading efforts into the Black Sea (finds at Samsun indicate their interests in central Anatolia). Mycenaeans were also settled at Miletus and at Iasus, further down the coast.

THE TROJAN WAR

The Greek account of the origins of the Trojan War, in a complex series of legends some of which are recounted in the *Iliad* and other epic poems, is of course quite different. The Trojan prince Paris (or Alexander) was appointed to judge a beauty contest of the three goddesses Athena, Hera and Aphrodite. Choosing Aphrodite, the goddess of love, who promised him the most beautiful woman in the world as wife, he gained the undying enmity of the other two goddesses for Troy. He then jilted his own lover, Oenone, to carry off Helen, the wife of Menelaus of Sparta. Because all the Greek heroes had sworn an oath to defend whichever of them gained Helen as a bride (for they all wanted her), they formed an expedition under the leadership of Menelaus' brother, Agamemnon of Argos (or Mycenae) to win her back.

The war lasted ten years. The *Iliad* covers a period of a few months in the last year, centring on the exploits of the greatest of the heroes, Achilles. The poem ends with the funeral of the Trojan prince Hector, killed by Achilles. After this, in the legend, events moved fast. Odysseus devised the stratagem of the Wooden Horse. The walls of Troy, which had been built by the gods Apollo and Poseidon for King Laomedon, could not be brought low by any mortal enemy; so the Trojans must be persuaded to dismantle them themselves. The episode of the Wooden Horse is described in Virgil's *Aeneid*: the Trojans, believing the great creature to be an offering to Athena, broke down their walls and dragged it within. When night fell, the Greek soldiers hidden inside leapt out, fired the city, and wreaked a bloody slaughter on the Trojans. King Priam was butchered at one altar, his daughter, the prophetess Cassandra, raped at another. The child Astyanax, Hector's son, was hurled from the walls. The men were massacred and the women taken into slavery. Troy was no more. Only – according to Roman legend – Aeneas escaped, carrying his father Anchises on his back, and leading his son Ascanius; he sailed westward and in due course reached Italy where he founded the settlement that was to become Rome.

It is impossible to know how much, if any, of this rich tale we can accept as historical. The archaeological record shows that the end of Troy VIIa was accompanied by destruction and killing, at a date probably around 1250 BC (though it must be emphasised that all our

The 'Trojan Horse': a modern reconstruction

dating of these millennia rests on shaky foundations). The second book of the *Iliad* contains a catalogue of the Trojan allies which may shed some light on their connections at this period. They include people from most of the cities of the Troad and Hellespont region: Sestos, Abydos, Zeleia, Larisa; the Mysians from the Bergama region;but also the Cicones and Paphlagonians further east, and the Lycians from the south (though these last were almost certainly not there in the 13th century BC).

It seems probable that an actual war has become the vehicle for a series of legends and folktales, filled out with later geographical detail and cultural elements, which give the Trojan War a resonance and significance far greater than that achieved by most real events. The drama of the end of Troy, the last great act of the Mycenaean Empire, is a fitting conclusion to an epoch in the history of Anatolia. Troy of the Dark Ages continued to eke out an existence as a humble village. All around it, the personnel of history were changing their positions for a new age.

CHAPTER THREE

From the Dark Ages to the Persian Conquest,
1250–494 BC

The Sea Peoples

The end of the thirteenth century and the beginning of the twelfth BC were a period of extreme disruption not only for Anatolia but for Greece and even parts of the Near East. These seventy-odd years saw the end of Troy, of Mycenaean rule in Greece, and of the Hittite Empire, as well as disruption in upper Mesopotamia and Cyprus. The disturbances consisted of a series of raids by the 'Sea Peoples'. These are first heard of in the reign of the Egyptian Pharaoh Merneptah, about 1220, when Egypt faced an attack by the Libyans accompanied by allies who included the Shardana and Lukka, the Ekwesh, Teresh and Shekelesh. A generation later, an inscription of the Pharaoh, Ramesses III, describing his preparations for their onslaught on his frontier in Palestine in 1186 BC, details the events:

> . . . as for the foreign countries, they made a conspiracy in their islands. All at once the lands were on the move, scattered in war. No country could stand before their arms. Hatti, Kode [Kizzuwatna], Carchemish, Arzawa and Alashiya. They were cut off. A camp was set up in one place in Amor [Amurru]. They desolated its people and its land was like that which has never come into being. They were advancing on Egypt while the flame was prepared before them. Their league was Peleset, Tjeker, Shekelesh, Denyen and Weshesh, united lands. They laid their hands upon the lands to the very circuit of the earth, their hearts confident and trusting: 'Our plans will succeed.'

Who were the Sea Peoples and where did they come from? Some of the names are familiar. The Lukka had been based for some time in

21

south-western Anatolia where they achieved a reputation for piracy. The Shardana, pictured with horned helmets, had been at Byblos in the fourteenth century. The Ekwesh have been connected with the Achaioi (Greeks), the Ahhiyawa of Hittite texts, and the Peleset are to be identified with the Philistines of the Old Testament. Most of the other names also echo those of familiar nations – sometimes more than one! The Shardana have been connected with Sardinia and with Sardis, the Denyen with the Danaoi (another name for the Greeks) or with the city of Adana in southern Turkey, or with the Biblical tribe of Dan. The Tjeker sound like the Teucri of Troy, and the Teresh also recall the name of Troy; the Shekelesh sound like the Sicels of Sicily. Only the Weshesh defy such linkage, though connections have been made with Wilusa, the Hittite name for – possibly – [W]Ilion or Troy.

It accords with the story at the end of our last chapter that many of these homeless, pillaging refugees should emerge from the region of the Troad, recently devastated in some violent attack. But we should not regard the Trojan War as the sole cause of this great movement of peoples to the south-east. The most authoritative study of the Sea Peoples, by N.K. Sandars, suggests that the over-centralisation of the thirteenth-century states and an over-specialised economy led to over-population and exhaustion of the land: 'What the economy fatally lacked was that balance based on exploitation of local resources that can sustain itself for long periods and survive short-term climatic change and even catastrophe.' The movements of the Sea Peoples, then, are an early episode in the trend which led to the creation of the first Greek colonies from 1100 onwards, the need for more land. The Sea Peoples cannot on the whole be localised more distantly than Anatolia (though Greeks and even Northmen have at one time or another been invoked). Their eruptions did not end at the Egyptian frontier, though some found homes here; some perhaps went west and became the first inhabitants of Sicily, Sardinia and Etruria. Their motivation and their legacy alike are to be found in the centuries of relative poverty that now descend on Anatolia.

The centuries from 1180 to about 875 are a Dark Age because there is almost nothing in the archaeological record. Some scholars suggest that this is because the period was much shorter than usually supposed; others however would prefer to see the Dark Ages extended over many more centuries. This book will follow the conventional view of the Dark Ages, and draw attention to the few glimmers of light that prick the darkness of these centuries.

The Hittite Empire left a remnant in various smaller kingdoms which the Egyptians referred to as Hatti; there were Hatti states located at Carchemish and at Milid. In their inscriptions they used a dialect of Luwian but wrote in a hieroglyphic script which has come to be known as Hieroglyphic Hittite. Luwian was the language of several parts of Anatolia including the Lukka lands and Kizzuwatna, and is closely related to Hittite.

The Hittites seemed to be retreating southwards in the face of the continuing attacks of the Kaška, to whose encroachments was added the arrival of the Muski, later known as the Phrygians, from south-eastern Europe. By the mid-twelfth century the Muski had reached the Upper Tigris and had launched a joint attack with the Kaška on Assyria. At the same time a new kingdom of Tabal, Luwian-speaking, emerged in central Anatolia and may have been the dominant power in the region.

Urartu

Slightly less shadowy than these powers is the kingdom of Urartu which emerged in eastern Anatolia around Lake Van. Vannic kingdoms are first heard of in Assyrian records in 1275, and the need to combine against repeated Assyrian invasions led to the formation of a unified state around 875 BC. The peoples composing Urartu were predominantly Hurrian and Anatolian. The kingdom of Urartu was founded by Sarduri I *c.* 835–25. It was able to resist Assyrian attack by Shalmaneser III (ruled 860–825) and rapidly extended its influence to northern Iran, northern Syria and Transcaucasia. The name is the same as that of Mount Ararat which is the focus of the region, and was given to the kingdom by the Assyrians. Assyrian influence was strong in Urartian life: costume, art, script and even language were Assyrian. Yet the few finds of 'non-official' art or folk art belong to a very different tradition from the formal near-eastern style, and suggest that, like the Hittites, the Urartian kings were a caste imposing on a people of essentially different nature and extraction. The same is true of Urartian religion, focussed on the god Teisheba, corresponding to the Hurrian Teshub, while popular religion is evident in the cult of trees and stones, notably in the form of that universal near-eastern symbol, the Tree of Life.

The successful century of expansion culminated in the foundation of the capital Tušpa (Van) late in the ninth century. Further expansion in the eighth century led to the foundation of Erebuni (Yerevan) in 782 and of Argishtihinili (Armavir) in 775. In the 750s Sarduri II penetrated almost as far as the Assyrian capital of Nineveh; but in the reign of the next Assyrian king, Tiglath-Pileser III (745–727) the Assyrians returned to the attack. Tiglath-Pileser subjected the Rock of Van to a long and exhausting siege; although he was forced to withdraw, Urartian expansion was over and a period of consolidation began.

BUILDING AND ENGINEERING

Urartian civilisation found one of its most successful expressions in building and engineering works. King Menua (810–785) was responsible for the construction of a canal 40 miles long to bring water from the Artos range to Van; this is known in modern Armenian folklore as the River of Semiramis, the legendary Assyrian queen to whom are attributed a number of constructions in the region of Armenia, not least the city of Van itself. The wealth of the kingdom is indicated in the quantities of finely-wrought bronze armour found at the city of Teishebaini (Karmir Blur) 150 miles from Van in Soviet Armenia. Finds at Toprakkale indicate that the Urartians also traded across Asia, as there are carbonised remains of silk, which can only have come from China.

Assyrian attacks continued, culminating in the sack of the temple of the chief gods at Haldi in Kurdistan, portrayed on a relief in the palace of Sargon II at Khorsabad, from which the Assyrians went away with vast amounts of plunder. Nonetheless, Urartu managed to outlive the Assyrian Empire which collapsed in 612, and only finally succumbed in 590 when it was conquered by the Medes.

Ionia

In western Anatolia (see map, pp. 72–3) the Greeks were steadily gaining a foothold, displacing native populations of Carians, Leleges and others. There had been Mycenaeans at Miletus and Iasus well before the Fall of Troy. Greek legends reflect such historical movements in a number of cases: one example is that of Mopsus, grandson of the Theban seer Tiresias whose daughter Manto had fled to Colophon. Mopsus, when he grew up, led a band of Greeks and Cretans from Colophon to Cilicia where he founded a settlement. The legend receives confirmation from the discovery of a late Mycenaean settlement (1200 BC) at Tarsus. Again, the leader of the Lycians in the *Iliad*, Sarpedon, was in Greek legend a brother of the Cretan king Minos who had been exiled by him to Lycia: the extraordinary longevity thus implied for Sarpedon indicates the anxiety of the Greeks to push back settlements dating from the time of the Trojan War to a much greater antiquity.

The sixth-century writer Pherecydes of Syros, who summarised the Greek traditions about the Ionian migrations, noted that several cities, including Miletus, Colophon and Priene, derived their founders from the Mycenaean kingdom of Pylos, destroyed in the twelfth century. There are strong links at other foundations (e.g. Ephesus) with Athens, in such matters as the month-names. Miletus had been settled before 1100, and the other cities were mostly settled by 1000 BC.

Thereafter there is no information about the region until the seventh century, when we find the Ionians engaged in warfare with each other and against Caria. Early in the century a war was fought for control over the Panionion, the religious centre for the Ionian peoples situated on the south side of Mt Mycale, which may have ended with Priene in control of the religious arrangements. Scattered anecdotes reflect the struggles for political dominance which characterised many Greek states at the period. At Erythrae (Ildır) for example, about 700 BC, King Cnopus was thrown into the sea by a group of oligarchs (upper-class supporters of rule by 'the few' – i.e.

themselves); but their coup was in turn crushed by Cnopus' brother Hippotes who resumed power. Over the next century and a half many such upper-class groups were ousted by 'tyrants' with a populist programme — a process which led in the Greek states to a greater participation in politics, even in non-democratic states, than had ever been known in the autocracies of the near east.

LAND HUNGER

The seventh century saw the first colonising movements from Ionia, the result of a land hunger which had already stimulated colonisation by the mainland Greeks. The Mycenaean connections with the Black Sea had lapsed and the next finds in the region are from Sinope, *c.* 600 BC. But from the early seventh century Miletus, pressed for land at home, was sending out colonists to the Propontis: Cyzicus, Proconnesus and Abydos were all founded between 700 and 675. These were followed by colonies of Megara (on the Greek mainland) at Astakos/Nicomedia (Izmit), Selymbria (Silivri) and Chalcedon as well as Byzantion (640–25) — the first appearance in Greek history of a city that later was to rule the region for more than a thousand years. The islanders of Samos founded Perinthus and other cities; the Aeolians of Phocaea the cities of Ainos (Enez) and Lampsacus (Lapseki: 654); Methymna on Lesbos founded Assos and Gargara in the Troad (675–50); and the Athenians Sigeion, also in the Troad.

Ionians also made settlements further afield, at Massalia (Marseilles), Olbia at the mouth of the Bug, and Naucratis in Egypt.

Land hunger is not the only explanation. These adventurers were displaying what has become a very characteristic Levantine fondness for trade. Neither should one neglect that very important mainspring of the Greek character, curiosity. Exploration may have been undertaken for its own sake. The first maps were made in Miletus (by Hecataeus, flourished *c.* 500 BC) and Phocaea. Ionian colonisation set the stage for that extraordinary first flourishing of the human intellect in the sixth century BC that has come to be known as the Ionian Enlightenment.

Phrygia

Further inland was the kingdom of Phrygia, centred on the city of Gordium. The Greeks believed that the Phrygians had reached Anatolia from south-eastern Europe before the Trojan War, and the Assyrian annals first refer to them, under the name of Muski, or Muski and Tabal, from about 1160. Their kingdom, which emerged in the eighth century, has left conspicuous archaeological remains, in the form of a series of royal burial tumuli at Gordium, minor settlements on Bronze Age sites such as Alaca Hüyük, Alışar, Kültepe, Pazarlı and Boğazköy, and a number of rock-hewn sculptures in the rocky uplands south-east of Eskişehir. The most impressive of all is a rock-hewn tomb in the form of a gabled building at a site called Yazılıkaya (Carved Rock) or, to avoid confusion with the Hittite Yazılıkaya, Midas Şehri (Midas' Town).

MIDAS

Midas was the name of the most important Phrygian king, known to the Greek historian Herodotus (fifth century BC) as the first foreign king to send offerings to Apollo at Delphi. A number of legends attached themselves to the name of Midas, notably his role as judge in the musical contest between Apollo and the satyr Marsyas, located somewhere on the River Marsyas (modern Çine). Midas judged wrong, and Apollo in his anger flayed Marsyas alive and caused Midas to grow asses' ears. Midas in his shame wore a special cap to conceal his ears, but could not keep the secret from his barber, who, desperate to tell somebody, whispered it to the reeds of the river, which then began to whisper eternally 'Midas has asses' ears'. Another legend of Midas also related to this westerly region. A grateful Silenus, rescued from captivity by Midas, gave him the power to turn everything he touched to gold. This was fine to begin with, but when Midas discovered that his food, his drink, even his daughter, were turning to gold, he begged the god Dionysus to relieve him of the curse. Dionysus commanded him to wash in the Lydian river Pactolus; it worked, but the river thereafter ran with gold.

These delightful tales are quite imponderable in relation to the real

Midas, whose name interestingly recalls the Muski king Mita who was a puppet or perhaps ally of the Assyrians. He is said to have married a Greek from the Ionian city of Cyme.

ART AND LANGUAGE

Phrygian was related to the Hittite-Luwian group of languages, but Phrygian art, from the eighth century, shows a marked Urartian influence replacing the preceding west Anatolian type. Phrygia is also the first state west of the Euphrates to develop an alphabetic script, which is likely to have been developed under Phoenician influence.

Phrygia emerges from darkness only to be eclipsed rapidly as a result of the invasion of the northern people, the Cimmerians of south Russia, who sacked Gordion in 714 BC. Midas is said to have committed suicide.

The Lydian Empire, 685–547 BC

No sooner do the Phrygians vanish from history than their place is taken by another, greater and more enduring empire, that of the Lydians.

The Lydians were probably related to the Hittites by race, and were established in Western Asia Minor in the second millennium BC (Herodotus mentions a king, Myrsilus, whose name could belong to a descendant of the Hittite Mursili). A number of settlements rose up around the gold-bearing waters of the river Pactolus which runs through Sardis. After some destruction in about 695 BC caused by the Cimmerian invasion, they were rebuilt in more substantial form. It is from this date that the historical record of the kings of Lydia begins with the legendary Gyges (685–57). Herodotus tells us that Gyges came to power because the reigning king, Candaules, did the remarkable thing of falling in love with his own wife. So overcome was he by her beauty that he wished Gyges, one of his bodyguard whom he liked, to admire her too, and arranged for him to spy on her naked. The queen discovered what had happened, and gave Gyges the choice of being killed, or killing Candaules and becoming king in his stead. Gyges took the obvious course and established a dynasty.

Gyges' successors were Ardys, Sadyattes, Alyattes and Croesus. Herodotus skates briefly over the reigns of the first three, which were largely devoted to a series of wars against Miletus. From this period dates the assemblage of great royal tombs, huge conical mounds which concealed a stone-built chamber, at Bin Tepe six miles (ten kilometres) north of Sardis: the largest is known as the Tomb of Alyattes.

CROESUS

The reign of Croesus was one of great prosperity. He subdued all the Greek cities of Ionia, and in due course all the lands west of the river Halys. Despite these wars, Lydia maintained close contacts with Greek civilisation: Lydian garments were worn in Greek lands, and pottery and other goods from Greece have been found at Sardis. The Lydians were the first people to mint coins in gold and silver; the gold-refining works have been excavated on the banks of the Pactolus, and some tantalising fragments of gold jewellery have also been found.

Lydian religion was basically Anatolian in character, centring on a mother-goddess who is represented on numerous dedicatory stelae and who had an altar near the gold-works as well as a temple in the city of Sardis. However, Croesus was devoted to the point of obsession to the Greek god Apollo, to whose shrine at Delphi he sent an enormous number of valuable dedications including, according to Herodotus, 117 ingots of gold all weighing well over one hundred pounds, and a golden lion weighing 570 pounds. Croesus was also an admirer of the oracular powers of the god, which he tested by sending messengers to ask the oracle what he was doing at a certain stated hour; the oracle replied, correctly, that Croesus was at that moment boiling a tortoise and a lamb in a bronze cauldron. In addition Croesus gave plentiful gifts to the great temple of Artemis at Ephesus which was being built during the 560s.

Croesus' wealth became legendary in his own lifetime. When the Athenian sage Solon visited him, Croesus asked him who was the happiest man alive, thinking that he himself must surely be that man. Solon replied that no man should be called happy until he is dead. 'The richest of men is not more happy than he that has a sufficiency

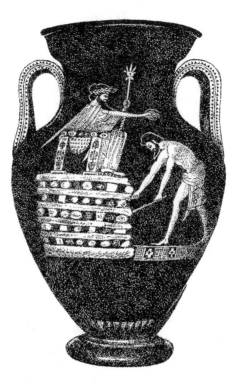

Croesus about to be burnt on the pyre
by Cyrus as depicted on this vase

for a day, unless good fortune attend him to the grave, so that he ends
his life in happiness.'

Croesus was annoyed, but after a couple of years the truth of the
Athenian's words began to be borne in on him. First, his favourite son
Atys died after an accident while hunting boar. After a two-year period
of mourning Croesus returned to political activity with an attack on
Cappadocia, partly to extend his territories and partly in revenge for
the dethronement by the Persian king Cyrus of Croesus' brother-in-

law Astyages, king of Media. Cyrus had challenged the rule of the
Medes in Iran about 550, and was to make himself the first king of
the Achaemenid dynasty of Media and Persia. Croesus consulted the
Delphic oracle about the proposed campaign, and received the
famously ambiguous reply that if he made war on Persia, he would
certainly destroy a great empire.

The two armies met at Pteria in Cappadocia; the Lydians were
worsted and retreated to Sardis. But now Cyrus' army attacked Sardis,
coming up the valley of the Cayster and scaling Mt Tmolus to descend
on the city from the south. They overwhelmed the mudbrick
defensive wall, 7 metres high, which had been built by Alyattes, and
took the king prisoner. Croesus built himself a funeral pyre and
ascended it with his wife and daughters. The conclusion is variously
told. According to Herodotus, Croesus in his adversity called out the
name of Solon; the Persian king, hearing him, was puzzled and asked
him to explain. When Croesus did so, the king was so impressed by
the Athenian's wisdom that he spared Croesus. A different version is
given by the poet Bacchylides, who recounts that Croesus stretched
up his arms in prayer to Apollo; and the grateful god, remembering
all his gifts from Lydia, sent a rainstorm which quenched the pyre so
that Croesus was saved.

Such colourful legends, however little historical truth they may
contain, make the Lydian empire an unforgettable episode in the
history of Asia Minor. Its successor, the empire of the Persians, held
sway for far longer and is the subject of considerably more real
historical information. But our story has already taken us beyond the
sixth century, and before considering the impact of Persia, we must
backtrack and look at the state of affairs in Ionia during these years.

The Ionian Enlightenment

The wars of Gyges and Alyattes against Ionia had resulted in the
conquest of Miletus, and subsequently of Smyrna (before 590) and
Colophon (effected by the treacherous murder of the nobles of
Colophon at a banquet at Sardis). Many of the cities were ruled by
semi-autonomous 'tyrants' (the Greek word means 'ruler'). The

population of Miletus under its tyrant Thrasybulus, who ruled *c.* 600 BC, became so polarised that under his successors there were two groups, known as the rich and the poor. The latter gathered the children of the rich into granaries and had them trampled to death by oxen; the rich retaliated by daubing the poor and their children with pitch and setting them alight. For a long time thereafter the men of Miletus were excluded from the oracle of Apollo (presumably that at Branchidae) for this dreadful crime. Similar struggles between rich and poor, and the emergence of tyrants, characterised other Ionian cities including the islands of Samos and Lesbos.

POETRY

But despite such political savagery, the Ionian cities reached a high standard of culture, with the emergence of some of the first and finest poets of western literature, men and women such as Terpander of Lesbos — who introduced the 'Phrygian' musical scale to the west — Arion of Methymna, Sappho and Alcaeus of Lesbos, Xenophanes of Colophon and Semonides of Amorgos. Xenophanes sneered at his fellow-Colophonians for their decadent Lydian ways; Sappho admired the Lydian headband worn by a girl of her entourage.

PHILOSOPHY

Even more important than such achievements was the remarkable movement which began in Miletus and inaugurated the scientific and rational approach to the world which we now think of as typically western. Aristotle wrote, 'When practically all the necessities of life were supplied, men turned to philosophy as a leisure-time recreation.' By philosophy he meant something like 'disinterested rational speculation'. To begin with, this took the form of speculation on what the world is made of. Thales of Miletus, who lived at the very beginning of the sixth century BC, famously proposed that everything is made of water. His younger Milesian contemporary Anaximander surmised that all physical objects are made of forms of what he called 'The Unlimited'. Then Anaximenes of Miletus proposed that all is made of air, through its condensation and rarefaction. A little later

Heraclitus of Ephesus attributed the physical universe to the successive changes of Fire.

The Pre-Socratic philosophers (as these thinkers are known) did not reflect only on cosmology. Thales was included in most lists of the Seven Sages of Greece: his life is dated for us by his prediction of an eclipse which took place in 585 BC. Another report of him has him buying up all the olive presses in Miletus in early summer, and then making a handsome profit by leasing them out when the olive harvest came round, thus being the first recorded Greek to make a profit by his wits and superior knowledge. He also had political views, proposing a political union of the Ionian cities with a centre of government at Teos (Sığacık). His contemporary Bias of Priene (another of the Seven Sages) had the more extravagant idea of a wholesale emigration of all the Ionians to Sardinia.

The scientific approach of these men derived in the first instance from Babylonian astronomy with which, through their eastern neighbours, especially Persia, they were familiar. The difference is that, though Thales could predict an eclipse, and Anaximander was credited with introducing the gnomon to Greece, their thought did not have a purely practical purpose. In fact, Greek science always fought shy of experiment or anything which hinted of the practical, which is one reason why they excelled in astronomy and mathematics. (Eudoxus of Cnidus, the fourth century mathematician and astronomer, was another Ionian.)

The most notable feature of their cosmological speculation is the absence of gods. Hesiod had constructed in his *Theogony* a world picture which relied on a complex hierarchy of gods and divine personifications such as Hunger and Strife; the Milesians looked for a physical principle. This became an explicit religious agnosticism in the thought of Xenophanes of Colophon (perhaps 570–480 BC) and Anaxagoras of Clazomenae (about 500–428 BC). Anaxagoras was in fact prosecuted in Athens for his doctrine that the Sun is 'a large fiery stone, about the size of the Peloponnese'.

Heraclitus of Ephesus, who was said to have been a pupil of Xenophanes, does not fit comfortably into this mould of thought. His cosmology is based on the principle of the unity of opposites, and his religion assumes that men's ideas of gods are pale approximations to God. In addition, his pronouncements were made in a poetic, riddling style, of which only fragmented examples remain.

Anaxagoras travelled to Athens and is said to have had among his students the scientist Archelaus and the dramatist Euripides. The ideas of the Pre-Socratics of Ionia and their contemporaries of South Italy were well known in Athens and instrumental in the development of the sceptical, relativistic thought of the age of the sophists and Socrates, and the reaction under the greatest philosopher of them all, Plato. Western Europe properly regards the Ionian philosophers as the first stirring of its own scientific and philosophical achievement.

ARCHITECTURE IN IONIA

The sixth century also saw the emergence of the characteristic style of architecture known as Ionic. The earliest temples in Greece had probably been made of wood, and their form resembled an artificial grove, the columns representing the trunks, surrounding a gabled dwelling for the god's statue. By the early sixth century temples were being built of marble, and ambition showed in the construction of temples of enormous size. The first of these (before 575) was the temple of Hera on Samos erected by the local architects Rhoecus and Theodorus, who may also be credited with the invention of the Ionic column, with its characteristic fluted surface and volute-capitals replacing the simpler cushion-like capitals of the Doric style. It was soon followed by the early temples of Artemis at Ephesus and of Apollo at Didyma. These temples represent the beginning of a long tradition in classical Greek architecture, though most of them had to be rebuilt more than once in succeeding centuries.

The Persian Empire

The intellectual achievement of these generations in Ionia sems to have gone on curiously undisturbed by the momentous political changes taking place around them. The Persian defeat of Lydia in 547 BC was the last stage in the advance of the Persians across Anatolia, which was to conclude with their conquest of the cities of Ionia and

Lycia in the years immediately following, and the establishment of Persian rule throughout Asia Minor.

THE MEDES AND PERSIANS

The Medes and Persians, two closely related Iranian peoples, first appear in 836 BC when they are listed among peoples paying tribute to Shalmaneser III of Assyria. The Medes dwelt in Media, with a capital at Ecbatana (modern Hamadan), and the Persians in the more southerly Persis, with a capital at Pasargadae. In 612 the Assyrian Empire was overthrown by the Median king Cyaxares, whose granddaughter Mandane married Cambyses of Persia. Their son was Cyrus who became king of Persis in 559 and, with Babylonian assistance, overthrew his father-in-law Astyages the king of Media (550) and became ruler of a united kingdom of the Medes and Persians. The Greeks always referred to the empire Cyrus founded as that of the Medes, but in modern literature it is customary to call it the Persian Empire.

On the fall of Media, Croesus of Lydia attacked the Persian Empire, as described above, and was defeated. Having taken Lydia, Cyrus naturally turned his attention to the western seaboard, some fifty miles on. Angry that the Ionian Greeks had not revolted from Lydia in his support, he began a campaign against their cities — except Miletus, which had promptly made a treaty with him.

The first act of resistance was a revolt by Pactyes of Lydia, whom Cyrus had put in charge of looting the kingdom. Cyrus sent his general Mazares to put down the revolt, and Mazares, having done so, enslaved Priene, plundered the Maeander plain and captured Magnesia.

Mazares died and was succeeded by Harpagus who undertook the conquest of the rest of Ionia. His first assault was on Phocaea (Foça), which he forced to surrender. The Phocaeans asked for one day's grace to consider the terms of surrender, and overnight the entire population took ship for the west, leaving Harpagus an empty shell of a city. The Phocaeans then settled in Corsica.

Next came Teos, whose people fled to Abdera on the north Aegean coast. Harpagus then quickly overcame Cnidus (whose people had tried to dig a canal across the isthmus to keep the Persians out, until instructed by an oracle to desist), Caunus, and the whole of Caria and Lycia. Contemporaries blamed the swift collapse of the Ionians on the complete lack of political unity among the Greek cities – a problem which was to bedevil Greek civilisation for another two centuries. However, the Persian army was strong enough to compel also the Lycians, who had never been subject to Croesus.

Persia maintained control by the installation of tyrants in the cities. The first of whom we hear is Histiaeus of Miletus, and by 513 there were similar arrangements in place in the cities of Abydus, Lampsacus, Parium, Proconnesus, Cyzicus and Byzantium in the Hellespont region, as well as in Cyme, Chios, Samos and Phocaea. In Lycia a dynasty was ruling in Xanthus by about 520, but this mountainous region was only partly under central control.

DARIUS THE GREAT

Cyrus was succeeded in 529 by his son Cambyses, who undertook the conquest of Egypt, and was succeeded in turn by Darius the Great (521–486). Darius was responsible for the consolidation of the Persian administration and of the system of post roads which marked a revolution in communications. The most famous of these was the Royal Road from Sardis to Susa, the essential artery of the whole western empire. Darius reorganised the system of satrapal government created by Cyrus, which decentralised control of the huge empire under a number of vassal rulers all owing allegiance to the Great King. He divided the empire into twenty satrapies: those in western Anatolia were at Sardis, Dascyleium on the Marmara, Celaenae (Dinar, near modern Denizli) and Caria, while to the east were the more extensive satrapies of Greater Phrygia, Cappadocia, Pamphylia and Armenia. Each satrapy was responsible for a stated tribute, the annual delivery of which is portrayed on the impressive friezes of the Royal Palace at Persepolis.

It is notable that Persian culture was kept within the confines of the satraps' palaces: there is little indication of any impact of Persian artistic styles on the arts of the region. Persia kept Ionia politically under its thumb, but exercised no such cultural imperialism as the Romans were to exert in the heyday of their Empire.

The Ionian Revolt

Greek resistance to Persian rule erupted in the Ionian Revolt of 499. Histiaeus, the tyrant of Miletus, had profited from his support by the Persians. He built a new city near the mouth of the Strymon and began to extend fingers into Thrace with its rich resources of timber and minerals. Soon it became apparent to Darius that he was becoming too big for his boots; and the king invited him in a friendly way to stay with him at Susa for a while. Histiaeus' place as ruler of Miletus was taken by his son-in-law Aristagoras. The latter was asked by some exiled Naxian aristocrats to help them retake their city. The tyrant asked for Persian help, and the king supplied a fleet of two hundred ships for the enterprise. Aristagoras was now commander of a powerful force. A delightful story in Herodotus has it that Histiaeus tattooed a message on a slave's head, let his hair grow, and sent him to Miletus. Aristagoras shaved the slave's head and read there the single word, 'Revolt.' So he did.

Aristagoras now took the initiative, capturing the pro-Persian tyrants in his fleet, and sending to Sparta, and then Athens, for support from the mainland Greeks. The latter city sent a force, and in 498 the army descended on Sardis, setting fire to part of the city before being beaten back by the satrap Artaphrenes.

Cypriots and Hellespontine Greeks now joined the revolt, but Cyprus was soon subdued and the remainder of Ionia saw defeat staring it in the face. Many of the Milesians fled with Aristagoras to Nine Ways in Thrace, where they were destroyed by the natives. Histiaeus now returned to the west, meeting a cool reception both from Artaphrenes, who said 'You have stitched the shoe, and Aristagoras has put it on', and from the people of Miletus, who threw him out again. Darius now decided to stage a final attack on the core of the revolt, Miletus. The decisive battle took place in 494 off the island of Lade (now a mound in the plain created by the silt brought down by the Maeander), and Miletus was sacked, the men killed and the women and children enslaved. The temple at Didyma was plundered and burned. The region was repopulated by Persians and Carians. The destruction caused shock-waves throughout the Greek world: the Athenian tragedian Phrynichus wrote a play called *The Capture of Miletus* which caused such consternation in Athens that he was fined a thousand drachmas.

The end of Histiaeus was not long in coming. After the fall of Miletus he mounted an expedition against the island of Thasos, but was soon captured by Harpagus. He was taken to Sardis, where he was crucified, and his head pickled and sent to the king at Susa. Darius, however, was not pleased at the disgrace inflicted on his former satrap, and had the head buried with proper honours.

The fall of Miletus marks the end of the Persian conquest of Ionia; but it also marks a beginning. It was as a result of the revolt that the Persians first became aware of Athens, and conceived the idea of a conquest of mainland Greece. The revolt also made such an enduring mark on Greek sensibilities that 'liberation of the Greeks of Ionia' became a political watchword for the next two centuries, until it was put into effect by Alexander the Great.

CHAPTER FOUR

The Persian Empire at War with the Greeks, 494–334 BC

The collapse of the Ionian revolt created a new situation for Persia. The satrap Artaphernes exacted an oath of loyalty from all the Ionian states at Sardis, and reassessed the tribute for them all at a rate which, according to Herodotus, remained unchanged some forty years later. At the same time, the tyrannies were replaced by democratic governments of the kind common in mainland Greece, especially Athens. There was clearly a danger that the Ionians might again identify their interests with those of Greece rather than of Persia, and this move will have been designed to counteract those inclinations.

This did not stop Persia undertaking further conquests in the northern Aegean and the Hellespont region. The longer-term plan, however, was to crush and punish Athens and the mainland Greeks for their part in the Revolt. Darius developed a plan for an expedition directed specifically against Athens and Eretria. A fleet of 600 ships and perhaps a quarter of a million men was assembled at Samos, under the command of Datis and Artaphernes, a nephew of Darius. Many Greek cities contributed to the Persian armament, including Athens' arch-rival Aegina; the exiled tyrant of Athens, Hippias, also joined the expedition.

The armies met on the plain of Marathon in Attica (September 490). Astonishingly, the clash resulted in an Athenian victory with very slight losses (only 192 slain). This heroic resistance became a watchword for a generation in Greece, and also entrenched in Athenian minds an image of Persia as the Great Enemy. For Persia, however, the defeat at Marathon meant the end of its Greek adventure, and its image as the Great Enemy was out of date as soon

39

as it was established. But the victory gave Athens a temporarily unassailable position as leader of the Greeks, which was resented by her main rival, Sparta. For the rest of the Persian Empire, however, the first part of the fifth century was a period of relative peace, and Anatolia remained undisturbed by any momentous events.

Lycia

This may be a good moment to pause and look at the condition of Lycia, one of the few states in the Persian Empire which had not previously been subject to Croesus.

The name of the people of Lycia bears a marked resemblance to that of the Lukka of the Hittite texts, who appear to have dwelt further north than classical Lycia, in the region of Caria. It is likely that this people, who spoke a Luwian language, were forced south in the wave of migrations that opened the Dark Ages. The Homeric poems have them already at home in the Xanthus valley. A curious feature of Greek tradition about the Lycians, however, is the strong ties they are given with mainland and island Greeks.

In Homer the Lycian leaders are Sarpedon and Glaucus. The latter is the grandson of the hero Bellerophon, who slew the Chimaera in its home on Mt Chimaera in Lycia by an airborne attack on the winged horse Pegasus. The former, according to Herodotus, was the leader of a group of Cretan immigrants to Lycia called Termilae (the Lycian name for themselves was Trmmili). This tradition created a huge chronological problem which was solved by the expedient of making Sarpedon live for three generations (and still be active to fight in the Trojan War at the end of them). Why were the Greeks so keen to make the Lycians Greeks? The question is unanswerable, but the answer may have to do with trading links in the region in the Mycenaean period.

A second unanswerable question is, If the Lycians were the Lukka, why did they call themselves Termilae? It is possible the Lycians of the historical period included more than one racial stratum, and that there was a Greek element as well as the Luwian. Certainly in the fourth century Lycia developed an indigenous artistic style with distinct Greek overtones; while its contacts with the Greek island of Rhodes from an early date led to a hellenisation which, again in the fourth century, produced some native writers of Greek prose (e.g the historian Menecrates).

Though Lycia was swift to succumb to Harpagus in 540 BC, it remained a remote region, enclosed by its precipitous mountains, looking always to the sea. (In Mycenaean times it had been notorious for pirates, and was to be again.) Some glimpses of its political history can be obtained from the inscriptions. Though the Lycian language has not been fully deciphered, bilingual inscriptions in Lycian and Greek reveal some information. A native dynasty seems to have been established in Xanthus by 520, and the inscriptions hint at various conflicts and rebellions in the fourth century. By 360 the region was under the rule of the Hecatomnid dynasts of neighbouring Caria.

One of the Lycian tower-tombs at Xanthus

A peculiarity of Lycian society is that it may have been matrilineal (name and inheritance descended in the female line) or matrilocal (the bridegroom moves to his bride's household, rather than vice versa). If this is so, it may be an intriguing relic of an Anatolian matriarchal society of the type that focussed its religion on a mother goddess. However, the evidence is conflicting and will allow us only to say that in some cases such measures were undertaken, perhaps with the aim of preserving families that might otherwise die out for lack of males.

The gods of Lycia also belonged to the old Anatolian groups, but became hellenised (the mother goddess turned into the Greek Leto) and also shared their honours with new Greek gods.

By the time of the Romans, Lycians had lost their Anatolian characteristics and could be regarded simply as Greeks.

HERODOTUS

The Persian peace of the early fifth century had one excellent consequence for us, that it enabled one man to travel freely throughout its domains and to record what he saw and to piece together the history of his time. That man was Herodotus, a native of Halicarnassus (Bodrum) in Caria. He was born in about 490, and completed his History (the Greek word means 'inquiry') probably not long before his death around 425.

Herodotus had travelled to Egypt and to Babylonia as well as to many parts of Greece, though he seems never to have visited the Persian heartlands beyond the Zagros mountains. He preserves an enormous amount of information about the way of life, geography, history, legends and lore of these regions; but the main aim of his History was a moral one, to record the great deeds of the Greeks in resisting the Persians, and to explain the moral causes of the war: the blame is put on Croesus for his excessive ambition in making war on Persia.

The Father of History, as he is often called, had few predecessors, though one of whom we should dearly like to know more is his older contemporary Hecataeus of Miletus, a geographer and mythographer as well as a recorder of oral historical traditions. His achievement is the invention of a kind of history, distinguished by a readiness to engage in intriguing digressions and to record piquant but unlikely stories. Though by the austere standards of scientific historians he is often found wanting, his is the armature on which we build our history of the early fifth century. And there is no one to put the Persian point of view. In these generations, the history of Asia Minor is a silent one but for Herodotus.

The Persian War on Greece

In 485 Darius died and was succeeded by his son Xerxes. Xerxes began his reign with a campaign against Egypt; however, his mind soon turned to Greece. Mardonius, who was eager to be satrap of Greece himself, urged the king to resume the plans his father had developed for an all-out war against Greece. Before long, a vast army was making its way along the road to Sardis.

The description of Xerxes' campaign against Greece forms the climax of Herodotus' work (Books VII to IX) and the wonderful narrative should be read in its entirety. The following account does no more than summarise the story with an emphasis on events in Asia Minor.

The enormous army reached the Hellespont in spring 480. The crossing was marked by acts of savagery and impiety, in Herodotus' view. First, the bridges which had been constructed from Sestos to Abydos were torn away in a storm. Xerxes, furious, not only had the engineers beheaded, but ordered the sea itself to be given three hundred lashes for obstructing his will. Next, one of his richest sponsors, Pythius of Celaenae, asked Xerxes, in return for the wealth he had provided, to allow one of his five sons to remain with him at home and not to join the army. Xerxes' response was to seize Pythius' youngest son; he had him cut in two, and the army marched out of Sardis between the two halves of the youth.

From Sardis the army marched northward through the Troad, Xerxes riding in a chariot or in a covered carriage, surrounded by a thousand noble spearmen and ten thousand native infantry, whose spears were all topped with a pomegranate (of gold for the first thousand, silver for the rest). At Troy Xerxes ordered a diversion to

A Persian warrior from the army of Darius' successor, Xerxes

visit the site of the Greeks' conquest of an Asian people. His army drank the Scamander dry, and the king sacrificed a thousand oxen to Athena of Troy, enlisting her support in this war which would redress the balance of history.

New bridges of boats had been constructed across the Hellespont and the army marched into Europe. The crossing took seven days and seven nights. Xerxes, as he watched, is said to have wept at the thought that, of so great an army, very many would before long be dead.

The army – later estimated at the impossible number of seven million – included contingents from every part of the Empire: the

Anatolian peoples represented were the Phrygians, Lydians, Pisidians, Paphlagonians, Cappadocians and Bithynians. In addition Xerxes had a fleet of 1207 triremes (the figure is Herodotus'), including ships from Cilicia, Pamphylia, Lycia, Caria, Ionia, Aeolia, the islanders, the Hellespont region, as well as from the oriental provinces of Syria, Phoenicia, Egypt and Cyprus.

THERMOPYLAE AND SALAMIS

The army marched swiftly through Greece, forcing its way through the Pass of Thermopylae despite the resistance to the death of Leonidas' band of Spartans. It descended on Athens where, after a siege lasting two weeks, it sacked and plundered the temples on the Acropolis. Despite consternation in Athens, Themistocles advised the Athenians to rely on their ships, and shortly afterwards the Greeks defeated the Persians at the naval battle of Salamis (480).

The news caused dismay in Susa. Xerxes held a council of war, which included Artemisia, the female dynast of Caria who was one of his naval commanders. She advised Xerxes to leave Greece to Mardonius, which Xerxes indeed did. Mardonius was subsequently defeated by a combined Greek force at the Battle of Plataea (479). Shortly afterwards the Persian fleet was defeated by the Greeks at the Battle of Mycale. The Persian threat to Greece had been routed; but it was not the end of Persian involvement in Greek affairs.

The Athenian Empire

Immediately after the battle of Mycale, according to Herodotus, some of the Greeks began to discuss whether they should resettle the Ionian Greeks in mainland Greece; however, triumphant Athens opposed the idea, and thus brought into her orbit the Greek cities of Ionia and Aeolia. Athens' naval supremacy put her at the head of a confederacy known as the Delian League which was devoted to continuing the harrying of Persia and capturing strategic cities (notably Eion on the Strymon, and the island of Scyros). The Athenian leader, Themistocles, was prescient enough to see that from now on Athens' true enemy would be her Peloponnesian rival Sparta, not Persia; but such opinions were seen by his fellow-citizens as pro-Persian sympathies, and he was exiled in 472. He ended his life as governor (under the Persian king) of the city of Magnesia on the Maeander, thus no doubt adding grist to the mill of those who saw him as a traitor.

The war under the Athenian general Cimon reached a climax at the combined naval and land battle of the River Eurymedon (469) at which both Persian forces were defeated, thus bringing all of southern Asia Minor under Athenian control. Cimon then captured several Hellespontine cities. Other important gains were the islands of Carystus, Naxos and Thasos, and the city of Erythrae (Ildır).

By 454 the confederacy had developed into an empire with Athens at its head. The treasury was moved to Athens, and the tribute from the members used to restore the destruction caused by the Persians and to create the splendours of classical Athens. Athens was the ruler of, and beneficiary of the wealth of, all the coastal cities of Asia Minor from Byzantium and Calchedon in the north to Aspendus in the south, as well as most of the islands of the Aegean. Inscribed stones recorded at Athens the tribute brought every year from the member states; in the strongest years the number of tributary cities reached 170.

This aggrandisement of Athens aroused the resentment of Sparta and was indirectly the cause of the Peloponnesian War between Athens and Sparta, in which all the other Greek states joined, and ultimately led to the re-emergence of a Persian role in the affairs of Greece.

The Satraps dictate to Greece

The Peloponnesian War broke out in 432. A peace negotiated in 421 led only to a temporary cessation of hostilities, and by 413 Sparta had occupied Decelea, at the very gates of Attica. Until this point the Persian King Artaxerxes (Xerxes had been murdered in 465) had been content to ignore the internecine squabble of the Greeks, and had allowed the satrap of Lydia, Pissuthnes, to make his own decisions and support whichever side suited him, for example in helping to liberate Notium from Athenian control in 430. In 424 Artaxerxes died and was succeeded, after a dynastic struggle, by Darius II. In about 413

Pissuthnes revolted against the king, and thus brought western Asia Minor into the forefront of Persian concerns again.

TISSAPHERNES

Pissuthnes' revolt was quickly put down by the king's emissary (and perhaps his son-in-law) Tissaphernes, who became the new satrap in Sardis. Tissaphernes was to become a figure of major importance in the Greek War, and for that reason we are relatively well informed on his career, through the history of the war written by the Athenian Thucydides. Tissaphernes, along with the satrap of Hellespontine Phrygia, Pharnabazus (the fourth generation in his family to hold the office), decided that it was time to bring Athens' Asian dominions back under Persian rule. However, they were not often in agreement about how best to do this.

Tissaphernes was regarded by Greeks as a prime example of Persian perfidy, changing sides whenever it suited him. But it should be remembered that Tissaphernes' loyalty was not to Athens or to Sparta, but to the king. He had also the benefit of advice from the Athenian aristocrat Alcibiades, who had changed sides and then been expelled from Sparta. He, according to Thucydides,

> advised Tissaphernes not to be in too great a hurry to end the war, or to let himself be persuaded to bring up the Phoenician fleet which he was equipping, or to provide pay for more Greeks, and thus put the power by land and sea into the same hands. Rather, he should leave each of the contending parties in possession of one element, thus enabling the King, when he found one troublesome, to call in the other. . . . The cheapest plan was to let the Greeks wear each other out, at a small share of the expense and without risk to himself.

Most of the time, Tissaphernes courted Spartan power and offered the Spartans help. Pharnabazus, by contrast, was more inclined to lend his weight to the Athenian side. He dreamt of restoring Persian sea-power, to which end Athenian sea-power would be more useful to him. In addition to these differences of approach, the two satraps inevitably became personal rivals, both jockeying for power in Asia

Minor and trying to keep in the good books of the distant despot in Susa.

The overriding aim of Persian policy was to recover the Greek cities of Asia from Athens, and to see Athenian power destroyed for good and all. Both satraps would follow whatever course seemed to lead to that aim at any particular time. The Spartans, having signed a treaty with Persia, regained control of Ionia and immediately took it upon themselves to start collecting the tribute from the former Athenian holdings in Ionia, in breach of their agreement with Persia. Tissaphernes stopped supporting Sparta financially until a new Spartan–Persian treaty was signed in spring 411.

Now Pharnabazus entered the scene with payments to the Peloponnesian armies. Both satraps found themselves involved in considerable expense, and minted magnificent series of silver staters bearing their respective portraits, to pay their mercenaries and the Greek states they favoured. It was not long before the war of attrition seemed the better and cheaper policy.

Tissaphernes had lost his trust in the Spartans and supported at least one anti-Spartan revolution (in Thasos). Furthermore, his position was becoming insecure owing to the enmity of the Persian queen. In 408 the king's son Cyrus was sent to the west as commander-in-chief of all the armies in the region, with specific instructions to assist Sparta. Though Cyrus was soon recalled again to Susa, it was the funds he brought which enabled Sparta finally to win the war against Athens and to impose a bloody dictatorship on the city.

'THE ANABASIS'

Before Cyrus reached Susa, the king was dead. The succession of his elder son, Artaxerxes II, was immediately contested by Cyrus, who returned to Asia Minor and began to assemble a huge force of Greek mercenaries with the ostensible purpose of putting down a revolt in Pisidia. The story of his expedition is the subject of the *Anabasis* (The March up-Country) by Xenophon, an Athenian general who took part in the march and eventually found himself in command of the remnant. Cyrus and his Ten Thousand (as they were known) set off eastwards in spring 401. Pretty soon it became apparent that their destination was not Pisidia but the Persian court at Babylon. The army penetrated deep into Mesopotamia before being cut off and defeated at the Battle of Cunaxa. Cyrus himself was killed, and the army without a cause began to make its painful way back to Greece.

Their march took them through upper Mesopotamia and the eastern reaches of Anatolia. Xenophon's account is often frustratingly poor on details of the route, but he describes vividly many of the peoples they encountered on the way – the underground houses of the Carduchi in Kurdistan (the first mention of the Kurds in history), the linen battledress of the Chalybes, the hair tunics of the Macrones – as well as such natural phenomena as the honey which when eaten caused madness (no doubt it was made from nectar of a poisonous plant indigenous to the mountains). Eventually the Greeks crossed the mountains and caught sight of the Black Sea near Trapezus (Trebizond, Trabzon). A great cry went up from the Greek army: 'The Sea! The Sea!' At last they were in reach of the element with which they felt familiar.

The army was eager to commandeer ships and sail the rest of the way back to Greece, but in the end they made the journey by land, reaching European territory in Thrace in late 400.

Meanwhile Sparta had turned against Tissaphernes. With Athens out of the way, and seeing the collapse of Cyrus' army as an opportunity to embark on a systematic programme of liberating the Greeks of Asia from Persia, she had embarked on a vigorous campaign to win the maritime empire for herself. In autumn 400 the Spartan general Thibron arrived in Asia. He immediately took into his service the remnant of the Ten Thousand and regained several small cities of Aeolia. But in autumn 399 he was recalled, fined on the charge of plundering the cities he was supposed to be liberating, and replaced by Dercylidas. Dercylidas immediately made a treaty with Tissaphernes and attacked Pharnabazus, gaining control of some further Aeolian cities. He was then ordered to Caria to attack Tissaphernes' headquarters. Pharnabazus meanwhile was developing a naval programme, having taken the Athenian admiral Conon under his wing.

In early summer 396 the Spartan king Agesilaus himself arrived in Asia, ostentatiously beginning his expedition with a sacrifice at Aulis, just like that performed by the Greek fleet against Troy in legendary times. Agesilaus was explicitly setting himself up as a successor to those commanders and as the avenger of the Persian conquests of a century before. His initial campaigns were so successful, conquering parts of Caria and Phrygia, that Tissaphernes, already out of favour because of his failure to intercept the Ten Thousand, lost his credibility at the Persian court and was beheaded. His successor was Tithraustes. Agesilaus made common cause with Tithraustes against Pharnabazus, but failed to take the latter's stronghold at The Lion's Head (now Afyonkarahısar). In 394, by the terms of his agreement with Tithraustes, Agesilaus had to retire from Asia, abandoning his grand plans of conquest. In August 394 the Spartan fleet was defeated at Cnidus by the Athenians under Conon, supported by the gold of Pharnabazus. The Athenians and Pharnabazus were now working hand–in–glove: Pharnabazus was paying for the reconstruction of the walls of Athens and was liberating the Asian cities for Athens.

The King's Peace

Sparta continued to harry the Athenian navy. By 387 Artaxerxes II had had enough of it all, and announced at a conference his final offer for peace. The treaty, signed in spring 386, and known as the King's Peace, provided that all the cities in Asia Minor should be the king's, and also the islands of Clazomenae and Cyprus; the other cities (and islands) were to be autonomous; the islands of Lemnos, Imbros and Scyros were to belong to Athens. The agreement was backed by the sanction of armed force against any who disputed it.

There can be little doubt that, whoever was winning the war, Persia had won the Peace. Though the Greeks continued to fight for several decades more, the position in Asia established by this Peace remained in place until the conquest by Alexander in 336. The final arrival of peace in western Asia Minor seems to have led to renewed urbanism, the first sign of which was the refoundation of the city of Priene in the 350s, on a new type of city plan – a grid plan as pioneered by the city planner Hippodamus of Miletus (who flourished 450 BC). This type of plan was to become the model for most of the Greek city foundations of subsequent centuries. Priene controlled the important religious centre of the Panionium in its territory, and the revenues of pilgrims in the years of peace no doubt contributed to the construction of the gymnasia, theatre and other buildings which catered for their needs.

However, the Persian grip on the region as a whole was weakening as Artaxerxes II's long reign went on. The result of the constant fighting in the region had been to usher in an age of warlords and mercenaries. Persia seemed to be falling into the old trap of trying to run a vast empire from a single centre, a neurotic approach epitomised by its attempt to gain total control of Cyprus, whose king Evagoras, though he had been enlarging his power considerably, was far from being in outright revolt. His aim was to hang on to Egypt which had been out of Persian hands since before the battle of Cunaxa. But when Athens sent ships to support Evagoras, the Persian response was to impose more direct control on the region by making Hecatomnus satrap of Caria (which had hitherto been an independent vassal kingdom) and making Autophradates satrap of Lydia and Lycia (which also had hitherto been semi-independent). These moves suggest a loss of grip on the region by Persia, which was exacerbated by a revolt of the Cadusii in 380, a bid for independence by Bithynia, the transformation of the Carian satrapy into a virtual dynasty under Maussollus (377–53) and the rise of dynasts in the Lycian cities of Telmessus and Limyra.

In 371 the septuagenarian Pharnabazus was finally replaced by Datames. The latter wasted little time in revolting against the king. Then Ariobarzanes the satrap of Dascylium also rebelled and was besieged at Assos (Beyramkale) by Autophradates and Maussollus. Heraclea also changed its allegiance.

The Satraps' Revolt

All these events culminated in 363 in the Satraps' Revolt, begun by Maussollus and Orontes. Orontes had been before Cunaxa the satrap of Armenia, and his name is plausibly Armenian; but at the time of this revolt he was satrap of Mysia and made his last stand at Pergamum.

Maussollus, dynast of Caria

Autophradates joined the rebels, while Tachos of Egypt also rose up with Spartan support. By 360 the revolt had collapsed, but when Artaxerxes died in 358, one of the first acts of his successor Artaxerxes III was to disband the mercenary armies of the satraps. However, disintegration had reached a stage where it could not simply be reversed. Maussollus, in particular, had consolidated a personal kingdom in Caria which included much of Lydia and Lycia as well, besides the islands of Rhodes, Cos and Chios and the cities of Erythrae and Byzantium. In 362 he moved his capital from Mylasa to

Halicarnassus, where he had a tomb built for himself (it was incomplete on his death and had to be finished by his widow and successor Artemisia) which was to become known, under the name of the Mausoleum, as one of the Seven Wonders of the World.

The Rise of Macedon

In the year 359 a new power came on to the scene in the Aegean world, as King Philip II of Macedon began to develop a formidable military power and to secure for his kingdom the mineral resources of Thrace. The largely tribal people of Macedon became urbanised and organised. It quickly became apparent to forward-looking politicians in Greece (such as Demosthenes) that Philip now posed a much more formidable threat to Greece than did Persia; and indeed his threat to Persia was just as great. Many Greeks, however, remained locked in a world view which could regard none but Persia as the great enemy. The result was that Philip made himself master of mainland Greece at the Battle of Chaeronea in 338.

The Persian king was occupied with a revolt among the Cadusii which had been simmering for thirty years, as well as with the reconquest of Egypt which was finally effected in 343. No doubt he welcomed a non-aggression pact with Philip. But in 341 Philip had laid siege to his recalcitrant ally Perinthus on the Hellespont. Artaxerxes ordered his satraps to repel the Macedonian king but it was one of his last acts, for in 338 Artaxerxes was murdered and succeeded by Arses.

However, it soon became clear that Philip had taken on the mantle of Agesilaus in his enthusiasm for a crusade against the Persian Empire. In 337 he was chosen to lead an expedition of Greeks to overthrow the Persian king and actually crossed the straits into Asia; but the following year he was assassinated at a theatrical performance in the Macedonian capital of Aegae. In the same year the new Persian king Arses (338–6) was killed and succeeded by Darius III. Darius however was to find his Macedonian rival more than a match for him: the new king of Macedonia was Alexander III, to be known as Alexander the Great, and he would destroy the Persian Empire.

Retrospect

Here, on the eve of Persia's conquest, let us look back and consider what, in the end, Persian rule had brought to Asia Minor. The answer seems to be, curiously little. There is little sign of Persian influence in the arts of the region; indeed, there is little art at all. The fourth century was a bleak period, in which what wealth there was was bled away to the treasuries of Persepolis and Susa, and constant warfare debilitated the cities. Persian government, however, had ceased to exist except for military purposes. The region was divided into a number of semi-independent satrapies, mostly under hereditary dynasties which functioned like royal ones. The populations were mixed, though in the west Greeks probably preponderated over natives and Persians; further east, a Persian ruling caste may have dominated the indigenous people; but our sources are silent on the eastern regions at this period. All in all, one has the impression of a region exhausted, waiting for a new beginning.

CHAPTER FIVE

Alexander the Great and his Legacy,
334–133 BC

It is not often that a single man can seriously be credited with having changed the course of history. In the case of Alexander the Great, it is undoubtedly true. Barely twenty when he succeeded to the throne of his father Philip, he was a remarkable being who combined the military genius and political vision of his father with a literary bent, a romanticism and a taste for adventure that led him to achieve what many others would scarcely have attempted – the penetration of the Persian Empire to its heart, and even beyond.

Alexander adopted with enthusiasm the watchword that had been the Greeks' for more than a century – Liberation of the Greek cities of Asia and revenge on Persia for the conquest of Greece. The Macedonians, in fact, were dubiously Greek by race, but their kings were allowed an honorary status as Greeks and could compete in the Olympic Games. Alexander was an enthusiast for Greek culture; the later plays of Euripides had been performed at the Macedonian court and an interest in Attic drama was maintained. Like any Greek, he was brought up on the poems of Homer, and in his invasion of Asia had a text constantly by him, to remind him of that earlier Greek war against the east.

In less than two years Alexander secured his rear in Greece and Thrace and assembled an army of about 50,000 men for the assault on Asia. Less than half were Macedonians, and less than a quarter Greeks. The importance of mercenaries is again underlined. A considerable fleet of warships and supply ships was also ready: Alexander showed himself from the beginning a master of commissariat and logistics – an army marches on its stomach. With him he took also a staff of scholars to record their discoveries in the distant east. From the beginning this was to be a journey of discovery as well as conquest; perhaps only the enthusiasm of youth could have set off so confident of great discoveries in distant hostile lands.

ONWARD TO ASIA

The army crossed the Hellespont in spring 334. Alexander made libations to the sea as he crossed (how unlike Xerxes' angry scourging of the same waters!) and, like the Homeric hero Protesilaus, leapt ashore on landing in full armour, casting his spear into the soil to claim Asia as spear-won territory. He then immediately made for Troy, then only a modest village, where he sacrificed to Athena of Ilium and to the Greek heroes of the war. Almost at once he had to join battle with the Persian army, at the River Granicus, whose steep banks precluded any frontal assault and could be expected to give the advantage to the superior Persian cavalry. However, the might of the Macedonian phalanx, advancing with its massed heavy spears like a cross between a tank and a porcupine, carried the day. The Persian commander Arsites committed suicide and the remaining Persian satraps regrouped on the Aegean coast.

Alexander left a commander of his own, Parmenio, in Arsites' palace at Dascyleium, and marched, via Sardis, which he quickly won with its precious wealth, to Ephesus where he was to meet the fleet. Here he found the Persian garrison had already run away and the city was in the grip of a democratic revolution. This he supported, making over the Persian tribute, not to his own coffers, but to the great temple of Artemis, to whom he also made a great sacrifice. These benefactions encouraged other Greek cities to offer their allegiance to Alexander, Magnesia and Tralles being among the first.

Alexander now marched on to Miletus, which offered resistance, and a siege was begun. Success was threatened when the Persian fleet arrived; but Alexander's ships, though inferior in numbers, prevented them making a landing on the coast at Miletus and, declining to offer battle, frustrated the Persian forces completely. Miletus was taken. In deference to their ancestors' part in the Ionian Revolt, the population was not enslaved, but a tribute was imposed on the city.

Alexander the Great

An equally tough struggle awaited at Halicarnassus, which was defended by the commander Memnon of Rhodes. The up-to-the-minute siege equipment of the Macedonians, including siege towers, catapults and rams, as well as sappers, came under heavy bombardment from the defenders, while repeated sorties were made to fire the siege towers. Eventually, however, Memnon gave the order to abandon the defence, and Alexander's army marched in and razed the town.

He had not finished off Memnon, who was to be a thorn in his side for some time to come. Politically, however, Alexander was satisfied. He left his general Ptolemy and a garrison to support the Hecatomnid princess Ada, to whom he left intact her authority over Caria. Indeed, she seems to have been eager to welcome him in her mountain fastness at Alinda, where she insisted on adopting him as her son and plied him daily with offers of food too abundant and delicious for a man on campaign: he parried — as many victims of Turkish hospitality have also had to do — with the excuse that 'he wanted nothing but a night-march to prepare for breakfast, and a moderate breakfast to create an appetite for supper'.

In barely six months Alexander had become the acknowledged ruler of all the cities of the west coast. His claim was to have liberated them, and to have given them autonomy. What exactly did this mean? First, democratic governments had been imposed to replace the Persian oligarchies. Autonomy may have meant no more than the privilege of using a new constitution imposed by Alexander; and certainly garrisons were inescapable. Tribute, however, was in most cases remitted. Alexander was already master of the wealth of Sardis, and this will have given substance to his support for the dedication of the new temple of Athena Polias at Priene (the stone bearing his name and dedication is in the British Museum). The people of Ephesus, however, declined his offer to pay for the building of a new temple of Artemis to replace one which had been burned down, according to tradition, on the night Alexander was born, by a madman named Herostratus who hoped thus (correctly, alas) to win an imperishable name in history. Their tactful excuse was that 'it was not right for one god to make a dedication to another god'. Contributions were, however, required from most other cities, to support the expenses of the campaign.

SOUTH INTO LYCIA

As winter came on, Alexander pushed south into Lycia. He annexed cities as he went, and had to trust that his Aegean conquests were secure behind him. Amazingly, he met no Persian resistance. By midwinter he was at Phaselis, and from there he sent his army over Mt Climax along a road specially constructed by Thracian pioneers, while he went with his staff along the coast. Here the waves beat right across the path; but the wind veered round and left an expanse of beach for his passage. This was interpreted by the court historian as a sign of the gods' favour to Alexander: even the elements drew back at his approach.

The Aegean holdings were being shaken by the activities of Memnon; but in summer 333 Memnon died, and even before that Darius had decided to concentrate all his forces for a great confrontation by land. Mercenaries and other forces were drawn from the Aegean to Babylon, and the danger in the west consequently receded.

THE GORDIAN KNOT

Pamphylia was subdued after a siege at Aspendus, and Alexander moved on leaving Nearchus of Crete as satrap in Perge. Alexander now turned inland and northwards to take control of Phrygia. His arrival at Gordium, the capital, was the occasion of one of the best-known events of his expedition. In the palace of the Phrygian kings was a wagon that had belonged to the legendary king Gordius, the yoke of which was fixed to the pole by a knot so cunningly made that both ends were invisible. Tradition said that whoever could loose the knot would make himself master of Asia. Alexander wasted no time in 'loosing' the knot in the simplest possible way, by cutting it through with his sword.

Alexander had little trouble making his way through the relatively disorganised tribes of Paphlagonia, who were assigned to the satrapy of Hellespontine Phrygia and excused tribute, and receiving the allegiance of the Cappadocians too. His army penetrated the Cilician gates, the one pass through the forbidding Taurus range, easily dislodging a slight Persian force, and arrived at Tarsus which was to be his base for the next three months. An illness brought on by an imprudent swim in the river Cydnus produced a temporary crisis, when his treasurer Harpalus fled to Macedon with the cash; but the king recovered and made ready to meet Darius' army at Issus.

THE BATTLE OF ISSUS

Issus (Dörtyol) is situated at the inmost point of the Gulf of Iskenderun, where the Asian coast turns southwards to the Levant. Here Darius assembled his huge army in September 333. It vastly outnumbered the Macedonian troops, and Darius confidently made the first move by sweeping around through the Bahçe Pass to cut off Alexander's communications with Cilicia. The exact site of the main battle is uncertain, as the water courses have probably changed in the intervening centuries, but may have taken place near the Kuru Çay, where the plain is about 4 km wide between sea and mountains. North of the river Pinarus, Darius had positioned his cavalry by the sea on the right; mercenary infantry occupied the centre, while Persian infantry extended up the foothills and bent around almost to encircle the Macedonians. Alexander's army faced northwards, and the formidable phalanx with its projecting spears moved forward, first slowly to preserve formation, and then at a charge. The light–armed Persians could not withstand the phalanx, but their cavalry was almost irresistible. However, the Persian centre could not hold. Alexander forged closer and closer to the enemy king himself. Suddenly Darius turned and fled. The Persian line lost its confidence, wavered, and was routed. The Macedonian pursuit resulted in a massacre: Persian losses were enormous, rated by some accounts as high as 100,000.

Alexander was now master of the Persian baggage train and quickly secured also the treasure at Damascus as well as capturing the wife and mother of Darius.

KING OF PERSIA

The rest of Alexander's expedition takes him beyond the confines of modern Turkey and may be more quickly told. He secured the Syrian coast, the most difficult campaign being the siege of Tyre, after which he is said to have crucified enormous numbers of the defenders. He marched into Egypt where he was hailed as a new Pharaoh and founded the first of many cities named Alexandria (another was founded near Issus, to be known later as Alexandretta, and now as Iskenderun). A final battle at Gaugamela in Mesopotamia saw the final collapse of Persia, and Alexander went on to capture the Persian capitals of Susa and Persepolis, with all their vast wealth. This was soon followed by the death of Darius, murdered by two of his subordinates. Alexander was now king of Persia. Greece was avenged.

Alexander had, perhaps, less talent for administration than for adventure. In the main he left the satrapal system of the Persian Empire intact, replacing the Persian rulers in most cases with Macedonians. The Greeks of Asia were forgotten as Alexander began to adopt the manners and ceremonial of the Persian king, to the disgust of many of the Greeks and Macedonians in his entourage. He also let it be known that he would welcome the offer of divine honours in Greece (to which Demosthenes retorted, 'Well, let him be a god if he wants to!'). He seems to have been prepared by 324 to regard the Greek cities as his personal fief, offering the Athenian general Phocion a choice of any one of four of them for his own. The Greek cities were privileged subjects, but subjects they were.

Alexander's mind, by the time he conquered Persepolis in 330, was fixed on further exploration and conquest. He made himself master of the eastern satrapies of Central Asia and then plunged on into Pakistan. A fleet was sent down the Indus to explore the sea-route to Mesopotamia, while Alexander led his army on a hazardous and largely disastrous march through the desert of southern Iran, on which many of his soldiers died. Reconvening at Opis he celebrated a mass marriage intended to cement Macedonians and Persians in to a single governing class. He was planning further conquests when he died, suddenly, perhaps of poison but more probably of fever, at Babylon in 323. He was thirty-two years old.

The Successors

Alexander had changed the face of the Greek world. A Greek-speaking caste now ruled from the coasts of western Greece to central Asia. Alexander's achievements had been so great that many did not baulk at calling him a god, and he himself claimed that at the Oracle of Ammon in Egypt he had been hailed as a son of Zeus. He had achieved power such as no man had had before him, and his cult in the Greek cities was a way of acknowledging his power that transcended any local autonomy. But for all his achievement he had made no provision for his succession. His young wife Roxane was pregnant, and when she was delivered of a boy, the infant was proclaimed Alexander IV of Macedon alongside Alexander's mentally defective half-brother Philip Arrhidaeus who was hailed as Philip III. The dual kingship could never be more than a façade.

Legend had it that Alexander on his death bed, asked who should be his successor, had replied unhelpfully, 'The kingdom shall go to the strongest.' A will was later produced which appointed Craterus ruler of Macedon, Ptolemy of Egypt, and Perdiccas and Antigonus of Asia. Even if it had been genuine, it provided no basis for agreement between the surviving warlords, and Alexander's empire was soon split by warfare between his generals. Twenty years were to go by before things began to settle down and the outlines of the Hellenistic world began to take shape.

CONTROL OF EGYPT

The simplest division of responsibility was Ptolemy's assumption of control of Egypt, where he established the royal dynasty of the Ptolemies which was to rule until the arrival of Julius Caesar. Antigonus (382 301), an exact contemporary of Philip II, was satrap of Phrygia, and was appointed by Antipater who had been Alexander's regent in Macedon as commander of the royal army in Asia. He put down opposition from the generals Alcetas and Eumenes, and when Antipater died in 319 stood a chance of reuniting the whole of Alexander's empire under his own rule. He continued to hold out against opposition from Ptolemy, from Cassander in Macedonia and from Lysimachus (360–281) in Thrace, defeating all three of them in a war ending in 311, though Babylon and the eastern satrapies were occupied by Seleucus in 312. In 306 both Antigonus and Lysimachus declared themselves kings and, in the following year, Ptolemy and Seleucus followed suit. There were now four self-styled kings vying for control of the empire.

THE SELEUCID REALM

Seleucus (358–281) was a minor general in Alexander's army, but had been made satrap of Babylonia. After Ipsus he retained the region, with a kingdom centred on Syria and Cilicia, where he built the cities of Seleucia on Tigris and Seleucia in Pieria (Silifke). He soon transferred his capital to Antioch (Antakya), however, another of his foundations (it was named after his father Antiochus). In 281 Seleucus defeated Lysimachus at Corupedium (near Magnesia ad Sipylum, Manisa), but Lysimachus' kingdom was broken up and did not become part of the Seleucid realm. The dominant powers until the coming of Rome remained the Seleucid and Ptolemaic kingdoms, while Macedon continued to control the affairs of the Greek mainland. The story of Asia Minor in these two centuries is that of the kingdoms of Antigonus and Lysimachus, and the fragments into which they were broken, and the Seleucid realm.

Antigonus and Lysimachus

The ancient sources portray Antigonus as an arrogant and ambitious man, obsessed (as indeed were the other successors) with the idea of obtaining control of the whole of Alexander's conquests for himself. In fact Antigonus never showed any inclination to dominate any further east than the Eastern Mediterranean region, which Alexander's general Parmenio had urged him to treat as the core of his empire. It seems to have been only in his last years that he became determined to eliminate all opposition. In the intervening years, he was occupied with establishing an administrative structure in Asia Minor and the Levant, and a model for Hellenistic kingship, which were both to be taken over in essentially the same form by those who succeeded him. Antigonus is thus in a real sense one of the main creators of the Hellenistic world.

His policy centred on an accommodation between the absolute power of the ruler and his military might, based in large part on mercenary forces on the one hand, and a genuine commitment to the 'autonomy' of the Greek cities on the other. In 311 Antigonus formally declared that all the Greek cities of the region were to be free and autonomous, and the details of this are spelt out in a letter he sent to the city of Scepsis in the Troad in that year:

> Know then that peace is made [between Antigonus, Cassander and Lysimachus]. We have provided in the treaty that all the Greeks are to swear to aid each other in preserving their freedom and autonomy, thinking that while we lived on all human calculations these would be

> protected, but that afterwards freedom would remain more certainly
> secure for all the Greeks if both they and the men in power are bound by
> oaths.

In fact Antigonus had the little city incorporated in the larger polity
of his newly-founded city of Alexandria Troas.

It was in the same spirit that Antigonus took steps to re-establish
the city of Smyrna as an independent state. However, just as
Alexander's declaration of the autonomy of Priene had not prevented
him from exacting a substantial donation from it, so too the
'autonomy' of the cities under Antigonus did not stop them being
liable for substantial taxes and tribute. Similarly Antigonus did not
hesitate to intervene with direct instructions in the matter of the
synoecism (coalescence of two cities) of Teos and Lebedus. The
tension in the position of the cities is nicely encapsulated in the
institution of ruler cult: the cities claimed to be autonomous, yet they
offered worship to the ruler as to a god (poor little Scepsis was among
the first so to honour Antigonus). Such cult did not so much
categorically make the cities unfree as acknowledge the king as a larger
power, not includable in any existing political structure.

The self-proclamation of the four rulers as kings in 306 (*see p. 62*)
led to a decisive battle at Ipsus in Phrygia in 301, as a result of which
Lysimachus, the Thracian ruler, inherited the kingdom of Antigonus
which included northern and Central Asia Minor. Lysimachus' power
remained centred in Thrace, and he made no essential changes in the
administration of his realm in Asia Minor, but was remembered for
over-authoritarian administration and oppressive taxation. All the
Successor kings were in desperate need of money to fund their endless
wars, and this explains not only high taxation, but their anxiety to get
their hands on the treasuries of Persia.

Seleucus I Nicator and Antiochus I Soter

Lysimachus' power lasted for some twenty years, until 282 when much
of Asia Minor went over to Seleucus, perhaps the most important
defection being that of Philetaerus, the governor of Pergamum.

Seleucus proved himself a more humane ruler than Lysimachus, and continued to support the Greek cities. He had already distinguished himself as a founder of cities, Seleucia on the Tigris being the first (312), soon followed by Seleucia in Pieria (Silifke) in 300 which was for a short time his western capital until he transferred that role to the newly founded Antioch (named after his father). (He also founded Apamea in Syria, named after his Bactrian wife Apama, and there he kept the stables for his army of elephants.)

Seleucus was murdered in 281, the year after his conquest of Asia Minor, and was succeeded by his son Antiochus (324–261), known as Soter (Saviour) for his defeat of the Gauls in 273 – the 'Elephant Victory'. Antiochus declared his father a god. He too was a great founder of cities, and achieved a solid peace with the Macedonian ruler Antigonus Gonatas, renouncing any claim to the Greek mainland. However, many parts of his kingdom began to slip from his grasp, notably Pergamum which won its independence in a battle at Sardis in 262, and Caria and Lycia. Antiochus' successors Antiochus II, Seleucus II and Antiochus III took on more and more the role of local dynasts, though their policies towards the cities continued to reflect those established by Antigonus. Antiochus III (223–187) proved himself a successful conqueror, campaigning even as far as Bactria, in search of gold; he reconquered Armenia under its king Xerxes; but in the end Antiochus fell foul of Rome which was extending its empire eastwards through Macedonia, and the Treaty of Apamea in 188 signalled the end of the Hellenistic kings in most of Asia Minor.

Cilicia and Syria (including Antioch) remained in the hands of further Antiochi until their annexation by Pompey in 63 BC. The later Seleucids were colourful characters: Antiochus IV Epiphanes was an ardent Hellenist and began the rebuilding of the Temple of Olympian Zeus at Athens. Two of the last Seleucids, Antiochus VII Sidetes and Antiochus VIII Grypus, became bywords for luxury and magnificence – Posidonius describes the feasts at Daphne at which Grypus (Hawknose) would present his guests with lavish gifts:

Presents were made of whole roast animals, as well as large geese, hares and deer. The gifts also included golden garlands for the diners and quantities of money, servants, horses and camels. Guests were obliged to climb on to the camel to drink, and then to accept the camel, and what was on it, and the boy who attended it.

Hellenistic Civilisation

The Hellenistic period was an age of cities. As has been indicated, all the rulers of the Greek lands proclaimed their allegiance to the principle of the independence of the Greek cities. The cities or city-states (*poleis*) were characterised by having their own code of laws and the forms of self-government including a council and magistrates and usually an assembly of the people. Their economic basis was agriculture and the cities were usually walled for defence, though few could now raise a citizen army as the city-states of classical Greece had done. military affairs were in the hands of the kings and their mercenaries. The latter offered a career to many inhabitants of the cities, so that Greek culture was spread far and wide through the travels of these soldiers and their eventual settlement often in specially created new cities, known as *cleruchies* (a Greek word meaning shareholdings).

Hellenistic Asia Minor contained not only the traditional Greek cities but many other kinds of political unit. One important type was the temple state, a community whose *raison d'être* was the service of a major cult centre: examples are Didyma (the oracle and temple of Apollo) and Magnesia on the Maeander where there was an important temple of Artemis. Such cities claimed a right of *asylia* or inviolability, i.e. they requested freedom from tribute and also freedom from any reprisals another city might wish to make against their own citizens. Both Teos and Magnesia made such requests in the later third century, though it is not clear whether all kings always granted such requests. Certainly the kings were happy to support the establishment of festivals with games on the model of the Olympic and Pythian Games in Greece, and these usually took place every four years. Sometimes such games were named in honour of the ruling king; and after 189 many games were instituted under the name of Romaea. Teos also claimed *asylia* and was the home of a prominent guild of travelling actors known as the Artists of Dionysus.

In addition to the existing city-states and the temple states there were the numerous new foundations of the kings, including in our territory Lysimacheia in Thrace, Stratonicea in Caria, named for the wife of Seleucus I, daughter of Demetrius the Besieger, Alexandria Troas (originally founded as Antigoneia by Antigonus), and Antioch and Seleucia. Antioch was established on a site close to another Antigoneia, and according to the legend preserved by the local chronicler John Malalas (sixth century AD), Seleucus had sacrificed on an altar at Antigoneia when an obliging eagle descended from the skies and carried off the sacrificial meat to deposit it on the site of the future Antioch, thus confirming the choice of site for the city.

ANTIOCH

Antioch is a good paradigm for these new foundations. A perimeter wall was outlined in grain and then built in stone; the streets were laid out on a grid pattern like that established in the fourth century by the town planner Hippodamus; and the city was adorned with numerous fine buildings through the generosity of the ruler. The city had her own protecting goddess, the Tyche or Fortune of Antioch, a seated goddess with a mural crown who was portrayed on the city's coins and became a famous type imitated in the Tychai of many other cities. The population was ethnically mixed, including Greeks and Macedonians, as well as a number of Jews, local Syrians and about five thousand Athenian settlers forcibly transplanted from Antigoneia. The usual city institutions were established, as well as a cult of the ruling dynasty. Similar patterns, on a necessarily less grand scale, pertained at other new foundations.

The Greek cities did not, on the whole, reach the level of artistic and intellectual culture that had characterised the earlier *poleis* of Greece. No doubt this was due in part to the siphoning off of their wealth for military purposes. The major exception was the Ptolemaic capital of Alexandria in Egypt, which acted as a magnet for scholars and writers from the earliest days of its existence. The nearest approach to this level of achievement in Asia Minor was that of Pergamum.

The Attalid Kingdom of Pergamum

The independence of Pergamum dates from 282 when Philetaerus, the governor installed by Lysimachus, revolted and joined the coalition against Lysimachus. After the latter's defeat at the Battle of Corupedium, Pergamum became a vassal of Seleucus. Philetaerus' successor Eumenes I broke away from Seleucus after defeating him in battle near Sardis in 262. His rule in Pergamum was marked by constant trouble with the invading Gauls from central Europe, who had crossed into Asia in 278/7. Eumenes' adopted son Attalus (241–197) refused to pay tribute to the Gauls and finally conquered them, some time before 230. His achievement was celebrated by the construction (in the reign of Eumenes II) of the magnificent Altar of Zeus (now in the Antikenmuseum in Berlin) which depicts a battle of gods and giants on its outer walls. The Gauls carved out a territory for themselves known as Galatia and ceased to be an aggressive power.

Attalus gradually made himself ruler of all north-western Asia Minor, as far south as Colophon and as far east as Aezani in Phrygia. His successor Eumenes II reigned for thirty-eight years and in 197 successfully resisted Antiochus' attempt at reconquest of Asia Minor, at the Battle of Magnesia. Eumenes allied himself with Rome in order to keep Antiochus at bay, and the kingdom continued in existence for nearly fifty years after the Treaty of Apamea (188) had given Rome a solid footing in the region. Perhaps it was because real political power now belonged to Rome that the last ruler of Pergamum, Attalus III (138–133) found time to devote to his strange hobbies, which included medical and zoological researches, testing poisons on criminals, and metalworking. It is said that he died of sunstroke while working on a bronze monument for his mother. He concluded his career by leaving his kingdom to Rome in his will.

The Attalid dynasty had presided over the greatest cultural centre in Asia Minor. Its magnificent buildings at Pergamum are an enduring testimony to its achievement. Little is left at the site of the Great Altar, referred to in the Book of Revelation (because of its chair-like shape) as 'the Throne of Satan', but one can still see the fine theatre, built in a natural hollow of the hill, the extensive sanctuary of the healing god

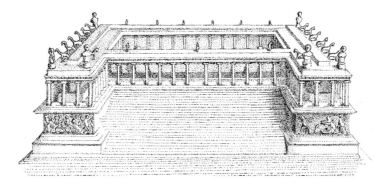

The altar of Zeus at Pergamum

Asclepius laid out in the early second century in the valley below the city, and remains of the walls and aqueducts created by Eumenes II. Eumenes also sponsored the construction of stadia and a gymnasium at Miletus, and Pergamene influence can be detected on the contemporary market building at Assos. Philetaerus was responsible for the building of the Sanctuary of Demeter on a spur of the acropolis.

THE LIBRARY

Most significant of all, perhaps, are the ruins of the Library, built in the reign of Eumenes II in direct emulation of the Library of Alexandria. It is said that when its contents were seized by Mark Antony as a wedding present for Cleopatra it contained 200,000 volumes. Because papyrus, the normal material on which book rolls were written in antiquity, was a monopoly of the Ptolemies, the books at Pergamum were written on a specially prepared goatskin (there were abundant goats in the region) which has become known, after the name of the city, as pergament or parchment.

SCHOLARS AND POETS

A library needs scholars to use it, and the Pergamene kings were sponsors of education at all levels, from the elementary (where inscriptions from Teos give details of their schemes) to higher education: the Pergamene kings directly supported the schools of philosophy at Athens. The scholars attached to Pergamum do not have quite the lustre of those associated with Alexandria, such as Callimachus, Theocritus and Apollonius of Rhodes as well as the great Homeric scholars; but they include figures such as the historian Antigonus of Carystus, Polemon the Periegete, an assiduous collector of inscriptions of historical interest, the geographer Demetrius of Scepsis, the critic Crates, the military engineer Biton, and the philosopher Panaetius of Rhodes (who later became associated with the circle of Scipio Africanus at Rome). The poet Nicander of Colophon was the author of some curious works on venomous creatures and on poisons and their antidotes. Thus most of the literary talent of Hellenistic Asia Minor was associated with Pergamum. (Two exceptions are Aratus of Soli, the writer on astronomy, and the historian Hieronymus of Cardia, both of whom found a home at the Macedonian court of Pella.)

SCULPTURE

Pergamum was also the home of the most famous and perhaps the most distinguished school of sculpture of the period. The highly distinctive and arresting 'baroque' style of the reliefs adorning the Great Altar was succeeded by a more realistic style including such famous works as the Dying Gaul, the Knife-grinder and many statues which subsequently found homes in the collections of Roman aristocrats. Attalus I, besides patronising artists, was also an art-collector himself; and Pergamum contained many copies of fifth-century works, notably the scale reproduction of the great Athena Parthenos from Athens, which was kept in the Library. Painting too was important, though inevitably less is preserved of its achievements.

CONCLUSION

The glories of Pergamum provide a kind of climax to a confused and often unedifying period of history. But despite the constant warfare, a solid administrative foundation had been created by the Hellenistic kings of Asia Minor, which was to serve very well the purposes of the Roman Empire for a millennium to come.

CHAPTER SIX

The Impact of Rome,
193 BC–AD 330

From about the middle of the third century BC the Greek rulers of Asia Minor had had to take account of a rising new power in the Mediterranean, that of Rome. The defeat of Antiochus' invasion of Greece in 193 put an end to the king's expansion westward; in 189 BC Manlius Vulso subdued the Galatians, a conquest which led to their abandonment of Gordium. Rome also took hold of mainland Greece as a result of the decisive battle of Pydna in 168, in which the Macedonian king was worsted, consolidating her rule over Greece by the demonstrative sack of Corinth in 146.

A World Power

The importance of Rome as a world power was recognised by Attalus, the last king of Pergamum, when he bequeathed his kingdom to the Romans, to whom it passed on his death in 133. These events, and the destruction of Carthage in the same year as Corinth, made Rome the master of the western Mediterranean, the culmination of an achievement which Polybius made the central subject of his history of the rise of Rome. Polybius was a Greek from Achaea who, while he may not have admired the action of the Romans in subduing his homeland, exhibited a traditional Greek curiosity in the rhetorical opening question of his History, 'Who is so indifferent or indolent that he would not want to know how, and under what form of government, almost every part of the inhabited world came under Rome's sole rule in less than fifty-three years, an unprecedented phenomenon?'

Greek and Roman Asia Minor

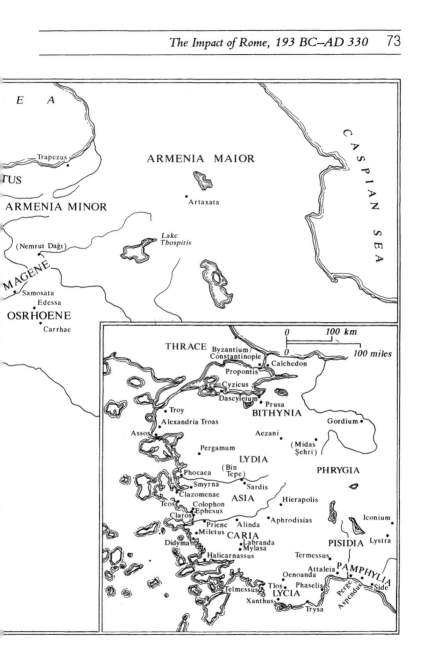

The brash militarism of Rome was an unfamiliar and alarming factor in the world of the Greek East which, despite the constant warfare of its kings, had reached a sophisticated level of civilisation, a thing for which the rough Romans to all appearances cared little. Conquest was what they were good at and it was to be their métier for the next four hundred years or more as they tried to push the border of their Empire eastward to the Euphrates and beyond.

CULTURAL CROSS-FERTILISATION

At the same time, as the poet Horace famously remarked, *Graecia capta ferum victorem cepit*, Captive Greece took her fierce conqueror captive: Romans recognised the cultural achievements of their subject Greeks and Roman poets and artists began to engage in systematic imitation of Greek literature, art and architecture. The story of Roman rule in Asia Minor and the other lands of the East is in large part the story of the interplay between Roman methods of military rule, civic government and administration, and Greek and Near Eastern artistic and philosophical brilliance, allied to the heterogeneous religious traditions of Greeks, Jews and Syrians. Cities sprang up all over the eastern Empire which built on Greek forms and models to produce a distinctive Roman-provincial city architecture; literature was written in Greek and Latin and Hebrew; religious cults and revelations interacted to produce new syntheses, one of the most lasting of which was Christianity, whose earliest roots were put down in Asia Minor.

However, it was not just the Hellenistic Greek world which found itself brushing up roughly against Rome. Rome's *Drang nach Osten* brought her immediately into conflict with two kingdoms further east, Pontus and Armenia.

Pontus

The centre of the kingdom of Pontus stretched inland from the Black Sea coast between the rivers Halys (Kızılırmak) and Iris (Yeşilırmak), a mountainous region with fertile coastal plains favourable to olives, nuts, grain and pasture. The kingdom had been founded, according to local tradition, in 337/6 by the first of six kings named Mithridates.

Mithridates was a Persian noble who claimed descent from Darius the Great; it was his successor, Mithridates the Founder (302–266), who established the capital at Amaseia (Amasya). The administration continued the Iranian structures that had been in force under the Persian Empire, with a feudal nobility and a population partly tribal, partly living in villages, groups of which focused around large temple complexes.

MITHRIDATIC WARS

Mithridates and his successors involved themselves in western politics, sometimes as allies and sometimes as opponents of the Seleucid kings and of Rome. Mithridates V Euergetes assisted Rome in her final struggle against Carthage in 149–6, and gained control of Galatia and Cappadocia; but his successor Mithridates VI Eupator, known as 'the Great' (120–63), came into conflict with Rome when he tried to annex the neighbouring kingdom of Bithynia, as well as Cappadocia under its king Ariarathes. The king of Bithynia, Nicomedes IV, was restored to power by Rome (90–89), to whom he was heavily in debt. Rome urged an invasion of Pontus to acquire resources to meet the debt, and thus began Rome's First Mithridatic War.

Mithridates invaded western Asia Minor, where he was not unwelcome as a deliverer from the exactions of Roman governors, who in this period were acquisitive and unscrupulous. Mithridates modelled his image, and his coin-portraits, on those of Alexander the Great, posing in this way as a liberator of the Greeks. He is said by the Roman encyclopaedist Pliny the Elder to have been able to speak twenty-two languages, the number spoken in his dominions. A peace treaty in 85, negotiated by the Roman general (and later dictator) Sulla, by which Mithridates gave up all conquered territory, did not deter Sulla's lieutenant Murena from initiating a second war against Mithridates in 81. In 74 Rome annexed Bithynia; Mithridates took the Bithynian side and found himself at war for the third time with Rome. Expelled from Pontus by Lucullus, he was decisively defeated at Nicopolis by Pompey and took refuge with the king of Armenia in 72. On Lucullus' defeat of Armenia in 69 (see below), his intention to commit suicide was thwarted by the fact that he had spent much of his life making himself immune to poison by the use of prophylactics, testing every known poison and its supposed antidotes on a plentiful succession of condemned criminals, and concocting a general 'antidote to everything'. So he had himself stabbed by a guard.

Pontus had thus become the property of Rome, and was made part of the Roman province of Bithynia-and-Pontus. Mithridates' notebooks on poisons also became the property of Rome and in due course came into the hands of the greatest doctor of antiquity, Galen.

Armenia

Armenia, lying further to the east in high mountainous territory around Lake Van, remained a thorn in Rome's flesh for far longer than Pontus. The Armenian kingdom which Rome encountered had been founded in 188 in the wake of the Treaty of Apamea which had divested Antiochus the Great of his possessions in Asia Minor. Artashes overthrew the reigning dynasty of the Orontids (sons of Ervand) and established the third Armenian kingdom under the Artaxiad dynasty. This for the first time brought all the Armenian cantons under a single ruler, whose kingdom stretched from the Euphrates to the Caspian Sea and Lake Urmia. The new kingdom was celebrated with the building of a new capital of Artashat (Artaxata, in the region of modern Yerevan), and classical writers record a tradition that the supervision of the building was undertaken by Hannibal after his flight from his Roman conquerors in 185 to the friendly court of Armenia.

TIGRAN I

In the first century Tigran I (or possibly II), whom the Romans called Tigranes, 'the Great' (95–55), became a formidable power in the region. He entered into alliance with Mithridates VI of Pontus and invaded Cappadocia in 93, but was driven back by Sulla in 92. He now turned his attention eastwards and began a series of campaigns against the Parthian king Mithridates II, annexing teritory as far afield as northern Mesopotamia and as far south as Syria and northern Palestine. He then built a new southern capital of Tigranocerta, probably at Farkin in the region of modern Silvan north-west of

Diyarbakır. To populate the city he moved, according to Appian, 300,000 inhabitants from Cappadocia and Cilicia alone, as well as the inhabitants of twelve Greek cities and a large number of Jews from Palestine. Tigranes set out to make his new capital a cultural centre, inviting Greek intellectuals to come and lend it lustre, as well as adorning it with the usual hunting parks and extensive mercantile quarters.

In 69 Tigranes was attacked by the Roman general Lucullus on the grounds that he was sheltering the defeated Mithridates of Pontus. A decisive Armenian defeat at Tigranocerta was aborted by Lucullus' sudden recall to Rome, but in 66 Pompey returned to finish the job and Tigranes became a Roman vassal.

Armenia remained however a famously unreliable ally of Rome. In 53 M. Crassus marched against Parthia. Tigranes' successor, Artavasdes II (55–34), offered alliance, but when Crassus spurned his advice to march via Armenia, Artavasdes took the Parthian side, and when Crassus was defeated at Carrhae (Harran), his head was brought to Artaxata and made a stage property in a performance of Euripides' *Bacchae* which was being staged to celebrate the marriage of the sister of Artavasdes to the son of the Parthian king. (D.M. Lang states that Artavasdes, an author himself of several Greek dramas, inherited his theatrical interests from his father Tigranes, 'father of the Armenian National Theatre'. Rarely has a theatrical tradition got off to such a striking start.)

ROMAN KING-MAKING

In 36 Mark Antony captured Artavasdes and inaugurated 200 years of Roman king-making in Armenia. In 1 BC the last Artaxiad king was removed by Augustus' grandson Caius Caesar. A series of Georgian intrigues led to the establishment of a new dynasty, the Arsacids, in AD 53. The first king, Tiridates I, was promptly attacked by Nero's general Corbulo, who captured Artaxata in 58 but failed to hold the kingdom. Nero then invited Tiridates to Rome and himself placed the Armenian crown on his head in 66.

Armenia, though it maintained an Iranian orientation in religion and culture, now fulfilled the role of a docile buffer state between Parthia and Rome. A series of Roman wars against Parthia in the second century AD, in which Armenia was constantly involved, achieved little for either side. Artaxata was repeatedly razed, but the summer palace at Garni rose up, like so many cities in this period, on a Roman plan. (It is now in Soviet Armenia.) Roman power thus made its impact even where it did not achieve decisive conquest.

Commagene

Another semi-Iranian kingdom was that of Commagene, which had gained its independence from the Seleucids in 162 BC. Its kings adhered to a hellenised version of the Zoroastrian religion of Persia. The most memorable of the kings was Antiochus I, builder of the vast monument that crowns Nemrut Dağı, incorporating colossal figures of the king, Zeus, Mithras and other deities. Antiochus surrendered to Pompey in 64 BC and Rome controlled the succession of the kings thereafter. The last king was Antiochus IV (AD 38–72). In AD 72 he was accused of seeking an alliance with the Parthian king and was deposed by the emperor Vespasian: his kingdom was annexed to the Roman province of Syria.

The monument of Antiochus I of Commagene at Nemrut Dağı

The Greek Cities of Asia Minor

The regions of western Asia Minor were incorporated with less difficulty into the Roman Empire. The kingdom of Attalus which he bequeathed to Rome in 133 BC became the province of Asia, which incorporated all the coastal regions as far south as Caria; on the north it was bounded at first by Bithynia, on the south by Lycia and on the east by Galatia. Lycia was annexed and incorporated into Asia in 84 BC; Bithynia was annexed in 74 BC; and Amyntas' kingdom of Galatia was annexed in 25 BC. The distinctive feature of Asia as a province was its division into numerous Greek city-territories or *poleis*. Rome established nine administrative and judicial divisions of the province, and a *koinon* or common council of the Greek cities was established. The *koinon* had the power to prosecute greedy Roman procurators, but with the establishment of the Principate (as the period of rule by an emperor, not by a republic, is called) their main function came to be the administration of the imperial cult. Asia was one of the 'senatorial' provinces, where the emperor did not have direct control through legates; but such events as the establishment of an imperial post (at the cities' expense) showed who wielded the overall power. Some of the cities retained a nominal autonomy, as they had had under the Attalids.

CONSPICUOUS EXPENDITURE

As the rapacity of the Republic gave place to the more self-disciplined administration of the Principate, established by the first Roman emperor, Augustus, in 31 BC, these Greek cities profited mightily from Roman rule. Political independence became a shadow, but that did not stop the upper classes of these cities from vying with one another for political position in the internal affairs of the cities. To a considerable extent such political power was wielded by conspicuous expenditure, a procedure whose technical name is *euergetism* (from the Greek for benefaction). City aristocrats would expend vast sums on such public services as games and shows, temples and other public buildings, as well as less glamorous benefits such as aqueducts and street lighting. From the reign of Augustus onwards we begin to hear of mysterious figures called the Asiarchs ('Rulers of Asia'): they have been supposed identical with the priests of Asia who presided over the *koinon*, but it appears more probable that Asiarch was an honorific title to be gained by precisely such acts of public benefaction. They certainly included many of the top men of the province, whom St Paul, for example, was careful to note among his acquaintance.

It is to such men that we owe the quantity of magnificent cities whose splendour, even in ruin, remains one of the chief attractions of Western Turkey to the historically minded tourist. The benefactions of the emperor Hadrian, who toured most of his empire in AD 123–4 and 129–131, and of Marcus Aurelius, who did the same in 176, also played their part in this development. This is not the place to enter individually into the histories of such cities as Pergamum, Ephesus, Miletus, Smyrna, Sardis, Mylasa, Tralles, Aphrodisias, Hierapolis, Phaselis and Aspendus, though each of them has its own notable achievements. From the point of view of the impact of Rome it is however instructive to consider their similarities.

CITY PLANNING

The form of the Roman city shows a remarkable degree of consistency from one end of the Empire to the other. The conservative architect Vitruvius (writing in the early first century, before most of the great imperial cities had been built) laid down precise rules for the choice of site, construction of walls, layout of street and disposition of public buildings within the city. Most cities did, over a period of a century or more, acquire a complete set of public buildings.

Vitruvius places first in the order of construction the layout of the streets in such a way as to minimise the harmful effects of prevailing winds; this would be followed by the layout of great public spaces such as the Forum or *Agora*. A modern authority on Roman architecture, William MacDonald, interprets Roman city planning in terms of 'armatures'. Cities are not planned on the rigorous grid-system popularised by Hippodamus of Miletus and exemplified in cities like Priene; neither do they follow the random arrangement of classical Greek public and sacred spaces as found in mainland Greece.

Public spaces in the Roman city are laid out in a harmonious diversity (the *Asclepieum* at Pergamum is a good example) and are linked by broad colonnaded streets which typically have a sharp bend near the central point of the city, a point marked by a monumental gateway or *tetrapylon* (gate with four columns) like those at Aphrodisias or in the Arcadiane at Ephesus.

In this armature are inserted the public buildings. Vitruvius has precise instructions on the placing of the temples to the different gods: Jupiter, Juno and Minerva (Zeus, Hera and Athena) on the highest point; Mercury (Hermes) in the Forum, to preside over trade and public intercourse; Apollo and Bacchus (Dionysus) near the theatre; Hercules (Heracles) near the circus or gymnasium; Venus (Aphrodite) at the harbour; Ceres (Demeter) 'outside the city in a place to which people need never go except for the purpose of sacrifice'. In addition, most cities in Asia Minor would have a major temple of their own presiding god. To consolidate their rule in the Greek cities the emperors, from Augustus onwards, had themselves declared gods and offered cult in a special temple in every city: for cities that were nominally independent, this was the most satisfactory way to incorporate acknowledgement of the emperor's superior authority over city institutions.

Besides temples, a Roman city would contain a gymnasium, baths, latrines, libraries, a theatre and probably also an *odeum*, a stadium (there is a magnificent one at Aphrodisias), and maybe an amphitheatre. The eastern provinces were less addicted than the western to the gladiatorial games and wild beast shows for which these were particularly designed, and the stadium could be used for such events in case of need, as it was for the burning of the martyr Polycarp at Smyrna in the mid-second century. Another form of public service might be the provision of such a service as a fire brigade; and it is revealing that Pliny, while governor of Bithynia in the early second century AD, wrote to the emperor Trajan about his anxiety that the establishment of such an institution at Nicomedia might be simply a cover for a political club.

CULTURAL LIFE

In visiting these Roman cities one gains the impression of a community life which was elevated by the application of fine building and attention to architectural detail, in even the humblest affairs of daily life. These are cities befitting and enhancing human dignity. The Greek cities maintained on this splendid architectural substructure a vigorous cultural life. Performances of the classics were staged in the theatres of Pergamum, Aspendus and Aphrodisias; fine book collections were assembled in the libraries of Pergamum, Ephesus and Nysa; a sculptural school of astounding accomplishment flourished at Aphrodisias from the reign of Augustus until the fifth century. The first and second centuries saw the rise of the travelling sophists or rhetors, who could pursue a career from city to city, giving displays of professional oratory which drew the crowds of Greeks – who always admired a good argument or piece of rhetoric – as much as any theatrical performance. The earliest of these was Dio of Prusa, known as Chrysostom (golden-mouthed) from his eloquence, who modelled his philosophical addresses on Plato and Xenophon, infusing them with Stoic content. His political speeches achieve a remarkable combination of Greek patriotism with allegiance to Roman rule. Another such was Aelius Aristides of Pergamum (*c.* 117–181), whose speeches included declamations on historical themes, prose hymns to the gods and political speeches (e.g. in praise of Rome) as well as discourses on religion. Aristides, a great hypochondriac, is remembered now mainly for his Sacred Teachings, an account of revelations made to him by the healing god Asclepius of Pergamum, which cast a remarkable light on pagan religious devotion.

GOLDEN AGE

Edward Gibbon was not altogether wrong to see the second century AD, the 'Golden Age of the Antonines', as a period of peace and prosperity for the eastern provinces, an age in which mercifully little happened to disturb this atmosphere of bourgeois comfort and artistic achievement. Needless to say, this did not last, and in the late second and third centuries Asia was troubled by a number of barbarian

invasions, which caused widespread devastation and economic collapse. The troubles of the third century made *euergetism*, and even the
expense of holding public office, less attractive, and the result was a
growing centralisation of political and military control on Rome. The
cities lost their significance.

But even in the earlier centuries there were some flies in the
ointment, one of the most significant of which was the impact of the
new religion of Christianity on Asia Minor.

Jews and Christians in Asia Minor

An important feature of the setting in which Christianity erupted was
the Jewish communities of Asia Minor. Many Jews had been settled
in the region in the years following 212 BC by Antiochus III, who had
transported them from Babylon to provide a pro-Seleucid presence
in his realm. Their numbers increased considerably during the second
century BC, and under Roman rule they continued to be allotted the
privileges that had been established under the Seleucids. Their
religious exclusivism brought them into conflict with the emperor's
requirement of universal allegiance to the imperial cult – Caligula had
affronted the Jews of Judaea to the point of rebellion by demanding
that his statue be placed in the temple at Jerusalem, while Philo of
Alexandria led a delegation of Jews to Caligula to protest against
similar incursions on the community in Alexandria – but Romans on
the whole respected a people who showed allegiance to an 'ancestral
religion', and in the reign of Claudius toleration was extended to Jews
throughout the Empire.

There were notable populations of Jews at Apamea and at Sardis,
where the synagogue is one of the showpieces of the Roman city,
cheek by jowl with both the gymnasium and the shopping centre.
Jewish religion proved attractive to many of the non-Jewish inhabitants of the region, and the discovery of a long inscription at
Aphrodisias has permitted the definition of a special class of *theosebeis*
or God-Worshippers, non-Jews who participated in Jewish ceremonies without, probably, undergoing the rite of circumcision. (The

Greeks, who exercised naked in the gymnasium, looked with scorn on a mutilated penis.)

PAUL OF TARSUS

The establishment of the Christian religion in Asia Minor in the first century AD was due to the extensive journeys of Paul of Tarsus. Though he is called the apostle of the Gentiles, he generally began his activities of conversion among the Jewish communities of the cities. Paul's journeys, which are described in the Acts of the Apostles, took him from Judaea via Cyprus to Antioch in Pisidia. This rather remarkable choice of itinerary can be explained by his having found

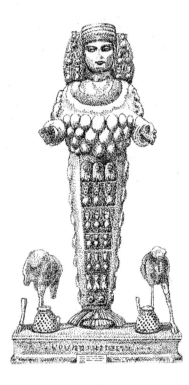

Artemis of Ephesus

favour with one of the notables of Paphos in Cyprus, who gave him an introduction to a relative who held an important position in Antioch. (One should not underestimate the extent of Paul's use, as a Roman citizen, of the inter-city aristocratic networks.) Here he and Barnabas preached first to the Jews and then to the Gentiles. Being driven out by the Jews, they went next to Iconium, where the pagans took them for gods in human form, while the Jews came and drove them out again. This pattern was repeated as Paul travelled westwards to northern Greece (where the Jews of Thessalonica again gave him a hostile reception), to Corinth, and finally to Ephesus, where in a famous episode it was the pagans, the silversmiths who made images of the goddess Artemis, who accused him of destroying their livelihood. Paul's Aegean period occupied approximately the years AD 53–58, and it was during this period that he wrote some of his most important epistles.

THE SEVEN CHURCHES

Christianity gradually took hold in Asia Minor, and led to the establishment of the Seven Churches referred to in the Revelation of John: Ephesus, Smyrna, Pergamum, Thyatira, Sardis, Philadelphia and Laodicea. Within a few years of their foundation these churches began to fall foul of the Roman establishment. The Roman historian Tacitus knew little of the Christians except that they originated in the troublesome province of Judaea and were conspicuous for their 'hatred of the human race'. Nero was able to blame them for the burning of Rome and to burn many of them in turn. Paul (Romans 13) urged Christians to accommodate themselves to the secular power; but Christians were disliked by the authorities because of their intransigence over participation in imperial cult. In addition many people believed the sort of charges that were contained in Celsus' work of *c.* AD 178, *Against the Christians*: that Christians habitually practised incest, that they engaged in indiscriminate ritual copulation, that they wrapped babies in pastry and sliced them up as a sacramental meal.

One of the first documents of trouble with Christians comes from

Pliny's dossier of letters to the Emperor Trajan when he was governor of Bithynia. He was uncertain

> whether it is the mere name of Christian which is punishable, even if innocent of crime, or rather the crimes associated with the name. . . . For the moment . . . if they persist, I order them to be led away for punishment; for, whatever the nature of their admission, I am convinced that their stubbornness and unshakeable obstinacy ought not to go unpunished. (Letters 10. 96)

Many governors had trouble with the 'obstinacy' of the Christians, who would not agree to place even a drop of incense on the altar of the emperor in order to be set free. Thus Christians came to be regarded as positively suicidal; Arrius Antoninus, governor of Asia in AD 183, asked a group in exasperation why, if they wanted to die, they could not hang themselves or jump off cliffs like anybody else.

CHRISTIAN PERSECUTION

Many Christians did none the less die appalling deaths by torture – dragging on sharp shells, being thrown to wild beasts, burning at the stake – at the hands of the Roman authorities. One of the first was the saintly Bishop Polycarp of Smyrna, whose burning body was alleged to have given off the sweet smell of incense. Official sanction was not always required for murdering Christians; the Jews of Smyrna joined in eagerly with the hounding of Polycarp. Paul's successor Bishop Timothy was said to have met his death at Ephesus through lynching at a carnival festival of an unidentified god.

In the face of such persecution, several important works of Christian apologetics came out of Asia Minor in the second century. The first of these was the *Apology* of Bishop Melito of Sardis, who intercepted the Emperor Marcus Aurelius on an eastern tour to deliver in person his plea for Christianity. Contemporary apologists, Irenaeus of Smyrna and Apollinaris of Hierapolis, also tried a conciliatory approach to Rome.

The last major persecution was that of Decius (249–251), to whose reign belongs the legend of the Seven Sleepers of Ephesus, who hid in a cave to escape the persecution, and woke up to find themselves living under the Christian Emperor Theodosius I.

THE FIRST CHRISTIAN KING

By the later second century Christianity was spreading more widely in Asia Minor. The first Christian king in history was Abgar VIII (176–213) of Edessa (modern Urfa), whose ancestor Abgar I was supposed to have maintained a correspondence with Jesus. The year 310 saw the conversion of Armenia as a result of the activities of Gregory the Illuminator. The latter was imprisoned by King Tiridates for preaching Christianity, but survived in a dungeon in Artaxata for fifteen years. Tiridates meanwhile was punished for his murder of a number of Christians by the divine infliction of a disease that made him grovel, like Nebuchadnezzar, on all fours like a beast. On his sister's advice he had Gregory released; the latter cured him and then baptised him. Gregory then experienced a vision of the Lord, who struck the earth with a golden hammer; a fiery golden column, topped by a cross, arose in the middle of Tiridates' capital of Vagharshapat, surrounded by other crosses on the spots where Tiridates' martyrs lay buried. These crosses formed an arch which became the base of a grand temple. When the vision was concluded, Gregory immediately began the construction of a church on the spot indicated in his vision, in the centre of Vagharshapat, which he now renamed as the holy city of Echmiadzin. From this time dates the history of the Christian church of Armenia.

In 324 the Roman Emperor Constantine was converted to Christianity, and in 325 at the Council of Nicaea (Iznik) it was proclaimed as the official religion of the Roman Empire. Five years later Constantine established his new capital of the Empire at Constantinople (formerly Byzantium), and the Byzantine Empire had begun.

Economic Conditions

These first centuries of Roman rule had been a period of prosperity for the cities. The perceived decline in standards of living in the third century was relative only to the enormous boom of the first and second centuries. Yet it is important to realise that this prosperity was very much a city phenomenon. In antiquity, cities were centres not of production but of consumption. They existed to provide an elegant ambience for the ruling élite and to administer the often oppressive collection of taxes from the peasantry. It was common for aristocratic landowners to live in the town and take part in civic life, visiting their estates only rarely and enjoying the fruits of their tenants' labour. The ruling class of the Roman Empire enriched itself at the expense of the producers.

In the third century the impoverishment of the entire empire, and the introduction of the poll-tax, had led to a flight from land. The Emperor Diocletian had responded to this reluctance to farm and pay taxes by making it illegal for the lower classes to pursue any occupation other than their father's. Peasants were thus unable to leave their farms, and became effectively tied to their smallholdings in a position closer to that of medieval serfs than of free peasants. In this state they came to be known as *coloni*, and the institution as the colonate. This ossified social and economic structure was inherited by the Byzantine Empire.

CHAPTER SEVEN

The Byzantine Empire, from the Foundation of Constantinople to the Battle of Manzikert, AD 330–1071

Constantine the Great and the Christianisation of the Empire

Constantine the Great's foundation of the city of Constantinople was the culmination of a career in which he had made himself sole ruler of the Roman world. Diocletian (284–305) had established the system of the Tetrarchy, with two senior rulers (Augusti) and two junior rulers (Caesars). After Diocletian's retirement the new tetrarchy had consisted of Galerius and Constantius. Though each had a Caesar, each also had a son who aspired to rule. Constantius' son Constantine defeated the son of the Caesar Maximin, Maxentius, at the Battle of the Milvian Bridge in 312. A new western Augustus, Licinius, defeated Maximin and was then defeated by Constantine in 324, so that the latter became sole ruler of the empire.

Constantine had been converted to Christianity, allegedly by a vision of the cross before the Battle of the Milvian Bridge, and set out to make the empire for the first time an explicitly Christian one, rather than simply practising toleration as his more recent predecessors had done. This adoption of Christianity marked a watershed in the history both of the empire and of that religion.

At the time of Constantine's reign the Church was racked with division over the Arian heresy. This was a doctrine proposed by Arius, presbyter of Alexandria, according to which Jesus Christ was not

89

Constantine the Great

consubstantial with the Father but was created by him for the specific purpose of the Incarnation. For this teaching Arius was excommunicated by a council of bishops; but his influence continued to grow. Riots took place over the distinction; graffiti execrated the rival theologies; and Arius' own popular songs enshrining his beliefs were whistled in the streets.

THE COUNCIL OF NICAEA

Constantine, to put an end to the dispute, called the first Council of the Church, the Council of Nicaea. This was held in the imperial palace at Nicaea (Iznik) from 20 May to 19 June 325. Constantine himself proposed the insertion in the draft statement of belief of the word *homoousios*, 'of the same substance', as a way of determining the relationship of the son to the father. Though this was in explicit contradiction of the Arian belief that the son was *homoiousios*, 'of like nature' with the Father, the theological debate over that letter iota sputtered on for another half century, until the second Ecumenical Council of Constantinople in 381 confirmed the Nicene Creed.

The Council of Nicaea also made explicit the relation of the emperor to the Church: he was head of the Church as well as head of the state. The administrative organisation of the church had already substantially taken shape, with its hierarchy closely modelled on that of the civil administration. Every city had its bishop, who was also the metropolitan of the province. Of the metropolitans, five – those of Rome, Constantinople, Alexandria, Antioch and Jerusalem – were pre-eminent, and by the fifth century were defined as patriarchs with jurisdiction over the other metropolitans in their areas. The clergy were exempt from taxation.

Constantinople

To mark the new beginning that his Christian Empire represented, Constantine founded a new imperial capital on the site of the ancient Greek colony of Byzantium. Named by him New Rome, it rapidly became known as Constantinople. The Emperor embarked on a programme of building and adornment designed to make it the first city of the empire.

He built a new land wall to encircle the city, some three kilometres to the west of the previous wall built by the Emperor Septimius Severus. This wall enclosed a city which, like the first Rome, was built on seven hills. He constructed the hippodrome and a forum, linked by the street known as the Mese (middle street), and a large public baths named after Zeuxippus. To adorn his city he imported statuary, columns and other works of art from all parts of the empire, but especially from Rome. The hippodrome was marked out with obelisks and other monuments including the serpent column from Delphi, and in the Forum of Constantine he erected a porphyry column

(*Çemberlitaş*) which was topped with an equestrian statue of the emperor wearing the radiate crown of the Sun god Helios. The Baths of Zeuxippus functioned as a gallery of pagan art. Christian tradition later claimed that Constantine imported these pagan works to be figures of fun for the citizens of the Christian city, but it is clear that Constantine was simply following the Roman tradition of ostentatious display. His Christianity was as yet only skin-deep (he was not in fact baptised until a few days before his death). Like every Greek city, Constantinople had its own protecting goddess or *Tyche*, whose image was carried through the hippodrome on every anniversary of the foundation of the city.

SERFDOM IN THE COUNTRY

While great men and churchmen debated the fate of the iota, and while the city populace of Constantinople enjoyed the bread dole and the partisanship of the chariot-racing factions, the peasantry of the countryside suffered a deep and significant change in their condition. The social changes imposed by Diocletian (see page 88) had tied the peasantry to the land in a condition of serfdom. Enormous inequalities began to emerge in the Byzantine Empire, with the wealthy *patroni* on the one hand dominating the lives of the ever poorer *coloni* on the other. In due course a class of landed magnates arose who vied constantly with the hierarchy of government in the capital for political power.

EMPEROR THEODOSIUS I

An important step in the Christianisation of the empire was taken by the Emperor Theodosius I who in 392 officially proscribed paganism, bringing to an end a thousand years of the Olympic Games, among other changes. Pagan temples began to fall into disrepair, aided by the vandalism of Christians. Festivals and ceremonies acquired a new Christian colour.

The death of Theodosius in 395 led to the final separation of the empires of East and West, as the empire was divided between his sons Arcadius and Honorius. Arcadius thus became the first Byzantine Emperor, while Honorius presided over the already moribund Empire of Rome. In the minds of the Byzantines, however, the empires were still a unity. The Greek-speaking inhabitants of the eastern empire continued to call themselves *Rhomaioi*, Romans; and indeed the modern Greek word for a certain kind of Greekness is *Rhomiosyni*, Romanness.

The Fifth Century

The next hundred years were occupied with battles against heresies on the one hand and with the threat from the Persian Empire in the east, and the Slav tribes on the Danube, on the other. The Nestorian heresy (which stressed Christ's human nature) was denounced at the Council of Ephesus in 431, and the Monophysite doctrine (that the Father and the Son have a single nature) at the Council of Chalcedon in 451. But Monophysitism, like Arianism before it, was the cause of constant riots and murders. In 481 the Emperor Zeno issued a decree, the *henotikon*, which stated the official view and led to a temporary cessation of hostilities. At the same time, the growing authority, and claims, of the Pope in Rome, were already leading to tension between the churches of east and west which resulted eventually in schism.

Monasticism began to emerge in the fourth century: the first anchorite had been Antony who retired to the Egyptian desert late in the third century. The fashion spread to Palestine and Syria, and in due course to Anatolia. The first convent in Constantinople was founded in the reign of Theodosius I by Isaac the Syrian, and some sixty years later a Roman named Studius founded the basilica of St John near the Golden Gate, to which he attached a small monastery. Further east, St Basil (329–79) established his retreat on the River Iris (Yeşilirmak), and instituted a monastic order which was followed by the monks who established themselves in the rock-cut hermitages of Cappadocia at Göreme.

Justinian

The reign of Justinian (527–565) is unusually well recorded for us in the writings of his court historian, Procopius. Procopius' works

include histories of his wars and accounts of the buildings Justinian
erected throughout the empire, as well as the dramatically different,
and highly scurrilous, *Secret History*, which finds some harsh thing to
say about the emperor to balance every favourable comment in his
other works. In large part this may be explained by the requirements
of the different genres in which Procopius was writing — official
military history or Suetonian scandal-mongering — but they add up
to an unusually complex, not to say contradictory, account of the
emperor.

SCANDAL AND RIOT

The scandal, though juicy, is of minor importance, and much of it
focusses on Justinian's choice as his wife in 525 of a former actress,
Theodora, who was reputed to perform nude shows in which she
sprinkled her pubic hair with grain and invited geese to come and
peck at the fragments. She and Justinian probably became acquainted
through their shared devotion to one of the two Circus Factions,
which had by now become important political associations in the
capital. Both were attached to the Blues (the other side were the
Greens, from the livery they wore in the chariot races).

It was the conflict of these two factions which led in January 532
to the Nika Riots. A brawl between the two sides had been quelled
on the emperor's orders by executions. This led to a major riot, as the
participants streamed through the city with shouts of '*nika!*' 'Victory!'
and set fire to most of the buildings along the Mese. The fires burnt
for five days, and Justinian had begun to contemplate flight when
Theodora urged him, like herself, to stand firm and act as emperor or
die. He summoned his general Belisarius, who put an end to the riot
with a slaughter in which, it was said, 30,000 people were killed.

RUIN AND REBUILDING

It was the ruin of his capital which gave Justinian the opportunity for
his great building programme which transformed the city. Before the
end of February work had begun on the Church of Haghia Sophia,
the Holy Wisdom, which stands today. This was the third church on
the site, the first having been built by Constantine's son Constantius,

Justinian dedicating his new
church of Haghia Sophia

and the second by Theodosius II. The present church of Aya Sofia (as it is now pronounced) is a landmark in the history of architecture and a monument to the Golden Age of Byzantine art and architecture. Its architects were Isidore of Miletus and Anthemius of Tralles. Its huge dome was the largest ever erected. Unfortunately its engineering was less than perfect, and in 558, weakened by earthquakes, it collapsed. Isidore was now dead and the younger Isidore was engaged to build a new, taller and more durable dome. Despite further earthquakes and repairs, the building we see today is essentially that of Justinian. The magic of that vast space and its glowing illumination can still take the breath away.

The interior of the church was covered with a mosaic of gold tesserae, spreading over an area calculated at some four acres, and a jewelled cross on a background of stars was spread across the dome.

Other churches built in Justinian's reign in Constantinople were the lovely little church of SS Sergius and Bacchus and that of Haghia Eirene. The new style was also represented in the Church of San Vitale at Ravenna with its unforgettable portrayals of the emperor and his empress, clad in their ceremonial robes and accompanied by the leading men of the court.

A COURT OF WRITERS

The cultural life of Justinian's reign was not confined to architecture. He was surrounded by a court of writers centred on the historian and epigrammatist Agathias. The chronicler John Malalas of Antioch and many others worked in Justinian's reign. A flourishing school of commentators on Aristotle was centred on the figure of John Philoponus. Romanus the Melodist, author of some of the most elaborate Christian hymns in the Greek language, was active in this period, as was the traveller Cosmas Indicopleustes, author of the *Christian Topography* which set out to prove that the world had the same shape and proportions as Moses' Ark of the Covenant.

One of Justinian's most important acts was the closure of the philosophic schools of Athens. The Christian schools of Constantinople, first established by Theodosius the Great, now had the educational ascendancy in the empire, and were an important force in the diffusion of Hellenic culture in Anatolia. But Justinian's most enduring achievement was the codification, carried out under his instructions, of the enormous body of Roman Law. This was enshrined in several works, including the Digest, a systematic compilation of excerpts from the earlier Roman jurists, carried out under the direction of the lawyer Tribonian, and the Institutes and Novellae (Justinian's own constitutions from 534 onwards).

MILITARY ENDEAVOUR

Justinian's reign was also a period of military achievement. His general Belisarius regained the western part of the empire, including North Africa, Italy and southern Spain, but fell victim to a jealous calumny of Theodora's which accused him of wishing to make himself emperor in place of his master. In fact his successes against the Goths had led them to seek the easy way to end their troubles, by offering him the Gothic throne, an honour he turned down. Belisarius was disgraced, removed from office, and his property confiscated. However, he was pardoned and partially restored to favour not long afterwards. The final victory against the Goths in Italy was achieved by his successor as general, the eighty-year-old eunuch, Narses. In 559 a Hunnish tribe, the Kotrigurs, invaded northern Greece and Thrace, approaching within twenty miles of the capital. Belisarius was given the command and drove them back. But in 562 the general was accused of joining a conspiracy against the now-ageing emperor's life: he was disgraced again and shorn of all his privileges. There is no contemporary evidence of the famous legend that he was blinded and reduced to beggary; in fact he was again restored to favour and died in tranquillity.

The emperor's last years were largely devoted to ecclesiastical affairs, notably the fifth Ecumenical Council of 5 May 553 which was devoted to the differences between the Patriarch and Pope Vigilius of Rome.

Heraclius and the Persian Threat

From the end of the reign of Justinian the Byzantine Empire took on the character of an empire under siege. Slav and Avar invasions from the north were followed by the rise of the power of the Bulgars north of the Danube, and their insistent pressure southward. But most crucial in the reign of Justinian and after was the Persian Empire.

The Sassanian Empire of Persia had been founded after a coup in the early third century. It had at once taken on a more aggressive character than that of the Parthians which it replaced. The Roman

Empire was nervous of the existence of this, the only major empire to threaten its borders, and deployed several legions to guard against it. In fact, though the Persians twice attacked Antioch in the 250s, they never succeeded in retaining any territory west of the Euphrates, which seemed to form a natural dividing line of the two empires. But in the sixth century clashes occurred because both empires took an interest in the regions around the headwaters of the Euphrates, between the Black and Caspian Seas. Armenia had been made part of the Byzantine Empire by the Emperor Maurice (582–602), but Lazica or Colchis, Iberia and Georgia fell under the Persian sphere of influence. Persian activities began in the reign of Justinian's father Justin as the regions were troubled by a brigand people called the Tzani. The king of the Lazes changed his allegiance from Persia to Byzantium, and the two empires clashed.

Justinian's first war ended with the conclusion in 532 of an 'Eternal peace' between Byzantium and the Persian king Chosroes Anushir-van, Khosrow of the Immortal Soul. Seven years later Chosroes, prompted by Armenia's rebellion against Roman control, began a second war, penetrating northern Syria and Commagene and finally laying siege to Edessa (Urfa) in 544. Despite attempts to make peace, the region remained an open sore and no lasting peace could be anticipated.

This was the situation inherited by the great emperor Heraclius (610–41). Early in his reign Syria, Palestine, Egypt and North Africa were lost to the Persians. These losses, combined with the rampaging of the Slavs and Avars through the northern empire, where they established agrarian hamlets under the walls of ruined cities, led to an economic crisis in the empire, since Egypt and North Africa were its main source of grain.

Heraclius' military solution was reorganisation. He divided Asia Minor into military administrative districts known as *themes*, the heads of which were *strategoi* (generals who wielded both military and civil authority). Heraclius then made peace with the Avars and in 622 began a brilliant campaign in the east against the Persians. But in 626 the Avars renounced their peace treaty and made common cause with the Persians in an attack on Constantinople itself. The Roman fleet succeeded in raising the siege, and in 627 Heraclius destroyed the Persian army at Nineveh, occupied the capital of Ctesiphon, and eliminated the Persian threat. All the Byzantine territory was restored.

The Rise of the Arabs

But already a new threat was looming to the south-east, with the rise of the Arabs under their leader Muhammad and his successors. As Gibbon wrote, 'in the last eight years of his reign Heraclius lost to the Arabs the same provinces which he had rescued from the Persians.'

As early as 647 the caliph Mu'awiya had penetrated Anatolia as far as Caesarea (Kayseri), and this was followed by the Arab seizure of Cyprus, several of the Greek islands and Cyzicus (Erdek). In 674 the Arabs laid siege to Constantinople, and were only driven off by the employment of the newly invented Greek fire, a kind of early version of napalm which was used to bombard and fire the ships and tents of the enemy. But this did not end the Arab threat, and fifty years later the Arabs were still making annual invasions of Anatolia. Their repulse from Constantinople in 718 was perhaps the decisive defeat which preserved the Byzantine Empire.

These military troubles were accompanied by demographic decline in the seventh century. The colonate had in practice disappeared, and had been replaced by a freer peasantry bound in a feudal relation to the landowners. The growth of immense landed estates in Central Anatolia led to the rise of a provincial magnate class who, over the next centuries, came into head-on conflict with the established ruling bureaucratic élite of Constantinople.

Many cities shrank or were abandoned in the course of the eighth century; the harbour at Ephesus had silted up by the ninth century, though a market on a reduced scale still took place there. A long period of decline set in which was only to be reversed in the eleventh century.

The Iconoclast Controversy

Such economic and military disasters did not reduce the enthusiasm of the old aristocracy and bureaucracy of the capital for argument over theological minutiae. The arguments over iota gave place in the eighth century to a controversy over the admissibility of images of Christ and the saints in Christian worship. There was a long tradition in the Roman east of reverence to aniconic images (blocks of stone and the like) as well as the well-known Jewish prohibition of graven images, followed now by the similar prohibition by Muhammad. This oriental suspicion of the image had its effect on Christian theology. The attack on images was begun by the Emperor Leo III, the Isaurian (717–41), who had risen to be emperor by his success as a soldier in pacifying the Arabs. The first step was taken in 726. Justinian's palace, the Chalke, which faced the east side of Haghia Sophia, had over its bronze doors a huge gold icon of Christ, one of the most prominent religious images in the city. Leo had this torn down. Riots followed, but Leo was not deterred, and four years later issued an edict against images.

Monasteries were ransacked, monks fled to the west with icons concealed in their clothing. Pope Gregory of Rome issued a public condemnation of iconoclasm. Many of the peasants, particularly those influenced by the Paulicians (who seem to have believed that Christ's body was incorruptible and the crucifixion had been a kind of conjuring trick), shared the peasant emperor's opposition to icons.

A church council at Nicaea in 787 restored icon-worship, but the controversy rumbled on for another hundred years. One need not be surprised that Byzantine art has little to show between the age of Justinian and the tenth century.

The Bulgars

The eighth century saw the emergence of a new enemy for Byzantium, the Bulgars, an Asiatic race originating from the lands around the Volga. In earlier centuries they had been ill-distinguished from the Huns, the short squat horse-riding people of the Steppes who so terrified the Romans. Gradually the Bulgars had settled in the region now known as Bulgaria, but their hunger for land brought them into conflict with the Byzantine Empire as early as the 490s. By 681 they had come south of the Danube. In 809 they captured the important Byzantine stronghold of Sardica, just three years after Harun al-Rashid had taken the southerly city of Tyana. It fell to the Emperor Nicephorus I to take the field against them.

PALACE POLITICS

Nicephorus had come to the throne as a consequence of what must be one of the most grisly series of events even in Byzantine history. (The narrative of this one event must serve to give a flavour of a form of palace politics that endured for a thousand years.) The Emperor Constantine V, who died on campaign against the Bulgars in 775, was succeeded by his brother Leo and then by his son Constantine VI, who came to the throne in 780 aged ten. Constantine's mother Irene, a woman of great determination, acted as regent. In 792 the two became co-emperors. Constantine's weakness of character, and his insistence on marrying his mistress, made him an embarrassment, and his mother had him deposed and ordered him to be blinded, a sentence carried out with such force that for a time it was thought the wounds might be mortal. Irene, however, despite reductions of taxes, failed to win support, being disliked both as a woman and as an iconodule (adherent of icons), and was exiled and replaced by the chief finance officer of the empire, Nicephorus.

Nicephorus attacked and destroyed the Bulgarian capital of Pliska, but on the return march his army was annihilated by the Bulgars. The Bulgar king or khan, Krum, had the emperor beheaded and his skull made into a drinking cup. Krum now began a fierce campaign against the Byzantine cities of the Black Sea coast, and in 813 encamped before the walls of Constantinople itself. The crisis was only averted by the sudden death of Krum in April 814. His successor, Omurtag, was willing to sign a thirty-year peace with the Byzantines. In practice peace was maintained for eighty years (until 894).

In the 860s the Byzantines and Bulgars found it practical to form an alliance aginst a new threat from the north-east, the Rus from the region of the Dnieper, who attacked Constantinople in 860. As a consequence of this alliance, Khan Boris of Bulgaria was baptised a Christian in 865.

The Ninth-Century Achievement

The ninth century, despite economic, territorial and demographic decline, the attacks of the Bulgars and the inroads of the Arabs, had seen some positive achievements. One significant feature was the rise of the border-lords or *akritai*, who controlled the marches between the Byzantine and Arab lands, and whose achievements were celebrated in a new genre of oral poetry which, while it is not Homer, is one of the most important flowerings of medieval Greek poetry. The cycles centre around the figure of Digenis Akritas, the 'twice-born border-lord', and his relations with the neighbouring emirs. While the poems as we have them date from a century or two later, they do convey a flavour of the troubles of life in eastern Anatolia in this uncertain period.

In the capital, the Patriarch Photius presided over a mini-Renaissance of letters and learning, including the compilation of his own encyclopaedia of classical Greek culture. Leo the Mathematician was the inventor of a number of useful devices including a telegraph system, and of some less useful ones such as the emperor's famous golden plane tree with realistic singing birds – the kind of quintessentially Byzantine 'artifice' celebrated by Yeats in his poems on Byzantium. Photius himself was an opponent of the zealots in the church, whose appeal to the Pope led to a schism (the 'Photian schism') between east and west in 867.

The Macedonian Dynasty

In 867 the Emperor Michael was murdered at the instigation of his groom, a Macedonian peasant named Basil, who the next day had himself proclaimed emperor. Basil founded a new dynasty which was to rule Byzantium for two centuries, in which the empire reached the height of its power. Its borders were extended to the Danube in the north and to Lake Van and Samosata (Samsat) in the east.

The period was dominated by the renewed attacks of the Bulgars (from 894). Attempts to reach an understanding with King Symeon were unsuccessful, and in 919 the commander of the fleet, Romanus

Lecapenus, the son of an Armenian peasant called (for some reason) Theophylact the Unbearable, staged a *coup d'état* and became regent, marrying his daughter Helena to the fourteen-year-old Emperor Constantine VII. Romanus' wars against the Bulgars were inconclusive, and Byzantium was saved by the sudden death of King Symeon in 927. Romanus could now concentrate on the reconquest of much of the east, the success of which led to a great increase in the power of the eastern provincial magnates who commanded the armies, and from whose ranks the next dynasty, the Comneni, was to arise.

Constantine VII spent his career as emperor without effective power, though he did accede to the throne for a few years after the death of Romanus in 944, only to be murdered in 959. Constantine, known as the Porphyrogenitus (born in the purple), devoted his long retirement to literary and scholarly activity, including works on Byzantine history, on the administration of the empire, and on the ceremonies of the Byzantine court, all of which are valuable sources of information for modern historians. All these works, though they appear academic studies of history and geography, were prepared as background material for the exercise of a power for which, in the end, he had little scope.

ARTISTIC RENAISSANCE

The tenth and eleventh centuries were a period of artistic Renaissance in the Byzantine Empire. Numerous churches were built. They are for the most part small, as befitted a state whose revenues were dwindling; but the style of mosaic decoration, as exemplified at churches such as that of Daphni near Athens, displays a classic strength and power. The period also saw the compilation of another great encyclopaedia of classical learning, the *Suda*. Constantine Cephalas compiled a large anthology of epigrams which is the basis of the Palatine Anthology of Greek poetry from the third century BC to the tenth AD. The poetry of Christopher of Mytilene is not negligible, and the history of Michael Psellus is one of the most readable of Byzantine histories. The lays of Digenis Akritas were also written down at this period.

On the religious scene, the major event was the final schism of the

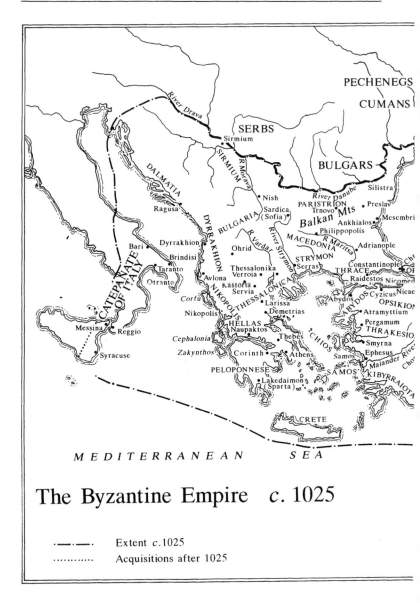

The Byzantine Empire   *c*. 1025

```
.—.—.        Extent c.1025
...........        Acquisitions after 1025
```

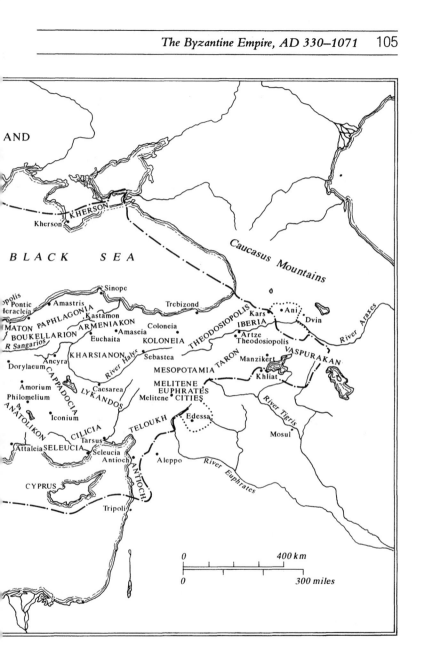

AND

KHERSON

Kherson

BLACK   SEA

Caucasus Mountains

opolis
Pontic
Ieracleia
• Amastris
• Sinope
Trebizond
PAPHLAGONIA
Kastamon
Kars
• Ani
Dvin
MATON
ARMENIAKON
Coloneia
THEODOSIOPOLIS
IBERIA
River Araxes
BOUKELLARION
Euchaita
• Amaseia
KOLONEIA
• Artze
Theodosiopolis
R Sangarios
KHARSIANON
River Halys
Sebastea
TARON
Manzikert
VASPURAKAN
Dorylaeum
• Ancyra
MESOPOTAMIA
Khliat
CAPPADOCIA
• Caesarea
MELITENE
• Amorium
LYKANDOS
Melitene
EUPHRATES
CITIES
River Tigris
Philomelium
ANATOLIKON
• Iconium
TELOUKH
• Edessa
Mosul
CILICIA
Tarsus
SELEUCIA
Seleucia
Attaleia
Antioch
ANTIOCH
Aleppo
River Euphrates
CYPRUS
Tripoli

0   400 km

0   300 miles

Orthodox and Catholic churches which took place in 1054. The differences were doctrinal, and were accentuated by the Patriarch's claim to authority over the churches of the Greeks in south Italy, which the Pope regarded as his domain. The Pope excommunicated the Patriarch as a heretic. The authority of the Patriarch was thereby immensely increased in the east, but diplomacy between east and west was made much more difficult.

The successors of Constantine had to contend again with the Bulgars. Notable successes were achieved by John Tzimisces in 971, but the final victory was due to Basil II, the Bulgar-Slayer. In 1014 he defeated the Bulgarian army decisively on the Strymon. Fifteen thousand prisoners were blinded on Basil's orders, every hundredth man being left with one eye in order to lead the rest back to the king. The king, Samuel, was so overwhelmed with horror when the remains of his army reached him at Prespa, that he died of shock. The Bulgarian state was destroyed and incorporated in the empire in 1018.

The Revival of Armenia

The Arab attacks of the seventh and eighth centuries had not only hammered at Byzantine control of the edges of the empire; they had loosened its grip on Armenia, where the Arabs established a limited control. The Armenians continued to dwell in their hills while the Arabs surrounded them in the valleys. Arab aggression resulted in the growth of a national consciousness for the first time since the days of Tiridates. Armenians had already reached prominent positions in Byzantine society, including more than one emperor (Basil I and his dynasty), and the partly-Armenian patriarch, Photius. At the same time, the energetic trading activity throughout the Arab dominions allowed the highland nobles to amass wealth and power. In the ninth and tenth centuries four dynasties emerged: the Bagratids in the Kars region and another line in Georgia; the Artsrunis east and south-east of Lake Van; and the Siounians of the regions south and east of Lake Sevan including Nagorno Karabakh (both part of the former Soviet Republic of Armenia). The Bagratids won the support of the Arabs by preying on their fear of the Artsrunis, and Ashot IV (806–26) won the title of 'Presiding Prince of Armenia.' Ashot's grandson Ashot V was High Constable from 856 and from 862 'Prince of Princes of Armenia, Georgia and Caucasus.' In 885 he took the title King of Kings and ruled as Ashot I of Armenia.

Though the caliphs showed the monarchs goodwill, there continued to be strife between the kings and the local emirs, culminating in the torture and death of King Smbat by Emir Yusuf in 914. Smbat's successors in the tenth century made Armenia a prosperous and powerful kingdom.

TREASURE AND PROSPERITY

It is from these dynasties that the great artistic treasures of Armenia date, the cathedral of Aghtamar built by Gagik II Artsruni (908–31) and that of Ani built by Gagik I Bagratuni (989–1019), as well as numerous castles. Aghtamar, like Ani cathedral, was based on a seventh-century model, but is adorned with friezes and bas-reliefs of exceptional richness, which portray both biblical scenes and scenes of the life of the Armenian kings.

The prosperity of Armenia was based on the fish of the lakes, horses and mules, timber, and mines of silver. The eleventh-century historian Aristakes of Lastivert is eloquent in his praises of the 'happy garden' of Armenia, with its happy citizens, its richly-clothed kings and the Christian piety of the people. To this age probably belongs the compilation of the heroic legends of the Armenians about David of Sassoun, first published in 1874. These heroic lays have a status in Armenian culture akin to that of Homer for the Greeks. The Christian 'Daredevils' mercilessly slaughter their heathen enemies; but, like the borderers of *Digenis Akritas*, they also interact both politically and socially with their Arab neighbours. The tales are probably very old, incorporating pre-Christian elements: for example, the name of the hero Meherr seems to be that of the Iranian god Mithras.

The later tenth century saw a diminution of Armenian power in the face of renewed Byzantine aggression, beginning with the annexation of the emirate of Malatya in 934 and the capture of Theodosiopolis (Erzurum) in 949. As the emirates collapsed Byzantine territory grew. Taron (around Muş) was acquired in 966. Basil II's

David and Goliath — relief from the cathedral at Aghtamar

defeat of the Bulgars was followed by an onslaught on Armenia (from 1021) which ended in the annexation of the Bagratid kingdom. Victorious Byzantium would have been in a position to advance on Syria and Iraq, but for the rise of a new enemy in the east, which in 1064 began to eat away at Armenia with the capture of Ani. These were the Turks.

The Rise of the Selcuk Turks

The Selcuk Turks were the first wave of the Turkic peoples who were eventually to make themselves masters of the Byzantine Empire and to give Asia Minor the name and ruling race it still has today. The Selcuks originated as one of twenty-four Oğuz tribes of Central Asia. The Oğuz may, like the Bulgars, be included under the general description of the Huns of late antiquity. Certainly Turks were known to Roman writers as early as the sixth century. By the tenth century the tribe tracing its ancestry to Selcuk had become established on the Lower Jaxartes. The Byzantines first noted their arrival in Armenia in 1016, where that always dubious region seemed as likely to throw its lot in with the Turks as to maintain its loyalty to Byzantium. In the 1040s the Selcuk leader Tuğrul Bey seized northern Persia, and quickly began to expand westwards into Armenia. In 1055 he marched on Baghdad and was accepted as his ruler and protector by the Caliph, who married Tuğrul's niece. In 1063 Tuğrul died and was succeeded by his nephew Alp Arslan.

Alp Arslan, though primarily concerned with the conquest of Herat, also turned his attention eastward, mounting a series of fierce raids on Armenia, followed by plundering raids on Antioch and Edessa (Urfa); in 1067 the Selcuks penetrated as far as Caesarea (Kayseri), and the following year Iconium (Konya). Soon they were at Chonae (Honaz), where the defenders, who had taken sanctuary in caverns close to the sanctuary of the Archangel Michael, were drowned in a flash flood. The disaster was taken as a divine sign, and the Byzantines awaited with trepidation the arrival of the Turks at Constantinople.

These ferocious horsemen were a new kind of enemy for the Byzantines, and the enlistment by the Emperor Romanus IV Diogenes of numerous mercenaries, including Pechenegs and even Turks, failed to halt them. In 1071 the two armies met at Manzikert in Armenia, and in a decisive battle the Byzantines were defeated, partly it seems due to the treachery of one of the generals, Andronicus Ducas, who retreated from the field, spreading panic in the Byzantine ranks. The emperor was captured, though he was later released. But the defeat had signalled the collapse of the empire. A civil war followed in which Romanus was blinded by Andronicus and Michael VII became emperor. More seriously, parts of the empire began to split away. Armenia took a separatist line; a new kingdom was founded in Cilicia by a Greek leader of the Armenians named Philaretus; while in the region of the Sangarius a Norman named Roussel established a short-lived kingdom of his own. Though these developments were impermanent, the last four centuries of Byzantium were dominated by the activities of the Selcuk, and later the Ottoman, Turks.

An Oğuz horseman

CHAPTER EIGHT

The Byzantine Empire and the Turks, 1071–1461

The Selcuk Empire

The Byzantines reacted with horror to the Selcuk conquest.

> The barbarians tread upon the boundaries of the empire of the Rhomaioi [wrote the historian Anna Comnena]. . . . Cities were obliterated, lands were plundered, and the whole land of the Rhomaioi was stained by the blood of Christians. . . . Terror reigned over all and they hastened to hide in the caves, forests, mountains and hills.

The picture is reinforced by another historian, Matthew of Edessa:

> Toward the beginning of the year 1079–80 famine desolated . . . the lands of the worshippers of the Cross, already ravaged by the ferocious and sanguinary Turkish hordes. Not one province remained protected from their devastation. Everywhere the Christians had been delivered to the sword or into bondage, interrupting thus the cultivation of the fields, so that bread was lacking. The farmers and workers had been massacred or led off into slavery, and famine extended its rigours to all places. Many provinces were depopulated; the Oriental nation [i.e. the Armenians] no longer existed, and the land of the Greeks was in ruins.

> (Both extracts cited from Vryonis 165, 172).

The successors of Alp Arslan rapidly secured control of most of Asia Minor, leaving to Byzantine rule only the Aegean regions and, later, a strip along the Black Sea coast which included the port of Trapezus (Trebizond, Trabzon). In 1078 they established a capital at Nicaea (Iznik) and by 1104 a secure Selcuk state was established. The Selcuk

Empire came to be known as the Sultanate of Rum (the land of the Romans, i.e. Byzantines).

The Sultanate of Rum

It has been suggested that much of the population welcomed the new Turkish rulers for the relief they brought from Byzantine taxation. From the quotations above it is clear that any such feelings can have been far from universal. Massacres, enslavements and forcible conversions were common. Churches were defaced and fell into decline from loss of revenue. The savagery of the imposition of Turkish rule continued for a century. Nevertheless, the Selcuks did bring some benefits to Asia Minor.

The establishment of a settled state with a permanent capital represented a marked change of lifestyle for the nomadic Turkish people. They set about ruling their empire, however, in an organised way. Provincial administration was in the hands of the emirs, military and civil commanders at once, while considerable power was wielded in the frontier provinces by the beys or leaders of the tribal groups.

MUSLIM BENEFITS

The Selcuks had been Muslims since the middle of the tenth century, and their social arrangements included such characteristically Muslim services as free hospitals, supported by the pursuit of medical learning. Educational institutions were also established. The advantages these offered will have played a part in the conversion of many of the Greek population to Islam, a process assisted by the confiscation of much of the church lands and the building of mosques and medreses (Islamic schools) as well as an active policy of conversion.

The thirteenth century was the high point of Selcuk civilisation in Asia Minor. The reigns of Keyhusrev I (1192–1210), Keykavus I (1210–19) and Keykobad I (1219–36), when the empire expanded to include (again) Antalya in the south and Sinop and Trabzon in the north, saw a flowering of military and artistic talent and the growth of a realm standing for civilised comforts of the kind celebrated by the contemporary Persian writer Omar Khayyam:

> —But come with old Khayyam and leave the lot
> Of Kaikobad and Kaikhosru forgot.

SELCUK ARCHITECTURE

Selcuk civilisation has left substantial traces in Turkey. The capital city of Konya contains a particularly fine collection of Selcuk buildings which exhibit the characteristic features of Selcuk architecture. This architecture was markedly influenced by the world of the tent. The simple, classical forms of Selcuk buildings, often octagonal or decagonal like the *türbe* of Kılıç Arslan II at Konya, seem to echo the design of tents; but their adornment represents something new in the art of the peninsula. Elaborate, formal decorations of abstract twirls and loops, most often carved in wood, but also made in stone or moulded in stucco, cover the exterior of many buildings, not only here but throughout Selcuk lands well into Iran. The roofs of mosques and other buildings are often supported by posts (like tents) which are similarly decorated. The interiors of buildings were decorated with tiles of glazed faience, which represent the first phase of development of the magnificent blue and white tiles which over the next centuries became a distinctive part of Turkish architecture. Mosques and medreses (theological schools) were commonly adorned with quotations from the Qur'an in Cufic script, inlaid in tiles or marble.

Whirling Dervishes

Konya was also the home of the mystic, philosopher and poet Celaleddin Rumi (1207–73). Rumi was the founder of the Mevlevis or Whirling Dervishes, one of the major dervish orders established during Selcuk rule. These mystics practise a distinctive form of fast rotation as a kind of dance to induce a religious trance. Many western observers have commented with fascination on these displays, which became widespread throughout the Ottoman Empire (another Mevlevi *tekke* or chapel was established in the Tower of the Winds in

Athens by the eighteenth century), and are still carried on in Konya itself, partly as a tourist spectacle.

THE ECONOMY

Selcuk rule reinvigorated the economy by the greater security it offered to agriculture and communications. Market gardening became widespread and represented an advance on the peasant subsistence economy. Perhaps an even more important contribution of the Selcuks to Anatolian life was the encouragement of trade. Roads were maintained and hans and caravanserais were established at convenient intervals along them; markets were set up in major towns, and there was even a system of shipping insurance to protect traders against pirates and brigands. In the early fourteenth century the Arab traveller Ibn Battutah described the division of towns such as Antalya into several quarters for the different races and religions – Muslims, Jews,

The Whirling Dervishes of Konya

and Christians — and the welcome that was extended equally to travellers of all nationalities.

All in all, the arrival of the Selcuks represented a sea-change in the culture of Anatolia. Many of the Greeks fled to the western regions, but others were absorbed into Turkish society and became Turkish-speakers (later known as Karamanlidhes, sing. Karamanlis). By the fifteenth century Asia Minor was almost entirely Turkish-speaking.

The Comneni

The inhabitants of Byzantium and its empire could hardly look on these developments other than with disfavour. In addition, Byzantium continued to be exposed to severe military threats from the north and north-west. When Alexius Comnenus (1081–1118), supported by the provincial aristocracies, established himself as ruler of Constantinople, he took control of a reduced and impoverished empire. His life is the subject of an almost hagiographic history by his niece, Anna Comnena, from whose pages emerges a portrait of an astute diplomat and successful conqueror. By 1118 Alexius had regained Trebizond as well as substantial other territories from the Selcuks.

The first threat he had to face was from the Normans under Robert Guiscard, who seized much of northern Greece in 1086 and had set their sights on Constantinople. Alexius secured the assistance of the Venetians by offering them the right to trade tax-free in the Byzantine Empire, a step which represented the beginning of Venice's maritime power.

Alexius tried to reform the military basis of the empire by grants of land for military service, a step which further enriched the wealthy landowning magnates, but provided the empire with a more reliable income from taxation.

The next threats came from two Turkic peoples, the Pechenegs (1091) and the Cumans (1094), followed by the Hungarians and the Serbs. Though all were quashed, Byzantium was weakened. The final century of the Comneni was dominated by the impact of the Crusades (see below), which resulted in immense losses of territory as the

Byzantine and Selcuk Asia Minor in the Eleventh and Twelfth Centuries

Boundary of the
Byzantine Empire
c. 1050

Crusaders established their own petty principalities, notably at Edessa and Antioch.

None the less, the Comnenian period was one of limited political and military revival, and also saw a notable output in the artistic field. Several new churches were built in Constantinople, and though all were destroyed in 1204, some idea of their style can be gained from the contemporary mosaic decorations of the cathedral of Cefalù and the Cappella Palatina at Palermo on Sicily, both probably carried out by Byzantine artists. In addition the period produced not only Anna Comnena, but one of the greatest historians of Constantinople, Nicetas Choniates (who wrote in the thirteenth century but described the events of the twelfth). Another important literary figure of the twelfth century was Eustathius, bishop of Thessalonica, who wrote a voluminous and often penetrating commentary on Homer as well as an account of the sack of Thessalonica by the Normans. Poetry was practised both by the so-called Theodore Prodromos, under whose name goes a substantial body of vernacular satirical writing, and by the scholar John Tzetzes, who also wrote long commentaries on Homer. Vernacular literature was represented by a remarkable revival of the novel, dormant since late antiquity.

The Cilician Kingdom of Armenia

After the Battle of Manzikert, the Byzantine Empire, as has been said, began to break apart. One of the most successful of the breakaway states was the Cilician kingdom of Armenia. Byzantine rulers had already resettled some Armenians in Cilicia in the first half of the eleventh century, and once Armenia had fallen to the Selcuks a Greek leader of the Armenians named Philaretus had established himself as ruler in Antioch, with a territory that incorporated Malatya, Maraş and Edessa. There were two main princely houses who began to vie for power, the House of Hethum led by Oşin and the House of Bagrat under Prince Ruben (1080–95). The latter founded a kingdom at the fort of Bardzrberd, while Oşin established himself at Lampron. Part of the Anti-Taurus was also held by Kogh Vasil (Basil the Robber). Gradually the Rubenids increased their territory at the expense of the

Hethumids. Ruben's son Constantine established his capital at Vahke and his daughter married the Crusader Count of Edessa. The kingdom was quick to establish trading relations with Genoa. As non-Orthodox Christians, the Armenians made common cause with the Crusader principality of Antioch against Byzantium, with whom they were engaged in a constant struggle for territory. The high point of the Cilician kingdom of Armenia was the reign of Levon the Magnificent (1185–1219) who was in effect a vassal of Bohemond III of Antioch. From his court in Sis he introduced systems of taxation and justice based on those of the Franks. Orphanages, hospitals and schools were founded, and the arts flourished; many of the Armenian castles (Anamur, Silifke) date from his reign.

In 1247 Hethum I the Great (1226–69) wisely submitted to the Mongols, actually visiting the Mongol court in Mongolia in 1253. Hethum won several victories against the Selcuks, gaining control of Silifke in 1263. However, the Mamluks were now gaining ground in the region: in 1260 they captured Damascus and by 1291 they controlled much of eastern Anatolia. In 1292 the Armenian city of Hromgla fell to the Mamluks, and a period of internal strife led to the collapse of the Cilician kingdom of Armenia.

MARCO POLO

An effective sketch of the kingdom at its height is given by the Venetian traveller Marco Polo (1254–1324) who visited the port of Lajazzo (Ayas) in 1271:

> The towns, fortified palaces, and castles are numerous. There is abundance of all necessaries of life, as well as of those things which contribute to its comfort. Game, both of beasts and birds, is in plenty. It must be said, however, that the air of the country is not remarkably healthy. In former times its gentry were esteemed expert and brave soldiers; but at the present day they are great drinkers, pusillanimous, and worthless. On the sea-coast there is a city named Laiassus, a place of considerable traffic. Its port is frequented by merchants from Venice, Genoa, and many other places, who trade in spiceries and rugs of different sorts, manufactures of silk, wool, and other rich commodities.

The Crusades and the Sack of Constantinople

The arrival of the First Crusade had introduced a new element into the Levantine balance, and the growing tension between the Byzantine Empire and the Crusader states was to lead to the greatest cataclysm Constantinople had yet suffered. The First Crusade, promoted by Pope Urban II to regain the Holy Places from the Turks for Christendom, was a cause that cut little ice with the Byzantines, though they were willing to join in with a movement that would re-establish their own political control of Asia Minor. The Crusaders defeated a Selcuk army at Dorylaeum in 1097, and in 1098 were at the gates of Antioch. The Byzantines had regained a number of cities, but their lands had also suffered from the passage of the motley army of the Crusaders. Bohemond the Norman established himself as prince of Antioch, while Edessa became the domain of Count Baldwin, and the Crusaders pushed on to capture Jerusalem in 1099.

Although the prince of Antioch nominally owed allegiance to the Byzantine emperor, both his principality and the Cilician kingdom of Armenia brought more trouble than reward to their lord. In 1138 the prince of Antioch renounced his allegiance to the empire, and this defection, combined with the constant threat from the Normans, preoccupied the Emperor Manuel I who came to the throne in 1143. Manuel seems to have dreamed of restoring the Roman Empire as Justinian had done, for in 1154 he launched a futile expedition to regain Italy from the Normans; in 1158 he marched against Cilicia and in 1159 made a formal entry into Antioch to proclaim the re-establishment of friendship with its prince.

THE SECOND CRUSADE

But in the meantime the Second Crusade had marched through Asia Minor (1146), and though the Byzantines had reluctantly allowed the Crusaders free passage to Antalya, they had caused considerable devastation in their disorderly progress.

In 1175 the Selcuk leader Kılıç Arslan was encouraged by Frederick Barbarossa, who was tired of the pressure placed on the Crusader States by Byzantium, to march against Constantinople. The armies met at

Myriokephalon, which became the scene of a Byzantine defeat (1176) almost as momentous as that of Manzikert a century before. In the ensuing weakness of Byzantium the various Balkan states finally left the empire, never to return. This debacle was followed by the Norman invasion of 1185, resulting in the sack of Thessalonica, the second city of the empire. The Norman army was however defeated before it reached Constantinople.

Meanwhile, in 1182, the governor of Cilicia, Andronicus Comnenus, marched through Asia Minor gathering the peasantry to his cause. When his forces arrived at Chalcedon, the resentment felt by the people of the empire against the Latins who were constantly marching through their territory and ruining them burst out in a massacre of the Latin population of Constantinople. In the wake of this the gates were thrown up and Andronicus welcomed as emperor. But Andronicus' populist and egalitarian policies were short-lived, for he was murdered in 1185.

THE THIRD CRUSADE

In 1187 the Third Crusade began its passage through Anatolia, having first taken Adrianople (Edirne) by force and caused great alarm in Constantinople. The Crusade was led by the German emperor, Frederick Barbarossa. The impact of this latest threat was somewhat diminished when Barbarossa was drowned while crossing the River Calycadnus at Silifke; but the successors of the Comneni, Isaac II and Alexius III, were unable to regain any territory, and a fourth crusade was already brewing, with the encouragment of the Doge of Venice who saw an opportunity to eliminate Byzantium, a major obstacle to her trading successes, for good.

THE SIEGE OF CONSTANTINOPLE

In 1201 the Fourth Crusade assembled at Venice, and the understanding was that they would take Constantinople before going on to the Holy Land. In 1203 they captured Galata, the suburb of Constantinople on the other side of the Golden Horn, and began to lay siege to the city.

The danger to the city led to the flight of Alexius III; Isaac was reinstated as emperor accompanied by his son Alexius IV. In January 1204 there was a a popular revolt, accompanied by a disastrous fire. Alexius IV was overthrown, and the statue of Athena by Phidias, which had once stood on the Athenian acropolis, was destroyed by the mob on the grounds that its outstretched hand seemed to be beckoning to the invaders. The new emperor was one of the sons-in-law of Alexius II, known as Murzuphlus (Bushy-Eyebrows), who now called himself Alexius V.

The replacement of the emperor and the destruction of the statue were alike unable to sustain the city. On 13 April the Crusaders breached the walls against the Golden Horn. The city had fallen.

The cruelty and lust of the invaders, wrote Gibbon, 'were moderated by the authority of the chiefs and feelings of the soldiers . . . but a free scope was allowed to their avarice, which was glutted, even in the holy week, by the pillage of Constantinople.' The city was stripped of its treasures, which if not stolen were wantonly destroyed. Bonfires were made with precious manuscripts, in which were melted the artistic treasures of a thousand years; jewels were ripped from the ecclesiastical plate; tombs were ripped open – even that of Justinian himself, according to Nicetas Choniates – and the sepulchral ornaments stolen.

The pretender Murzuphlus was captured and, as described by the chronicler Villehardouin, was taken to the top of the Column of Arcadius and made to leap down in the sight of all the people; 'every bone in his body was broken as soon as he reached the ground'.

Sir Steven Runciman has justly written:

> There never was a greater crime against humanity than the Fourth Crusade. Not only did it cause the destruction or dispersal of all the treasures of the past that Byzantium had devotedly stored, and the mortal wounding of a civilization that was still active and great; but it was also an act of gigantic political folly. . . . It upset the whole defence of Christendom.

The Crusaders gave up the idea of marching to the Holy Land. Satisfied with their prize, they crowned Count Baldwin of Flanders the first Latin Emperor of Constantinople. The Byzantine Empire was no more.

However, three successor states were quickly established under relatives of the last rulers of Byzantium: the Empire of Nicaea under Theodore Lascaris, from which the Byzantine Empire was in two generations to be restored; Michael Angelos established the Despotate of Epirus in northern Greece; and two grandsons of Andronicus I, Alexius and David Comnenus, established in the far corner of the Black Sea the Empire of Trebizond. Only the first and third concern us in this book.

The Last Empire of Constantinople

The half-century during which the emperor in exile declared his headquarters at Nicaea (Iznik) relied for its continuity with the preceding empire on the continuing authority of the Orthodox Church over the inhabitants of the region, including those who were now ruled by the Latins. The Venetians quickly signed a trading agreement with the new empire similar to that they had had with the old. However, the period was one of constant warfare between the Greeks and the Latins, in which the Emperor John III Vatatzes (1222–54) scored some notable victories. John's son and successor, Theodore II Lascaris was a scholar and has left a number of letters describing the conditions of the time (and bewailing the decline of the great Greek cities of the empire, such as Pergamum). He reigned only four years. The next emperor but one, Michael VIII Palaeologus, made Nicaea the dominant power in the region. In 1261 the Nicaeans recaptured Constantinople and Michael was crowned a second time in Haghia Sophia.

DECLINE OF THE SELCUKS

This reassertion of Byzantine power coincided with the gradual weakening of the Selcuk state. This was due primarily to the arrival in Anatolia of the Mongols under the successors of Genghis Khan. In 1241 the Mongols captured Erzurum and in 1242 they defeated a Selcuk army under Keyhusrev II (1236–46) at Kuzadağ. The destruction and wanton cruelty wreaked by the Mongols caused anarchy and famine in Anatolia. Turkoman uprisings in the east sacked

Selcuk cities, and in 1246 the sultan was strangled by a group of notables. Order of a kind was established by the Mongol leader Hulagu, and for the next thirty years the Selcuk sultans were puppets of the Mongol khan.

In eastern Anatolia the Mamluk dynasty of Egypt took advantage of the confusion brought by the Mongols to establish itself, in the process overthrowing the Crusader kingdoms, a process complete by 1291.

In 1276 Keyhusrev III (1264–83) conspired with the Mamluk leader Baybars and defeated the Mongols at Elibistan, recapturing the capital of Konya. But this was the last gasp of Selcuk power. Already Osman and his sons were making their presence felt in Byzantine lands, and soon their descendants, the Ottoman or Osmanlı Turks, were to eclipse completely the Selcuk state.

Michael VIII, now emperor in Constantinople, hastened to stabilise his political position by marrying his daughters (who were conveniently numerous) one each to the tsar of Bulgaria, the emperor of Trebizond, the despot of Epirus, the Mongol Khan and the ilkhan of Persia. He improved the defences of Constantinople and re-established trade with Genoa. Anxious to gain the support of western Europe, he actually tried to enter into discussions with the Pope on the reunification of the Catholic and Orthodox churches, but his approaches were not taken seriously. In 1281 Michael was excommunicated, and a new crusade which would have damaged Byzantium was only aborted by the episode of the Sicilian Vespers in 1282 which resulted in the collapse of the Crusade's leader, the Sicilian ruler Charles of Anjou.

The successors of Michael continued to involve themselves with the religious question, until at the Council of Florence in July 1439 an agreement on the Union of the Churches was finally reached. But by now it was of scarcely any political importance. The Byzantine Empire, weakening as a trading power with the rise of Genoa and Venice, and a victim of declining revenues due to economic problems, was only to last another fourteen years. The main reason for this was the rise of the Ottoman Turks, who by the 1420s had deprived Constantinople of all its territory other than the city itself, with inevitable loss of manpower and economic resources. But before we turn to the rise of the Turks we should say a word about the positive achievements of the last dynasty of Constantinople.

THE PALAEOLOGAN ACHIEVEMENT

Despite its economic weakness, Palaeologan Constantinople was the scene of a last tremendous flowering of art and scholarship. Between about 1315 and 1321 Theodore Metochites,a friend of the Emperor Andronicus II (1282–1328), was responsible for the rebuilding, restoration and decoration with frescoes and mosaics of one of the jewels of Byzantine architecture of any age, the Church of St John in Chora (in the Fields), otherwise known as the Kahriye Camii. The artists of this church, contemporaries of Giotto, whose work they almost certainly did not know, produced a new Byzantine style which is humanist without being realistic: it relies on modelling much more than the earlier linear styles, and carries an emotional charge as great as the awesome mosaics of the tenth century, though it speaks of human passions more than of the divine. Colouring is no longer chosen for symbolic purposes as in earlier art, but red horses and purple trees occur for the sake of harmony and emphasis. The churches of the Peribleptos and Pandanassa at Mistra in the Peloponnese also belong to this phase of Byzantine art.

Scholarship was hampered by the wholesale destruction of libraries by the Crusaders in 1204, but the emperors of the reduced empire took an interest in scholarship and literature: Manuel II was hailed by the scholar Demetrius Cydones as a living example of the Platonic 'philosopher-king'. Cydones made a translation of the works of Thomas Aquinas into Greek, while his contemporaries George Acropolites and Maximus Planudes were respectively responsible for the reconstruction of an education system in Constantinople and for the compilation of an immense anthology of Greek epigrams, among other scholarly work. Many Greeks had also fled to the west after 1204, and the trend continued; the arrival in Italy of such talented men as Manuel Chrysoloras (*c.* 1350–1415) introduced the west to Greek literature and language and was instrumental in the Renaissance of classical learning in western Europe. Byzantium had handed on the torch in the nick of time.

The Rise of the Ottoman Turks

During the twelfth and thirteenth centuries the court culture of the Selcuks, the first Turkish tribe to establish a settled state, had been counterbalanced by the nomadic culture of the Turkoman tribes who had established dynasties on their borders. These Turkomans were known as *gazis* or warriors of Islam. There were emirates of Aydın (centred at Izmir), of Saruhan (at Manisa) and of Karesi (at Balıkesir). In northern Phrygia a dynasty was established in 1280 by Osman (1288–1324). Osman claimed descent from Ertuğrul, the son of Süleyman Şah who had fled from northern Iran in the face of the Mongols in the early thirteenth century. In fact the tribe of Osman had probably arrived in the general westward movement of the Turkomans after the Battle of Manzikert. The tribe of Osman was known as the Osmanlıs, later westernised as 'Ottomans'.

Osman extended his rule eastward to the river Sakarya (ancient Sangarius), and westward to Mudanya (captured 1321) and Prusa (captured 1326) which became the Ottoman capital under the name of Bursa. In the early years of his reign he paid tribute to the Mongol ilkhans, but with the waning of Mongol influence and the decline of Selcuk power his descendants were able to establish the second stable Turkish state in Anatolia.

Osman's successor, Orhan Gazi (1324–59) made a series of rapid conquests of Byzantine territory, capturing in the 1330s the major cities of Nicaea (Iznik), Nicomedia (Izmit), Scutari (Üsküdar) and Karesi. In 1346 he captured the Black Sea coast north of Constantinople, and his daughter married the Emperor John VI Cantacuzene. He established a European base at Gallipoli and conducted raids into Thrace and against the Serbian Empire of Stephen Duşan.

MURAT I

The next sultan, Murat I (1360–89), conquered Thrace, Macedonia, Bulgaria and Serbia, routing the Serbs at a battle on the river Maritsa in 1364, and finally destroying their empire at the Battle of Kosovo in 1389 (also known as the Battle of the Blackbird Field). These rapid conquests in Europe were offset by tensions in the east, with the emirate of Sivas, the territory of the Turkoman nomad tribe of the Akkoyunlu (White Sheep) in eastern Anatolia and north-west Mesopotamia, and the kingdom of Karaman with its capital at Konya. His campaign against the latter was notable in two respects: first, as being the first use of Christian mercenary troops against a fellow-Moslem power, and secondly for being the first occasion on which cannon and muskets were used by the Turks.

At the end of Murat's reign it could fairly be said that the Ottoman Empire was established. To a large extent the Turks continued the administrative arrangements that had been put in place by the former Byzantine rulers. The fiefs remained intact as did the system of taxation. The court also borrowed many details of Byzantine ceremonial. Marriage with Greek princesses cemented the interaction of the two cultures.

ENERGY AND EFFICIENCY

Orhan instituted the army system that was to endure for centuries, taking over the Selcuk system of *devşirme*, i.e. the 'collecting' of Christian youths to be brought up as a slave army (*kapıkulları*) with exclusive loyalty to the sultan, as a counterweight to the power of the great nobles. He added a new force of infantry to the predominantly cavalry (*sipahi*) Turkoman army: this new force was known as the *Yeni Çeri*, westernised as 'Janissary'. A system of provinces or *sancaks* administered by *sancakbeys* took over the Byzantine fiefs or *pronoiai* under the name of *timars*. At the same time much captured land was established under religious trusts or *vakıf*, and the income used to establish baths, hotels and other amenities. The energy and efficiency of Turkish rule may well have come as a relief to the inhabitants of the increasingly demoralised Byzantine Empire.

These institutional changes were further developed by the next sultan, Bayezit I (1389–1403), known as *Yıldırım*, 'Thunderbolt', because of the speed with which he switched between his fields of operation in the west, against the Balkan powers, and in the east. In

1395 he laid siege to Constantinople in support of one rival claimant to the Byzantine throne against another, but as ever the walls proved impregnable. In 1397 he built the fortress of Anadolu Hısar on the Asiatic side of the Bosphorus, to control the sea-traffic and thus curtail Byzantine activity yet more severely.

TAMERLANE

Ottoman expansion was interrupted by the meteoric irruption of the Tatar leader Timur, known to the west as Tamerlane or Tamburlaine (1336–1405). Having come to the throne at Samarkand in 1369, he rapidly conquered Persia, Georgia and the Karakoyunlu (Black Sheep) Turkomans of northern Iran (1394). In 1402 the Tatar and Ottoman armies met near Ankara, and the Ottomans were defeated; Bayezit, as legend has it, was imprisoned by his conqueror in an iron cage and taken around with the conquering army. The death of Tamerlane in 1405 relieved Anatolia of the Tatar threat, which melted away, and after an interregnum the empire was reunited under Mehmet I (1413–21) and his successor Murat II (1421–51).

MEHMET THE CONQUEROR

The next sultan, Mehmet II (1451–81), known as *Fatih*, the Conqueror, was an ambitious man. He decided that he would establish himself as the leader of Islam by capturing Constantinople. Thus he would create a world empire and eliminate once for all the threat of Crusades from the west. His first act on his succession was to have all his brothers murdered to eliminate possible rivals, thus setting a precedent which was to become standard practice on the accession of a new sultan. He built the castle of Rumeli Hısar, facing Anadolu Hısar on the European side of the Bosphorus, in the space of barely a year. The stage was set for the momentous conquest.

In Constantinople, the people and the emperor watched his preparations with alarm. His predecessor, Murat, had been disposed to let Byzantium alone while he concentrated on the Balkans. Previous sieges of the city had been held at bay by its splendid walls and incomparable natural defences. But this time, everyone sensed that the empire was going to be fighting for its life.

The Conquest of Constantinople

In February 1453 the siege began. Some 7,000 defenders faced an Ottoman army of 60,000, including 10,000 janissaries. The Turks had 14 batteries of artillery including four cannons, one of which, the work of a Hungarian craftsman, was the largest gun yet built. The Emperor Constantine XI Palaeologus, who liked to call himself Dragaş or Dragases after his Serbian mother, had come to the throne in 1449. When Mehmet ascended the Turkish throne, he had sent urgent embassies to Italy to drum up support for a new crusade against the Turks, and to Venice with pleas for assistance. But to no avail. Byzantium was on its own.

Constantine XI, the last emperor of Constantinople

The Turkish forces were drawn up facing the land walls of the city. The tremendous impact of the guns caused damage which can still be seen on the tottering fortifications. But from the sea, Constantinople was protected by a boom fixed across the Golden Horn. When the ingenious Turks built a path over the hill of Galata to drag their ships into the Golden Horn above the boom, panic set in. Eventually, on 29 May 1453, the guns breached the walls near the gate of St Romanos and the Turks poured in. The emperor, according to tradition, threw away his finery, seized weapons and disappeared into the mêlée, to fall fighting to the death for the empire of which he was the last representative. His trampled body was never identified, and Greek legend has it that he still sleeps, like King Arthur, until the day when he shall wake to lead the Greeks back into their city.

The Turks poured through the city and made for the great church of Haghia Sophia to desecrate it. The Patriarch was celebrating mass, the legend runs, and as the Turks entered the priests and deacons disappeared into the walls, whence they, too, will re-emerge, when the city becomes Greek again.

The Empire of Trebizond

One last outpost of Byzantine civilisation survived the Ottoman conquest for a few brief years. This was the Empire of Trebizond, founded in the Black Sea region by the Comneni after the Latin conquest of 1204.

The Comneni were familiar with the region of north-east Asia Minor from which their family originated, and had family connections with the royal house of the Caucasian kingdom of Georgia. Trebizond had been an important city for many years, and was a natural choice of stronghold for the members of the deposed imperial family. Situated on the Black Sea with the Pontic Alps as its hinterland, the city was favourably placed for trade (it had been one of the major Greek colonies since its foundation in the eighth century BC) as well as for agriculture and horticulture.

The city became a vassal kingdom of the Selcuks and, with the arrival of the Mongols, depended for its existence on their favour, though their influence evaporated with the death of Hulagu in 1265.

The commercial success of Trebizond is reflected in the abundance of its coinage, which was widely used also in the neighbouring kingdom of Georgia. Many of the foreign trading nations had establishments there, the Genoese house being the first to be founded. In 1319 the empire signed a treaty with Venice also; arguments over trading terms were to continue with both these cities over two centuries, an indication of the increasing importance of western trade in the economy of Asia Minor.

PROSPERITY AND PEACE

The prosperity of the city was shown in the building works of the emperors; Alexius II built new walls in 1324, and in the great age of prosperity under Alexius III (1349–90) monasteries were founded – notably the refoundation of Soumela – both nearby and in distant Mount Athos. This period also saw the city exposed to attacks from the Turkmens and, from 1368, the Ottomans. In the fifteenth century the city was a broker of peace between the two major Turkmen nomadic tribes, the Karakoyunlu (Black Sheep) and Akkoyunlu (White Sheep), and managed to retain its independence during the invasion of Tamerlane (1402). The relations of the Greeks of Trebizond, and of the Georgians, with the Akkoyunlu, are the latest strand in the national epic of the Turks, the *Book of Dede Korkut*, which also incorporates tales dating from up to 700 years earlier concerning the Oğuz: its completion probably belongs to the late fourteenth or early fifteenth century.

The frequency of western travellers has preserved for us some vivid glimpses of Trapezuntine life. In 1404 Clavijo, the ambassador of Henry III of Castile, passed through Trebizond, and described the splendour of the reigning emperors, who 'wore tall hats surmounted by golden cords, on the top of which were cranes' feathers; and the hats were bound with the skins of martens.'

The cardinal and humanist, George Bessarion, was born at Trebizond in 1395, and composed a long encomium of his native city which dwells on the beauty and convenience of the landscape, the magnificence of the fortifications and buildings, and above all the palace, with its ceilings gilded and painted with flowers, its walls painted with portraits of the kings and with scenes of the creation of the world, and the church full of more paintings and rich dedications.

In the 1450s Trebizond, like the rest of the Greek states, became subject to attacks from the Ottomans. A siege which lasted a month ended ignominiously with the capitulation of the city. The last emperor, David, was put on board ship to Istanbul, and the empire of Trebizond was at an end.

CHAPTER NINE

The Ottoman Empire I: The Age of Expansion, 1453–1699

With the conquest of Constantinople, henceforth to be known as Istanbul, Anatolia became for the first time exclusively the land of the Turks. Though Turkey was but one part of the much larger Ottoman Empire which at its height stretched from the Balkans to Egypt, the land came now to be known to Westerners as Turkey.

Restoration and Reorganisation

Mehmet's first task on conquering Constantinople was to restore the decayed and neglected Byzantine city. Attention was given to the roads, aqueducts and sewers; the souk was constructed to encourage commerce; and the splendour of the new ruler was represented by the building of the Old Palace, the Topkapı Palace and the Mosque of Fatih Mehmet. The population of the city had declined in recent years, and one result of Mehmet's activities was to increase the number of its inhabitants, to about 100,000, of whom perhaps half were Muslims, a quarter Greeks, and the remainder Jews, Armenians and others. However, the city did not become the capital of the Ottoman Empire until the rule of Selim I (1512–20).

Mehmet had been quick to secure Greek support by appointing a new Patriarch, Gennadius Scholarius, and giving him civil as well as religious authority over his fellow-Greeks. Thus was created the characteristic Ottoman *millet* system of autonomous government. *Millet* means nation, and each national group in the Ottoman Empire was thus ruled by its own authorities under the overall command of the sultan. Religious authority was exercised by the *ulema*, or learned class.

THE DEVŞIRME

Millet rule by no means meant independence, however. The sultan as a Muslim took responsibility for what were known as his 'flock', the *rayas*. Though regarded as naturally inferior to the Muslims, the Christian subjects had certain important obligations. Most significant — and later, most resented — of these was the *devşirme*, literally 'collection', a system by which a certain number of boys were taken each year from Christian families and brought to the court to be brought up as Muslims and to form a slave army for the sultan. The most talented of these were educated in special military schools and

Mehmet II, the Conqueror

went on to become members of the élite corps of the Janissaries (*Yeniçeriler*). The *devşirme* was a system taken over from the Selcuks, and the Janissary-system had also been part of Ottoman rule from the beginnings. The Janissaries became an increasingly threatening power-broker in the empire, rising in number from 12,000 under Mehmet II to 40,000 under Süleyman the Magnificent, until their final abolition in 1826.

Trade Regeneration

Mehmet devoted energy to the economic regeneration of his new territories, with the establishment of industry, particularly in textiles, and with the opening of trade relations with the west: trading privileges were given to Venice and Genoa and thus established for the first time a channel for European ideas to enter the Ottoman lands. Mehmet also made the first attempt at solving that perennial problem of the Ottoman Empire, land reform. Landholdings were confiscated and given to Turkish *timar* holders who instead of salaries collected revenues direct from the peasants; in exchange they owed a duty to serve as cavalry officers (*sipahis*); if they failed in their duty the *timar* was forfeit, and in no case was it hereditary by right. A system of provincial administration was introduced, with the province (*vilayet*, governed by a *vali*) subdivided into regions (*sancaks,* governed by a *sancakbey*). Tax registers were compiled and new taxes introduced, notably the heavy burden of the poll-tax (*cizye*) on non-Muslims.

The revenues thus created were needed to finance the extensive wars of conquest of the rest of Mehmet's reign. These began with further forays into the Balkans, where Serbia was subdued with the exception of Belgrade, and the submission was finally obtained of George Scanderbeg in Albania and Vlad IV the Impaler, who became vassal prince of Wallachia. By 1460 Greece had come under the Ottoman sway. The conquest of Trebizond in 1461 led to an eleven-year battle to subdue the Turkoman tribe of the Akkoyunlu (the 'White Sheep'). In 1475 the Crimea was conquered, in 1478 Albania, and in 1479 the prolonged siege of Rhodes resulted in the conquest of that island.

The wars continued under the successors of Mehmet, Bayezit II and Selim I. The reign of the latter saw the construction of shipyards on the Golden Horn, as a result of which Turkey became for the first time a major sea power. At the same time Selim devoted some attention to cultural matters by building a school in Galata. The cultural impetus reached its apogee under his son and successor, Süleyman the Magnificent, known to the Turks as *Kanuni*, the Lawgiver.

Süleyman the Magnificent

Süleyman the Magnificent (1520–66) came to the throne unopposed because of the custom instituted by his father of killing all rivals to the throne: Selim had put to death his four brothers, all his nephews, and all his sons except Süleyman.

Süleyman became a byword in the west for the opulence of his court and the splendour of his public festivals: the celebration of the circumcision of his five sons lasted for three weeks of carnival. Every day the sultan wore a new outfit, and never wore the same one twice: he dined off gold and fine porcelain. The dress of his courtiers became more ostentatious and fantastic, and was vividly evoked by the Fleming Ogier Ghiselin de Busbecq, the envoy of the Emperor Charles V to the Ottoman court, who described

> the immense crowd of turbanned heads, wrapped in countless folds of the whitest silk and bright raiment of every kind and hue, and everywhere the brilliance of gold, silver, purple, silk and satin.

Such ostentation naturally impressed the western nations with whom the Ottomans were in increasing diplomatic contact, as well as the ambassadors from Persia who gave no ground to the Ottomans in their own opulence of attire.

AN ARTISTIC GOLDEN AGE

In the reign of Süleyman the arts flourished. In the visual arts the most striking feature is the large number of manuscripts adorned with brilliant miniatures. The earliest Ottoman illustrated manuscript is a

Süleyman the Magnificent

copy of the romantic poem *Hüsrev and Shirin*, dating from 1499. The style of illustration is derived directly from the Persian tradition, but is more gaudy. Silver and gold is used in abundance, while the colour-palette is narrower but the hues stronger. The strength and brightness of Turkish painting as against the Persian is closely analogous to the difference in pattern and colouring between the carpets of the two peoples, where Turkey has strong geometric patterns while Persia is prone to use more delicate, fluid and often floral designs. Both Turks and Persians paid no attention to the Islamic prohibition on the representation of the human form, and in addition to the manuscript illustrations there was a flourishing Turkish school of portrait painting. Action was central to Turkish art, in contradistinction to the more contemplative scenes of Persia.

Few Turkish painters are household names: among the most important of the later sixteenth century are Sun'i, Reis Haydar 'Nigari', the painter of a well-known portrait of Khaireddin Barbarossa as well as one of Süleyman himself, and the Persians Şahkulu and Velican. The illustrated manuscripts contain texts of works of history, such as the *Şahinşahname* and the Persian legendary *Şahname*, of poetry and of sciences such as divination and astrology. In this connection it is worth mentioning Piri Reis, the author of one of the earliest maps of the Atlantic Ocean and its coasts (made in 1513), as well as the numerous illustrated town plans included in historical books.

POETS AND VERSE

Poetry in this period continued the Selcuk traditions of divan poetry and poetry sung to the accompaniment of the *saz*, of which the most famous representative is the thirteenth-century Yunus Emre. In the sixteenth century a mastery of versification lent the mystical poetry of Baki a classic quality. At the same time the dervish orders produced popular poets such as Pir Sultan, who was eventually executed for rebellion, while wandering troubadours (*aşıks*) performed both short poems and epics to the accompaniment of simple instruments: this tradition was still alive in the early years of the twentieth century.

The most permanent monument of the magnificence of Süleyman's reign is in the work of the master architect Sinan.

SINAN, THE MASTER ARCHITECT

Sinan (*c.* 1491–1588) was born of Christian parents in Karamania and taken into the sultan's service as part of the annual *devşirme*. After experience in the Janissaries as a military engineer he was appointed Süleyman's chief architect (*c.* 1538). The official record states that Sinan built, throughout the empire, 81 large mosques (including 42 in Istanbul), as well as 55 medreses (theological schools), 32 palaces, 22 public baths and numerous other structures to a grand total of 323. Eighty-four of his buildings still stand in Istanbul, including, besides the Süleymaniye mosque, the Şehzade Camii (1544–8), Kara Ahmet

Paşa Camii (1555), Kılıc Ali Paşa Camii (1571–2), and Sinan Paşa Camii (1556), a copy of an older mosque in Edirne. The most important characteristic of Sinan's mosques is the incorporation of the lessons and the forms of the church of Haghia Sophia in structures which nevertheless breathe the spirit of Islam and serve its particular purposes. The four-square domed plan associated with so many Turkish mosques is the legacy of Sinan.

THE GRAND VIZIER

The reign of Süleyman saw the rise to importance of the grand vizier, the head of the government administration in what westerners knew as the Sublime Porte (Bab-i Ali), part of the Topkapı Palace complex.

Mosque of Sultan Selim II at Edirne, by Sinan

Süleyman's first grand vizier, Ibrahim Paşa, had married a daughter of Selim I and used his position to advance his power. After Ibrahim was strangled in 1536 – the sultan regarding his growing power and the adherence of the *devşirme* men as a threat to his own supremacy – his successor was Lütfi Paşa, who was closely associated with the composition of the Kanunname (1539–41), a comprehensive code of justice and finance, for which Süleyman is best remembered among the Turks. In 1543–8 a further Kanunname (the word means law book) was devoted to the organisation of the *ulema* (Muslim clergy) and to frontier administration.

War and Conquest

Concurrently with these domestic developments, Süleyman was engaged in several wars, both against rebels in Anatolia and against Hungary (from 1526) and Mesopotamia (conquered 1533). The rise of the Hapsburg Empire provided the sultan for the first time with an opponent of comparable weight. The conquest of Belgrade (1521) and of Rhodes (1522) gave the Turks beach-heads by both land and sea for advances in Europe. The Ottomans extended fingers further and further west, and their sea power became a formidable threat under the corsair leader Haireddin Barbarossa, a renegade Greek from Mytilene who, with his brother Horuk, established naval supremacy in the Aegean and harassed shipping in other parts of the Mediterranean. Their power damaged the trading supremacy of Venice, which in 1540 had to sign a humiliating peace surrendering its holdings in Greece, but received a confirmation of its trading privileges. Similar privileges, however, now known as Capitulations, were extended to the French, so that Venice lost its monopoly.

The magnificence of Süleyman also had its down side, in the financial burden placed on the empire. The population of the empire had rapidly doubled to about 22 million, resulting in rural overpopulation and a flight to the cities where unemployment became a problem. Food was short, prices rose. Taxes were raised and there was unrest throughout Anatolia, a situation to which the government responded by the placing of Janissary garrisons and increased police activity. In Rumeli (northern Greece) there was a rising by a pretender known as the Second False Mustafa (the first had been a claimant to be son of Bayezit I, executed in 1423). Süleyman's own sons engaged in a war which left the survivor, Selim, as the sultan's official heir.

INTERNAL DIVISIONS

The empire inherited by Selim II (1566–74), known as the Sot, was one which was increasingly divided internally as a result of the immense power wielded by the *devşirme* class and its own internal politicking. Few rulers arose of the calibre of Mehmet II or Süleyman, and they always ran the danger of being figureheads or puppets manipulated by the grand vizier. 'The heade beinge soe longe sicke hath weakened all the members,' wrote Sir Thomas Sherley, a member of the important English diplomatic family who was in Istanbul around 1600. The harem became an important centre of intrigues. In addition, much of the sultan's energy was diverted into its pleasures so that he had a less effective role in government; while his sons, his heirs apparent, were also immured in the harem – in the so-called 'cage'– so that they acquired no instruction in the arts of government or experience of the wider world, and were less and less fitted to rule when one of them did accede. In addition, the quasi-feudal structure of the empire was ill-equipped to compete on equal terms with the rising nation-states of Europe and their mercantilist expansion.

The Janissary corps became corrupted, partly because the abandonment of celibacy left its career open to the members' sons, who were free Muslims. Its ranks swelled to some 200,000 by the mid-seventeenth century, and most of them avoided military service and simply drew pay while pursuing trades or crafts of their own. In the further reaches of the empire the Janisasries became virtual local rulers. The dead weight and reactionary nature of this group had a major impact on the decline and inertia of the Turkish government.

Inflation affected the *timar* holders and they did their best to avoid their military obligations: so the number of *sipahis* also declined, leading to a loss of fighting strength. None the less, the Turkish army continued to be greatly feared in Europe.

THE BATTLE OF LEPANTO

The Ottoman Empire remained, for western Europe, a fearsome and alien power, constantly threatening to overrun Europe and institute Muslim rule over the Christian nations. The siege of Malta in 1565 had been followed by the brutal conquest of Venetian-held Cyprus in 1570, at the conclusion of which the Venetian commander Bragadino had been captured by the Turks, flayed alive, and his skin, stuffed with straw, paraded through the streets of Famagusta. Such horrors gave the Turks no favourable reputation in Europe. Thinkers from the humanist Erasmus to King James I of England were supportive of the idea of a new Crusade against the Turks, which took some of its colour from an incipient Philhellenism or desire to liberate the Greeks – whose ancient culture was the basis of European education – from alien domination. Hence the extraordinary rejoicing with which the news of the Battle of Lepanto (1571) was received, when the Christian powers under Don John of Austria defeated the Turkish fleet for the first time.

This event put a temporary halt to the Ottoman adventure in Europe, and from 1575–90 the empire was engaged in warfare with Persia. War with the Hapsburgs from 1593–1606 gave place to further wars with Persia, culminating in the capture of Baghdad by Shah Abbas I of Persia in 1624, with the assistance of some Janissaries who had defected from the sultan, and whom the shah rewarded for their treachery by boiling them in oil.

THE QUEEN AND THE SULTAN

Sultan Murat III (1574–95) epitomised the style for which the Ottoman Sultans were to become famous: he had his five brothers put to death on his accession; his harem consisted of 40 concubines and he had 130 sons plus uncounted daughters. His reign saw the development of further links with the west in the establishment by a group of English merchants, at the instigation of Elizabeth I, of the Levant Company. This company in Smyrna (Izmir) provided an important base for western travellers, merchants and diplomats, and gradually acquired a diplomatic role of its own. Queen Elizabeth's

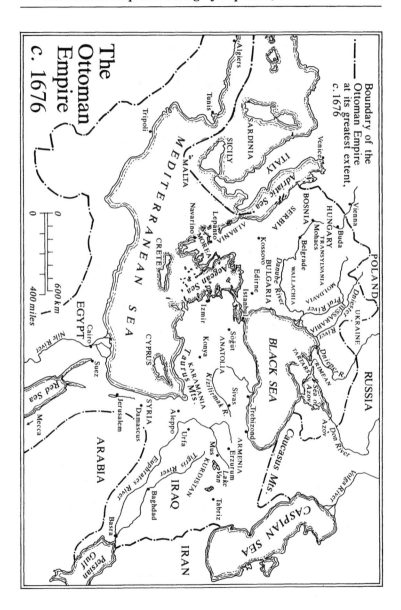

The Ottoman Empire c. 1676

Boundary of the Ottoman Empire at its greatest extent, c. 1676

A corridor lined with tiles in the harem

enthusiasm for eastern trade continued in the reign of the next sultan, Mehmet III (1595–1603), when she ordered the building of an organ by the well-known organ builder Thomas Dallam and had it delivered in person by Dallam himself to the sultan's court. Dallam's diary of his visit is a naïve and delightful account of his experiences: his audience with the sultan

> did make me almoste to thinke that I was in another worlde. The Grand Sinyor satt still, behoulding the presente which was befor him, and I stood dashinge my eyes with loukinge upon his people that stood behinde him.

The organ, fortunately, turned out to be a success. It was upon such odd amusements that the sultans increasingly found their time expended.

Evliya Celebi

A wider ranging account of the Ottoman Empire in the early years of the seventeenth century was written by Evliya Celebi (1611–84), the son of a goldsmith who entered the service of the sultan but was called by the Prophet, in a dream on his twenty-first birthday, to devote his life to visiting the tombs of the Muslim saints. From 1640 he travelled through nearly every part of Anatolia, and his descriptions of the cities he visited are informative and important, while being laced also with delightful anecdotes and extraordinary accounts of the magic talismans erected by ancient philosophers – to keep, for example, fleas away from Istanbul, or of the flocks of angels he encountered while swimming at Eyüp.

Evliya, who has become a 'standard author' in modern Turkey, is at his best in vivid descriptions like his account of Bursa.

> The inhabitants being fair, the air good, the water full of holiness, contribute altogether to render Bursa one of the most delicious spots on earth. . . . There are nine thousand shops. . . . The market of the gold-smiths is outside the *bezestan,* and separate from it; the shops are all of stone. There are also the markets of the tailors, cotton-beaters, cap-makers, thread merchants, drapers, linen merchants, cable merchants, and that called the market of the bride, where essence of roses, musk, ambergris etc. are sold. . . . None of the provisions at Bursa are sold by infidels, but by true Muslims. . . . There are seventy-five coffee-houses each capable of holding a thousand persons, which are frequented by the most elegant and learned of the inhabitants; and three times a day singers and dancers execute a musical concert in them.

PALACE POLITICS

If bourgeois life in the prosperous towns corresponded to this idyllic description, the politics of the ruling class became increasingly vicious. Some cultural achievements can be associated with the reign of Ahmet

I (1603–17), who was himself a poet and was responsible for the building of the best known mosque in Istanbul, the so-called Blue Mosque, as well as the establishment of a number of schools and hospitals; but his successor Mustafa, brought up in the seclusion of the harem, lasted only a year on the throne before being displaced by Osman II (1618–22). Osman attempted to reform the ruling class and strengthen the army by getting rid of the *devşirme* and establishing a peasant militia in its stead, and generally Turkifying the administration. The result of these reforms was a major revolt of the Janissaries in 1622, in which the grand vizier and the chief eunuch of the harem were torn to pieces, Osman was killed, and Mustafa briefly reinstated.

Little improvement took place in the following reigns. Murat IV

The Blue Mosque, Istanbul

(1623–40), who came to the throne as a boy of fourteen, attempted to impose law and order in the empire by massacring bandits, prohibiting coffee and tobacco and introducing dress regulations, and even used to prowl the streets at night in order to murder malefactors in person. The *cadi* of Istanbul was executed because there was a shortage of butter. Spies were everywhere. A continuation of this sort of thing under the brutish Ibrahim the Mad (1640–8) led to a further Janissary revolt in 1644, and the strangling of Ibrahim by order of the *şeyhulislam*, the leader of the clergy.

The next sultan, Mehmet IV (1648–87), was six-years-old when he came to the throne, with the inevitable result that power lay elsewhere. The first three years of his reign were known as the Sultanate of the Ağas, during which the Janissary leaders controlled events and manipulated court officials. The period was brought to an end by the execution of the leading Ağas. As the reign went on, inflation and famine led to further unrest, grand viziers were changed or executed with great rapidity, and in 1656 the Janissaries staged their largest revolt yet, in protest against their pay being made in copper. They hanged thirty leading officials in front of the Blue Mosque. At the same time eastern Anatolia was subject to the constant peasant revolts of the *Celalis* ('provincial rebels') which had been gathering momentum for half-a-century as a result of economic and agricultural decline. (The population had grown from *c*. 12 million in 1525 to 25 or 30 million in 1600.) It was at this disastrous moment that a figure emerged with the capacity to control the situation, in the form of the grand vizier Mehmet Köprülü.

Mehmet Köprülü had been a *devşirme* boy and had risen through the palace hierarchy from cook and clerk to *sancakbey* (regional governor) of Amasya. Friends who had the ear of the Queen Mother succeeded in getting him appointed grand vizier, and his ruthless confiscations and executions succeeded in imposing a measure of stability in the capital, while the revolts in Anatolia were crushed by massacres of some 18,000 rebels. His son Ahmet who succeeded him has gone down in history for successfully bringing to a conclusion the long war with Venice for Crete which had been going on since 1645: in 1669 Candia was finally taken. The English merchant Bernard

Randolph, in his *Present State of the Islands of the Archipelago* (1687), included some eyewitness accounts of the long siege, in which the Greeks had used grappling hooks to fish up the Turks as they sapped the walls; sometimes, he alleged, the inhabitants had eaten the besiegers they hooked.

But Turkey's attempts to expand into Europe were drawing to a close. In 1664 an Ottoman army was defeated at St Gotthart, and in 1683 the siege of Vienna, commanded by Ahmet Köprülü's brother-in-law Kara Mustafa, which filled all Europe with terror, was lifted by the Polish commander John Sobieski. Turkey was now on the run. The Hapsburg army advanced, and in 1697 the Ottoman army was dstroyed by Prince Eugene at Zenta. Two years later the Treaty of Karlowitz provided for the withdrawal of the Ottomans from Europe. The Ottoman Empire had reached its natural limits. From now on it was going to learn from Europe rather than fighting it, and the eighteenth century saw attempts at new kinds of reform, liberalisation and intellectual activity, accompanied none the less by seemingly unstoppable political decline.

The Inğra of Süleyman the Magnificent

CHAPTER TEN

The Ottoman Empire II: The Sick Man of Europe, 1699–1909

In the aftermath of the Treaty of Karlowitz, the government lay in the hands of a fourth Köprülü grand vizier, Hüseyin Paşa, who attempted to revive the demoralised army and navy. However, Hüseyin Paşa Köprülü was soon toppled from power by the Şeyhulislam, and a seizure of Istanbul by rebel Janissaries led to the enthronement of Sultan Ahmet III (1703–30). In 1718 Ibrahim Paşa became grand vizier, and brought to an end the smouldering warfare with Russia and Europe. In the same year the Treaty of Passarowitz was signed, which defined the borders of the Ottoman and Hapsburg Empires.

Ibrahim Paşa recognised the importance of Europe, and of peace with Europe. European arts and culture were beginning to be known in the empire, and Ibrahim made use of this influence to consolidate his own power and divert the emperor with the arts of luxury on the model of the court of Louis XIV of France. The period of (somewhat rococo) enlightenment thus introduced is known as the Tulip Period.

The Tulip Period

Sultan Ahmet III was a sophisticated sovereign who devoted the wealth of his empire to indulging his aesthetic tastes, most prominently in the building of a number of new palaces. The summer palace of Sa'adabad in Istanbul was based on the French château at Marly, whose plans had been brought back by his ambassador to Paris. Other palaces sprang up, by the Sweet Waters of Europe and of Asia, along the Bosphorus, and elsewhere. The Persian love of gardens was reflected in these palaces, and added a distinctive flavour to what was first of all an imitation of Europe. Festive illuminations were devised for the city, and fêtes and shows were arranged, of which one of the most significant was the spring Tulip Festival.

The tulip is a native of the Asiatic steppes and had accompanied the Turks on their westward migration. The flower (*lale* in Turkish) was cultivated by the earliest sultans and was nicknamed 'turban', from which derives the European name which was given it when the ambassador Ogier Ghiselin de Busbecq brought the flower to the Austrian court in the sixteenth century. The European craze for tulips which developed thereafter was in due course exported back to Turkey, and in the seventeenth century fortunes could be spent on rare bulbs. But Ahmet III was the first to import the flowers in quantities, from Holland and also from Persia. For the spring festival the Seraglio was carpeted with tulips, and when night fell on the music-making, turtles with candles on their back were sent wandering through the gardens to illuminate the varied colours of the flowers.

The frivolity of this kind of hedonism accompanied a real, if limited, awakening of the intellect. An ambassador, Mehmet Çelebi, was sent

Beylerbey Palace

to France to gather ideas for the enhancement of Ottoman civilisation. With western furniture and clothing came the custom of painting portraits of the sultans (portraiture being forbidden under the strict rule of Islam) and, most significant of all, the establishment of the first Turkish printing press in Istanbul.

This press was set up in 1727 by a Hungarian, Ibrahim Müteferrika (1674–1745), and began to turn out works in Ottoman Turkish (the Christians and Jews had of course been printing their own books for some time before this), including maps, a dictionary, works of history, geography and science – anything except religious subjects.

This period of enlightenment continued under Ahmet's successor, Mahmut I (1730–54), who brought in a French adviser on military affairs as well as building libraries and supporting the press. A generation of peace from 1740 to 1768 paradoxically interrupted the development of such arts as it left more leisure for the pursuit of political rivalries: corruption increased and the press fell into disuse. The self-satisfied stagnation of the Ottoman élite was jolted by the renewal of the threat from Russia under Catherine the Great.

Rivalry with Russia

The Treaty of Karlowitz of 1699 had left the Ottoman Empire for the first time in a position of weakness *vis-à-vis* the western powers; from now on the sultan would negotiate from weakness not strength, and as the eighteenth century went on the Ottoman Empire was increasingly eyed by the western powers as a candidate for dismemberment. The question became, not how to resist the Ottoman aggression, but who would benefit most from its weakness. To the existing powers in the equation – France, Austria, and presently Britain – was added a new element: Russia.

Rumblings of warfare with Russia in the 1730s had died away, to be renewed with a vengeance when Catherine the Great determined in 1770 to win back Russia's fellow-Orthodox country, Greece, from Ottoman control. Revolts were fomented in the Balkans, and in March 1771 the Morea (Peloponnese) rose in revolt. Russian troops were quick to arrive, and the Russian and Ottoman fleets met at

Çeşme, opposite the island of Chios, where a disastrous Ottoman defeat opened the Mediterranean to Russia.

One year later Russia succeeded in occupying the Crimea, and forced the Ottomans to sue for peace, which was agreed at the Treaty of Küçük Kaynarca signed on 21 July 1774. The Crimea was declared independent, but both empires were given religious rights: the sultan as caliph was to be the religious head of the Crimean tribes, while Catherine won the right to build an Orthodox church in Istanbul. A heavy tribute was also imposed on the sultan.

The Ottomans once again engaged European advisers to help reform their army, among them the Hungarian Baron de Tott and a Scotsman known (ironically) as Ingiliz Mustafa. The navy was rebuilt and modernised under the grand admiral Gazi Hasan Paşa, with French assistance, and a naval engineering school was established. France continued to offer support and co-operation to the Ottoman Empire, as a safeguard against the threat that Russia and Austria might carve it up. But Russia soon returned to the attack, with the annexation of the Crimea in 1779, a status confirmed by the Peace of Jassy in 1792. Catherine, it appeared, had dreams of reviving the Byzantine Orthodox Empire. (Her second grandson, born in 1779, was named Constantine – a clear hint of a return to the throne vacated by the last Constantine of Byzantium.)

THE FRENCH REVOLUTION AND AFTER

Another momentous event cast its shadow over these years. Sultan Selim III (1789–1807) came to the throne in the year of the French Revolution. The great impact of this event was reflected in the genuine desire for reform evinced by the new sultan. Selim restructured the scribal bureaucracy in an attempt to wipe out corruption and nepotism. The army and navy were reorganised and a naval medical service was set up which used both the knowledge and technical products of Europe. The arts of Europe began to be known in the empire and Selim even invited theatrical groups to his court; but there was little growth in any native arts. Society, meanwhile, was if anything more ossified as peasants were forced to remain on their land and each class was compelled to wear an allotted form of dress (the idea being that everyone would 'know their place' and this would eliminate social conflict). But the situation of the empire was already critical. In Egypt the Mamluk dynasty established in 1681 was showing little more than nominal loyalty. Separatist movements were active among the Arabs and among the Druze of Palestine and Syria; while in Epirus (northern Greece) Ali Paşa of Ioannina, the bloodthirsty charmer immortalised by Lord Byron in his letters and poems, had begun in the 1790s to establish a mini-kingdom which was for all practical purposes independent of the sultan.

The aftermath of the French Revolution and the rise of Napoleon raised a direct threat to the Ottoman Empire from the hitherto friendly France. Meanwhile, in England, the younger Pitt had reversed that country's previous pro-Russian policy with the formation of a triple alliance of England, Prussia and Holland to preserve the Ottoman Empire. In 1797 the Treaty of Campo Formio secured peace between Napoleon and the Austrian Empire: Napoleon acquired the Venetian dominions including the Ionian Islands, so that he now had a common frontier with the Ottomans. However, he did not attempt to attack the empire, expecting it to collapse under its own inertia and declaring, 'We shall see it fall in our time.' Instead, he mounted an expedition to Egypt. This short-lived adventure did clean out the ruling class of Egypt and improve its administration, setting it up for the reforms introduced by Mehmet Ali in his long reign (1805–48).

The Nineteenth Century

Napoleon's expectation of the collapse of the empire did not lead to European action, because it suited the western powers to preserve the corrupt and inefficient Ottoman Empire as a buffer and a balance to their own rivalries. In the nineteenth century the western powers made frequent attempts at reform in the empire, but primarily for their own ends (as for example in the restructuring of the national debt).

In 1805 Selim recognised Napoleon as emperor of France. He was still anxious for friendship with France to strengthen his position against Russia, but both France and Russia were indifferent to Selim except in so far as they could make use of him. In 1807 Selim was overthrown by a revolt of the Janissaries who had become increasingly restive under his attempts at reform. Under the Sultan Mahmut II who came to the throne in 1808 the empire was saved by the good fortune of Napoleon's invasion of Russia, which forced the tsar to agree the sultan's terms for peace in 1812.

The Greek War of Independence

Mahmut's reign was, however, troubled by other crises. The growing power of Ali Paşa in Ioannina had provoked a large-scale invasion by the sultan. The Greek secret society the *Philike Etaireia* (Friendly Society) determined to attack Turkey while this conflict was in progress. A force commanded by Alexander Ypsilantis crossed the Pruth into Ottoman territory in February 1821, but was quickly defeated. A month later, however, the standard of revolt was raised by Bishop Germanos of Patras and the Greek War of Independence had begun.

The sultan's first response was to hang the Patriarch of Constantinople from the doors of the Patriarchate. But to begin with the Greeks had considerable success, and in 1824 the sultan called in Ibrahim Paşa, the son of Mehmet Ali of Egypt. The atrocities wreaked by Ibrahim in the Peloponnese were added to the passionate entreaties and personal involvement of European Philhellenes like Byron and Trelawny, and the English foreign minister, George Canning, secured the support of France and Russia for the idea of autonomy for the Greeks. (Until now the western powers had hung back, reluctant to make common cause with their rivals, even against the Turks.) The Turkish navy was decisively defeated by these western allies at the Battle of Navarino in 1827, an event which showed that the era of Turkey's European power was drawing to a close. It also established the base for the continuing hostility of Greece to Turkey and vice versa.

TREATY OF ADRIANOPLE

Russia meanwhile was on the attack again. In 1828 the tsar took Kars and Erzurum. The fall of the entire Ottoman Empire seemed imminent. Russia held back because of the hostility this event would provoke in the western powers. By the Treaty of Adrianople (Edirne: 14 September 1829), these cities were returned to Turkey, though Turkey had to agree to extensive losses of territory in Georgia and Armenia (including Yerevan) as well as to Russian control of the Danube ports and to the autonomy of Serbia and Wallachia as well as Greece. Turkey had also to pay Russia a huge war indemnity. A further Russian-Ottoman treaty, that of Hünkar Iskelesi (1833), temporarily ended the threat of further aggression and incursions from Russia, but Turkey was left in an enormously weakened international position.

THE LOSS OF EGYPT

A further severe loss was that of Egypt. Since the end of the Greek war Mehmet Ali had been attempting to secede, and in 1838 he refused to pay further tribute: this was tantamount to a declaration of independence, and the Ottomans were defeated in the attempt to regain this important province. Mehmet Ali's success emphasised the growing weakness of Ottoman rule.

The Tanzimat

Sultan Mahmut II had recognised the need for reform and had built on the slight foundations put down by Selim III. The reign of his successor, Abdulmecit I, is associated with the period known as the Tanzimat (Turkish: 'reform'), but the achievements of the period would not have been possible without Mahmut's reforms of the 1830s.

The way was cleared for reform by the final abolition of the Janissaries. In June 1826 they revolted in protest against military reforms proposed by Mahmut and the introduction of a new corps within the Janissaries themselves. The grand vizier summoned loyal troops and the Janissaries retreated to their barracks at the Et Meydanı. These were set on fire and the rebels were burnt to death. This was followed, at last, by the abolition of the corps, an act known in Turkey as the Auspicious Event. Their supporters, including the bektaşi dervishes, were also abolished, and the stage was set for real reforms in the years that followed.

REAL REFORMS

The army was reorganised. Military bands were established, and trained by Giuseppe Donizetti, the brother of the composer. A new system of military education was introduced and the navy was reformed (too late to influence the defeat of Navarino). The first Turkish newspaper was established, in 1831. The government was divided into ministries and the office of the grand vizier was redefined as that of prime minister (*baş vekil*), thus sowing the seeds of struggle between palace and Porte. The turban was abolished and replaced by the fez (headgear has always been an important index of political allegiance in Turkey); a fez factory was established in Izmir to meet the country's needs. Western ideas were imported along with western clothes, and Prussian influence made itself felt for the first time with the arrival of General Helmut von Moltke to undertake such military tasks as mapping the empire, building fortifications, and modernising the army. Municipal government was extended and secular schools were introduced in addition to the traditional Islamic ones.

RESCRIPT OF GÜLHANE

All these reforms were further extended by the Men of the Tanzimat, of whom the leader was Mustafa Reşit Paşa (1800–58), who had already had a career as ambassador in Paris and London and as foreign minister from 1837–8. The first political statement of the Tanzimat was the Rescript of Gülhane (3 November 1839), which fell short of being a constitution but none the less bore many resemblances to the French Declaration of the Rights of Man of 1789.

STRATFORD CANNING

An important figure throughout the reign of Abdulmecit was the British ambassador, Stratford Canning, a nephew of George Canning, who was in the post in Constantinople from 1842–58. His time in office was a period of growing rapprochement between Turkey and Britain, while Canning's friendship with and influence over the sultan and Reşit helped maintain the power of both and hence the momentum of reform.

The other leading figures of the Tanzimat were Reşit's protégés Mehmet Emin Ali Paşa (1815–71), secretary to Reşit and ambassador to London 1841–4, and Keçecizade Mehmet Fuat Paşa (1815–69). When the sultan began to resent the increasing power wielded by these men of the Porte, it was Stratford Canning who by his intrigues and diplomacy kept Reşit in power. The younger generation of the Men of the Tanzimat comprised the dominant figures of Ahmet Cevdet (1822–95), the first minister of justice and author of a history of the Ottomans, and Midhat Paşa, a vigorous reformer of provincial government and in some ways a proto-Atatürk.

Clock Tower, Izmir

CONTINUITY AND PROSPERITY

The new bureaucratic institutions associated with the Tanzimat ensured a measure of continuity in policy and pushed to one side the political jockeying that had previously made Ottoman government so unstable. Power was centralised and there was far greater control over provincial and local institutions. Tax collection and local security were improved, as were education, agriculture and communications, so that the Ottoman Empire became a rather more comfortable, and certainly a more prosperous, place to live. In Istanbul the Ottoman Steamship Company was established in 1851, a police force was set up and the Galata Tünel was built. Post, gas supplies, railroads and the Golden Horn bridge all were legacies of this period. Banks were established, including the Ottoman Bank, set up in 1856 with British capital. In the same year the poll-tax was abolished and full equality declared between Muslims and non-Muslims. New taxes (stamp tax, customs; tobacco imports; grape juice tax) were introduced and salt was made a government monopoly. All these measures put the empire on a firmer financial footing.

Commerce was stimulated by allowing foreigners to own property in Turkey. Newspapers and theatres began to operate. Napoleon's expectation that the Ottoman Empire was about to fall apart could hardly have seemed further from fulfilment. Yet in 1853 Tsar Nicholas I of Russia could pronounce: 'We have a sick man on our hands – a man gravely ill. It will be a grave misfortune if one of these days he slips through our hands, especially before the necessary arrangements are made.' With these words the tsar showed that the Russian desire for Ottoman territory was far from dead, and Russian ambitions were expressed in the Crimean War of 1853–6.

The Crimean War

The Crimean War is perhaps the most important war ever to have begun by accident. The dispute began with a renewal of Russian claims to authority over the Christian subjects of the Ottoman Empire, and in particular over the relative rights of the Roman Catholic and the Orthodox guardians of the Holy Places in Jerusalem and Bethlehem. In 1850 Prince Louis Napoleon instructed his ambassador to demand from the Porte the execution of the grants to the Latin Church, made in 1840, which would allow the Latin monks of the church at Bethlehem a key of their own to pass through the church, rather than having to apply to the Orthodox for the right of passage. In 1852 Nicholas sent an ambassador – with a warship – to Constantinople to demand a Russian protectorate over the Orthodox subjects of the empire.

Stratford Canning had been briefly recalled to London. In April 1853 he returned, now Lord Stratford de Redcliffe, to exercise his diplomatic skills at this moment of crisis. He persuaded the sultan to reject the demand. Each side called the other's bluff, and the result was war. The Ottoman army crossed the Danube in October 1853, and Russia responded by destroying the Ottoman fleet in harbour at Sinop. In March 1854 Britain and France joined in the war, and quickly forced a Russian withdrawal. The remaining two years of the Crimean War were fought mainly through the enthusiasm of Palmerston to put down the Russians, and Turkish troops were scarcely involved. When the war did end in February 1856 the integrity of the Ottoman Empire was guaranteed (including Kars which had been temporarily lost to Russia in November 1855), and the Black Sea, Danube, and Straits were declared neutral. Redcliffe's bluff, which has been criticised as precipitating the war, had proved successful in consolidating Ottoman strength. None the less, the war had imposed a severe strain on Turkey, and the refugees produced by the war caused further disruption within the empire.

Provincial Unrest

One result of the Crimean War was a slowing in the rate of the reforms associated with the Tanzimat. Dissatisfaction with its achievements led to the emergence of a group known as the Young Ottomans who in effect represented a liberal, yet relatively conservative, opposition to Ali and Fuat. Their main demands were for a constitution, a parliament, and Ottomanism. The latter implied a rejection of the secularist values of the Tanzimat, which they regarded as having removed the moral basis of Ottoman society without putting anything in its place, and a preference for the values of Islam and the old empire, rather than the more 'Turkish' values of the Tanzimat. (Turkism versus Islamism continues to be a leitmotif of Turkish politics, ever since the decisive turn to Turkism by the Young Turks at the end of the nineteenth century and its development by Atatürk.)

Concurrently with this movement, many of the provinces had been evincing nationalist aspirations, perhaps encouraged by the series of European national revolutions of 1848. The problems this produced came to be known as the Eastern Question.

The Eastern Question

Lebanon was the first to revolt (1840–6), and a further crisis led to massacres in 1860. The growing autonomy of Egypt represented a further problem. In 1866 the island of Crete revolted, and was bloodily suppressed after three years. There were numerous risings in Bosnia-Hercegovina and in Montenegro from 1858–69 and in 1875. Western opinion was horrified by the brutality of the Turkish repression of a rising in Bulgaria in 1876; the events became known as the Bulgarian Atrocities, and led to the Balkan Crisis with Austria, Russia and Turkey on the brink of war. The bloodiness of the Turkish action led to a a permanent change in the attitude of the European powers to Turkey, which was now perceived as a savage and barbarian nation. This perception was to have a direct influence on European policy towards Turkey over the next half-century. Turkey was by now too weak to maintain the balance of power, and became instead a carcase for picking.

To all this was added a period of drought and famine in Anatolia, and winters so severe that wolves were seen prowling the streets of Istanbul. The empire plunged into financial crisis, mainly from collapse of the mechanisms for collecting the taxes. The result was a growth of political opposition to the sultan. In the summer of 1876 a major demonstration of theological students led to the deposition of the Sultan Abdulaziz. His successor, Murat V, proved of unsound mind and was deposed on 31 August. His successor, Abdulhamit II (1876–1909), who ascended the throne at the age of thirty-four, was to dominate the remainder of the century and to preside over the abolition of the sultanate itself.

The Reign of Abdulhamit II

The first demand the new sultan faced was for a constitution, a demand made alike by the Young Ottomans and the theological students: Abdulhamit appointed Midhat head of a commission to formulate it, and it was signed by the sultan within months of his accession. Its

Abdulhamit II

major features were as follows. The sultan retained his essential authority both as head of state and as caliph or head of Islam: he even had the power to suspend the Constitution. The grand vizier was no more than first among equals in the Council of Ministers. Parliament was divided into two houses, a Chamber of Deputies and a Chamber of Notables, while the Council of State established under the Tanzimat continued its role as supreme court and in the drafting of bills. The equality of all Ottoman citizens was restated, confirming the declaration of the Tanzimat. Secular courts were instituted for non-Muslims (of course in disputes between Muslims and non-Muslims the Muslim law prevailed, which was naturally perceived as a source of injustice by non-Muslims).

INSECURITY AND AUTOCRACY

The Constitution represented a real advance, but much of its liberalising force was negated by the autocratic tendencies of the sultan himself. His insecurity resulted in mistrust of the bureaucracy, while the efficiencies of the administration were now used to give Abdulhamit personal control of almost every aspect of government. The staff at Topkapı Palace were reduced while Abdulhamit developed a scribal staff in his new retreat at the Yıldız Palace, from which he seldom emerged. He had personal control of the secret police, which spied on everyone including other policemen. The invention of the telegraph lent speed to the activities of spies and to the ruthlessness with which follow-up action could be taken. Censorship of the press was firmly enforced.

CONFLICT WITH RUSSIA

On the international scene Abdulhamit soon had to face conflict with Russia, which declared war on 24 April 1877, and invaded the empire simultaneously in Europe and from the Caucasus. Abdulhamit promptly dismissed parliament. Britain, by now the dominant western power, looked apprehensively on as the Russian army marched towards Istanbul, and took up a threatening position so effectively that Russia ceased her advance. Instead she imposed terms on Turkey, at the Treaty of San Stefano (3 March 1878), which effectively dismembered the Ottoman Empire in Europe. However, the arrange-ment was unacceptable to the western powers. In June 1878 a secret bilateral treaty was signed between Britain and Turkey, by which Britain leased from Turkey the island of Cyprus, and in exchange offered to defend Turkey in the event of a Russian attack. By the same agreement, known as the Cyprus Convention, the sultan promised to Britain to respect and protect the rights of Christian citizens of the empire. These provisions were further ratified in the Treaty of Berlin (July 1878), by which Russian influence in the Balkans was greatly reduced.

The result was a growth of nationalist activity both in Bulgaria and Albania, where there seemed to be a chance of shaking off the Ottoman yoke, and in the east among the Armenians.

The Armenian Question

Since the Middle Ages the Armenians had been effectively assimilated in Ottoman society. In the large cities, notably Istanbul, Armenians had risen to positions of prosperity and power as merchants and had important roles in the recently established banks. In the east it was different: in the historical territories of Armenia, these Christian Ottomans had been treated as second-class citizens like other non-Muslim minorities. Abdulhamit's constitution had not intro-duced any tangible change to their status and rights. The Cyprus Convention seemed to offer the promise of change under the aegis of the western powers; at the same time the Orthodox Christian nation of Russia over the border was willing to play on Armenian aspirations for its own purposes.

Armenia, like the other provinces of the Ottoman Empire that had been threatening insurrection, had learnt new aspirations from the growth of nationalist sentiment throughout Europe in the wake of the 1848 revolutions. The sultan, by contrast, as caliph as well as emperor, held to the view that his was a Muslim Empire, and made little attempt to heed the provisions of the Cyprus Convention.

After the Treaty of Berlin Britain maintained a number of consuls in Asiatic Turkey, who were able to report at first hand the treatment of the Armenians. They suffered not least at the hands of marauding Kurds — another minority unpopular in Constantinople, whom it suited the sultan to keep at loggerheads with the Armenians — as well as the legal restrictions and governmental injustice mentioned above.

THE HUNCHAK PARTY

In 1885 the first Armenian political party was formed, the Armenakan. This was followed by the formation in 1887 in Geneva of the socialist revolutionary Armenian party known as the Hunchaks (from the name of their journal, *Hunchak,* The Bell). Other parties sprang up and were federated in an umbrella organisation known as the Dashnaktsutiun (Dashnaks for short); but the Dashnaks developed a nationalist policy while the socialist Hunchaks split away from the federation.

In June 1890 a petition was drawn up in Erzurum for presentation to the sultan. But the Hunchaks fired on Turkish soldiers and a ferocious battle followed which ended with 15 Armenians dead and 250 wounded. A month later a similar gathering took place in the Armenian Cathedral in Kum Kapı in Constantinople and ended in a similar fracas between Armenians and Turkish soldiery. The petition did not reach the sultan.

Massacre

The revolutionaries decided that more drastic action was needed. Further disturbances over the next three years were aimed in part at provoking a violent reaction by the authorities which would force the western powers to intervene. The reaction came in summer 1894 when local Armenian officials in the region of Sasun — the heartland of Armenia's heroic legends — refused payment of taxes unless the Turkish authorities put an end to Kurdish depredations (which were certainly being encouraged by the central government). This was treated as insurrection and the response was a military one. Soldiers and Kurds pursued the Armenians who had retreated to the mountains and slaughtered all they could find, smashing children against rocks, mutilating pregnant women, and, in the words of the British delegate at the commission of inquiry, hunting down the Armenians 'like wild beasts'.

The massacre did indeed provoke intervention by the great powers. A commission was set up. However, witnesses were tampered with by the Turks, and anyway no follow-up action was taken. Instead, it became the settled policy of the Porte to carry out a series of indiscriminate massacres of the Armenians, as a way of destroying the revolutionary activities. In October 1895 close on a thousand Armenians were killed by Turkish troops, accompanied by Laz brigands and others, in Trebizond. A week later there was a smaller massacre at Akhisar, followed by others in Erzincan, Bitlis, Gumuşhane, Urfa and Erzurum. November saw the extension of the action to Malatya (3,000 dead), Van (1,500 dead), Amasya (1,000 dead), and other cities. In December a second massacre in Urfa culminated when some 3,000 Armenians took shelter in the cathedral; the Turks then set fire to it and all those in it were burnt alive. A particularly chilling feature of these massacres is that the beginning and end of each action were signalled by a bugle call, lending an appearance of military precision to the orgy of killing.

The last event in this sorry chapter was the seizure of the Ottoman Bank in Istanbul by a group of Dashnaks on 26 August 1896: they were ready, they said, to destroy the bank, all the money it contained, its employees and themselves, if Armenian demands for reform were not met. Strenuous efforts by the Russian embassy brought the incident to a peaceful conclusion, but it was quickly followed by systematic murders of Armenians throughout the capital. Western opinion was outraged, and William Gladstone (now eighty-seven) made an impassioned and influential speech, but the foreign secretary, Lord Salisbury, recognised the difficulties of imposing reform on the sultan. A reform scheme devised in February 1897 by the ambassadors of the six powers in Constantinople was never put into effect. However, the massacres did soon die away. The Armenian struggle was swallowed up in a larger political conflict which was to lead to the deposition of the Sultan.

The Young Turks

Abdulhamit's 'problems' with the Armenians were compounded by losses of territory in other parts of the empire. Tunis was lost to the French in 1881, Egypt was occupied by Britain in 1882. Crete had begun a revolt as early as 1875, and with Greek support in 1897; though this was unsuccessful, Greece did win some territory in Thessaly. Macedonia was also a bone of contention between several regional powers at this time.

All this military activity had placed a strain on the empire's finances. Action was taken to ease this by the Decree of Muharrem in 1881, which provided for the restructuring of the National Debt and an injection of foreign capital. From 1889 a number of German shipping lines were established, and in 1903 the Baghdad railway concession was finalised.

Modernisation continued slowly, with the founding of schools, the development of mines and a cotton industry, increased foreign trade, and the introduction of streetcars and street paving. Even libraries were set up, and newspapers were established, though censorhip was still rigorously enforced. Ahmet Midhat (1855–1912) wrote a large number of historical and educational works designed to improve the level of information of the masses, while other newspapers were edited by one of the founding fathers of Turkish scholarship, Şemsettin Sami.

Such developments provided the conditions for the the rise of a liberal opposition, and this duly emerged in the form of the group known as the Young Turks, after the title of their journal *La Jeune Turquie*. The title was an explicit rejection of the Islamism of Abdulhamit and the Ottomanism that had characterised the empire hitherto. Nationalist ideas had infected the Turks too, who now began to emphasise their links with their brothers in other Turkic races of Asia. Ottomanism seemed to be a spent force as it proved incapable of holding the empire together, and the future was seen as belonging to a state which would identify with the Turkish nation.

Though their ideas were thus opposed to those of the sultan, he did find room for some of the Young Turk leaders in government. However, more powerful forces were at work outside his borders. A group of young officers was beginning to develop revolutionary ideas, and among these was the young Mustafa Kemal, who was posted in Damascus, where he set up the Fatherland Society (*Vatan*). In Salonica the Young Turks developed into a political movement known as the Committee of Union and Progress (CUP). Its most prominent figures were Enver Bey and Niazi Bey. The Young Turk Congress in Paris in December 1907 included, remarkably enough, a representative of the Armenian Dashnaks.

RECALL OF PARLIAMENT

Disaffection from Abdulhamit's regime grew stronger. An attempted coup by the Young Turks in Macedonia in May 1908 was put down, but in July Abdulhamit none the less announced the recall of parliament after its thirty-year suspension. Elections were held, and on 17 December the new Turkish parliament was opened by the sultan.

The main aim of the Young Turks was to improve the government, not to replace it. A Committee of Seven was despatched to Istanbul to work alongside the existing grand vizier, Kamil Paşa (from August 1908). Many reforms were introduced; but hopes for better things were jolted by events of October 1908, when Bosnia-Hercegovina was annexed by Austria, and Crete by Greece. The CUP was losing as much territory as the old sultan had. On 13 April 1909 the religious leaders staged a counter-revolution; an Armenian uprising in Adana was quelled with the massacre of some 30,000.

THE END OF THE SULTAN

At this point some of the Young Turk officers in Salonica gave up on the CUP as a means of progress. Two of them, Mahmut Şevket Paşa and Mustafa Kemal, marched at the head of an army to Istanbul. They were met by a large number of the parliamentary deputies, and it was agreed to depose the sultan. Martial law was introduced on 24 April and three days later Abdulhamit was sent on a train to Salonica. The sultan's rule was at an end.

CHAPTER ELEVEN

The Atatürk Years, 1909–1938

The early years of CUP rule saw a number of reforms and efforts at modernisation, such as the introduction of electric trams and the modernisation of the army, and the introduction of education for women; but progress was hampered by the struggle for dominance between the CUP in the cabinet and Mahmut Şevket as military commander of Istanbul.

The new sultan, Mehmet V (1909–1918), retained a constitutional position and had the right to dissolve parliament or to call on a political leader to form a government. The dominant figures in the CUP, apart from the grand vizier Sait Halim Paşa, the nominal leader, were Talat Paşa (1874–1921), Cemal Paşa (1872–1922) and Enver Paşa (1881–1922). Talat served as minister of the interior, while Cemal and Enver were more military figures. Cemal in particular had a vision of himself as a heroic leader, and this led to the exclusion from a position of dominance of the other leader of the 1909 coup, Mustafa Kemal. This cold-shouldering only acted as a further spur to Kemal, who would, in due course, establish himself as the undisputed leader of Turkey and take the name *Atatürk*, Father-Turk.

Kemal (1881–1938) was born in Salonica and made his career in the army, where his first posting after college was in Syria. He had been posted to Salonica in 1907, in time to lead, with Şevket, the Young Turks' revolutionary march on Istanbul. In 1911 he served as a major in the Libyan war against Italy, an out-of-the-way place in which to hope to make a reputation; but better things were to come.

The Balkan Wars

The Balkan Wars of 1912–13 which resulted from Austria's annexation of Bosnia-Hercegovina began badly for the Turkish government. All Turkey's European territory was lost to the Albanians, Greeks and Serbs; the Bulgarians advanced to the gates of Adrianople (Edirne). Furthermore, Tripoli and the Dodecanese were occupied by Italy. The defeats shook the position of the CUP, which had already had to concede control of government to the opposition Liberal Union. A peace conference chaired by the British foreign secretary, Sir Edward Grey, attempted to draw a frontier, which would give Edirne to Bulgaria. At this point the CUP intervened, and Enver led an army band directly into a cabinet meeting and forced the resignation of the government leader, Kamil Paşa. At the treaty of London Turkey was granted Thrace, including Edirne, but lost Crete and the islands. Şevket became grand vizier after Enver's coup, but was assassinated soon after.

The CUP was now in full power, but the second Balkan War of 1913 led to a further redrawing of frontiers, in the position they have today, except that Bulgaria was granted Dedeağaç (Alexandroupolis), which it lost again after the First World War. The loss of territory acted as a spur to ideas of Turkish nationalism, which were vigorously promoted by the writer and scholar Ziya Gökalp (1876–1924).

ZIYA GÖKALP

For Gökalp, the folk (*halk*) was the repository of national culture and identity, and religion was regarded as an earlier stage in the development of the people. Gökalp promoted the appreciation of folk literature, such as the heroic lays of Dede Korkut and the humorous tales of Nasreddin Hoca. This secularist approach to culture has remained the basis for the Turkish ideology as established by Kemal Atatürk. The trend of Gökalp's thought is represented in the title of his collected poems, *Kızıl Elma* (Red Apple): in Turkish folklore, the Red Apple Tree is the ideal home of the Turks, the city to which destiny is always leading them. Gökalp also argued for the replacement of Ottoman Turkish, with its admixture of Arabic and Persian words, with a purer Turkic language containing replacement vocabulary from Çagatay, Uzbek, Tatar, Kirğiz, Abkhaz, Gagauz and Uiğur.

MODERNISATION OF THE ARMED FORCES

Enver, who became a virtual dictator as the Ottoman parliament met more and more rarely, was anxious for friendship with and assistance from foreign powers. The army was brought up-to-date with the help of the German Liman von Sanders, while a British admiral oversaw the reconstruction of the navy. Enver was particularly keen on alliance with Germany, which he saw as the most likely defence against Russia in the event of war, and an alliance between the two powers was

Enver Paşa

signed on 2 August 1914. This was the position when the First World
War broke out.

The First World War

On the outbreak of war Turkey was awaiting delivery of two warships
which had just been completed in British shipyards. On 3 August these
were abruptly commandeered by Winston Churchill, first lord of the
admiralty, for use by Britain. Shortly thereafter, two German cruisers,
pursued by the British navy, took refuge in officially neutral Ottoman
waters. The Turkish government refused to intern these but, by a
fictitious sale, made them part of the Turkish navy. In September they
entered the Black Sea to bombard Russian ports, and on 2 November
Russia declared war on Turkey, to be followed on 5 November by
Britain and France.

Turkey's first action in the war was a disastrous winter campaign in
the Caucasus, in which three-quarters of the troops were lost. This
led to an open declaration of support for Russia by the Armenian
leaders. The Armenians had to be swiftly removed from the scene.

GENOCIDE

What followed is still the subject of angry debate between the Turkish
government, who deny that there was an official policy of massacre,
or indeed that systematic massacres took place, and the rest of the
world who are content to accept the documentary evidence that Talat
did order the extermination of the Armenians and the eyewitness
accounts of the concentration camps and forced marches in which
more than a million Armenians died by the end of the war.

Officially the Armenians were to be deported *en masse* to places
where they could not interfere with the progress of the war. In
practice, they were rounded up, village by village, beginning in
November 1914, and forced to walk, mostly in the direction of Syria
where camps awaited them in Deir-ez-Zor and elsewhere. Enormous
numbers died of hunger, thirst, exhaustion and exposure, or through
the brutality of their Turkish commanders. At the same time, an
alleged uprising in Van was brutally put down, and massacres took

place in Bitlis (15,000 dead), Muş, and Sasun. In June 1915 enormous convoys left Erzincan on the journey to Mesopotamia. The men were killed as they left the city; the remainder, perhaps 10,000 or more, marched on to the Kemakh gorge of the Euphrates, where they were pushed in at bayonet point. The same pattern was repeated in many other cities. Only the inhabitants of the villages of Musa Dağ escaped slaughter: holding out in their mountain fastnesses from July to September 1915, they were at last seen by a French vessel in the Black Sea, and over 4,000 Armenians were taken off to safety. Those who reached the concentration camps of Mesopotamia were, as eyewitnesses described them, no more than living skeletons. At Deir-ez-Zor many were crowded into underground caves where they were crushed or, in some cases, doused with petrol and burnt to death. By the end of 1916 the genocide was over, though it was to be renewed with somewhat less intensity after the war had ended.

BRITISH INTERVENTION

The first British intervention in Turkey took place in February 1915, when a British squadron attempted to pass the Dardanelles to capture Constantinople and thus remove the Ottomans from the war. However, the straits were mined and gun batteries had been placed on the shore. After a month, and a fierce battle on 18 March, Admiral de Robeck lost his nerve and the British force retreated, ignorant that the Turks had also despaired and abandoned their positions because of the short supply of ammunition. Churchill tried to persuade the admiral to fight on; if he had done so, he would have had control of Constantinople in a matter of days. Instead, the Turks had time to gather their forces and mount an impressive and sustained resistance to the Gallipoli landings a month later.

GALLIPOLI

It was at Gallipoli that Mustafa Kemal established his reputation as Turkey's leading general. As the British and Anzac troops poured ashore, Kemal issued his most famous order: 'I am not ordering you to attack; I am ordering you to die.' 'I cannot believe,' he said, ' that there is anyone in the troops I command who would not rather die than suffer again the disgrace that fell on us in the Balkans.' This heroic fervour, coupled with the error of the Anzacs in landing on the wrong beach, Ari Burnu (Anzac Cove) which crammed them in a small space and made advance almost impossible, ensured the slaughter of the invading troops and the complete success of Kemal's division. In the aftermath Kemal was promoted to colonel; and in August he was made commander of all the troops in the Anafarta hills, where he again succeeded in checking the combined British and Anzac forces after the British landing at Suvla Bay. In the fighting Kemal was hit by a piece of shrapnel: it had struck him over the heart, but his life was saved by a pocket watch, which was smashed. It seemed like an omen.

Kemal was less successful in his next posting, to Syria, where he

View of Anzac Beach, Gallipoli

was to carry out Operation *Yıldırım* (Thunderbolt) against the allied army in Iraq. His troops never reached Iraq; he was forced back by the lightning speed of General Allenby's advance and capture of Baghdad and Jerusalem in 1917. Kemal resigned his command in 1917 and returned to Constantinople.

ARMISTICE

After these losses, Talat and Enver resigned and advised the sultan to reach terms with the allies. An armistice was signed at Mudros, on the island of Lemnos, on 30 October 1918, which incorporated a total surrender by the Ottoman Empire. On 13 November a British fleet sailed into Istanbul and occupied the city. The sultan and his associates were for co-operation with the allies, but many CUP members and others disagreed. To silence them, parliament was dissolved on 21 December. The forces of resistance soon began to gather in eastern Anatolia.

The time had now come for the carve-up of the Ottoman Empire which had been foreseen in the secret agreement between Sir Mark Sykes, assistant secretary of the British War Cabinet, and François Picot, the French consul-general in Beirut, of 16 May 1916. The Middle East was to be divided between Britain and France under government by mandate; a Jewish state was to be established in Palestine; and, closer to home, the Greek prime minister Venizelos had persuaded the British prime minister, Lloyd George, of the Greek claim to the coastline of Asia Minor with its considerable Greek population. These provisions were embodied in the Treaty of Sèvres which was finally signed on 10 August 1920. The allies, moved by the horrors to which the Armenians had been subjected, were also determined on adequate protection for the Christian subjects of the empire.

The War of Independence

The resistance movement quickly gathered strength in the east, including even communist elements, supported by the Bolshevik rulers who had come to power in Russia in 1917. The sultan made no determined effort to put down their activities. In March 1919, Kemal's associate Ali Fuat Cebesoy arrived in Ankara to command the Twentieth Army corps, and in April Kiazim Karabekir (1882–1948) took command of the Fifteenth Army corps at Erzurum. Unrest among the Greeks led the British to threaten total occupation of the country; Kemal's name was then put forward as the commander best suited to restore order in the country, and he was granted a visa by the British to travel to Samsun to command the Ninth Army. He arrived on 19 May, a date he later decreed his official birthday, and which still remains a public holiday in Turkey. So far from restoring order, he had come to organise the resistance. The War of Independence had begun.

NATIONAL CONGRESS

As soon as the British discovered what he was doing, they demanded his dismissal. Kemal promptly resigned, thus making himself officially a rebel against the government. The Istanbul government ordered Kiazim to arrest Kemal; he refused, thus branding himself a rebel as well. On 21 June Kemal, with Ali Fuat Cebesoy, Rauf Orbay, the former navy minister, and Refet Bele, an army commander, signed the Amasya Protocol, which called for a struggle for independence and the formation of a National Congress. An independent congress in Erzurum, which drafted what became known as the National Pact, the manifesto of the nationalists, was followed by the meeting of the National Congress at Sivas in September. Elections were held by the Sultan, and inevitably in the east nationalist members were elected, thus gaining a place in parliament. In January 1920 a telegram from Kemal was read to parliament, in which the nationalists claimed to be the rightful government of Turkey. The allies now determined to suppress the nationalists. Martial law was declared in Istanbul.

ALTERNATIVE PARLIAMENT

In March 1920 Kemal established an alternative parliament in Ankara under the name of the Grand National Assembly, with Kemal as president and Ismet, his chief lieutenant, its Chief of Staff; a Constitution was proclaimed on 20 January 1921; and the country was divided. The allies refused to allow the grand vizier to send troops, which would begin a full scale civil war. In June the provisions of the Paris Peace Conference, later codified in the Treaty of Sèvres, became known. The acceptance of these terms in August by the Istanbul government led the nationalists to brand them traitors. When the nationalists came to power they never ratified the treaty.

GREEK OFFENSIVE

Further, the support of the Greek claims in Asia Minor led to a fierce Greek offensive through Thrace as far as Aydın in June and July 1920; they were repulsed at the Battle of İnönü near Kütahya on 10 January 1921, but began a new offensive in March, which was again repulsed at the İnönü on 7 April. The Greeks carried out a brutal massacre in Izmit. The nationalist forces under Ismet fell back on the River Sakarya, where by 13 August they had put the Greeks to flight. Unfortunately for the Greeks, they could no longer rely on British support, for in autumn 1920 the young king Alexander had suddenly died as a result of a bite from a pet monkey. The resulting return of the pro-German Constantine I led to the fall of Venizelos and the loss of his influence with the British government. The Greeks were on their own.

In September 1920 the Kemalist troops began an assault on Armenia. Armenia had declared itself a Republic under Russian protection as early as May 1918. In October 1920 Kars was taken. A month later President Wilson of the USA made an offer of territory for an independent Armenia; but this was whistling in the dark, as was the Sèvres stipulation of an independent Kurdistan.

FIRE AND DESTRUCTION

Kemal's response to the Greek invasion was long delayed. Finally, on 26 August 1922 the Turkish army under Kemal advanced, and on 1 September his rallying cry was 'To the Mediterranean!' The Greek army was in full rout. They retreated through Anatolia, setting fire to towns and generally causing what destruction they could as they went. When the Turkish army reached Izmir a series of atrocities began as Greek and Armenian inhabitants were raped, mutilated and murdered.

By the end of 13 September Smyrna was in flames. The Turks have always insisted that it was the Greeks and Armenians of the city who started the fires; the Greeks and Armenians insist that eyewitnesses saw Turkish soldiers with cans of kerosene starting the fires, which spared the Muslim quarter while destroying the Christian quarter. The fires forced the Christian inhabitants on to the quay, where they stood between the devil and the deep sea. Allied ships stood by, observing strict neutrality and declining to take any part in rescuing the refugees as they hurled themselves into the sea to escape the flames. Many smaller boats did what they could to rescue the victims. In the end an American named Asa Jennings became the hero of the disaster, commandeering a number of foreign ships, and finally a Greek fleet, to take off more than 60,000 exiles to Greece.

The Turks had won their war. The Çanak crisis of October 1922, which almost led to British troops firing on Turks who demanded the instant removal of Greeks from Thrace, was resolved by the signing of the armistice at Mudanya on 11 October. The nationalists put the seal on their power by abolishing the sultanate – and thus the Istanbul government – on 1 November. (The caliphate was however not abolished until 1924.) In November a peace conference began at Lausanne, at which the Turks were represented by Ismet, now with the name of Inönü to commemorate his victories against the Greeks. Playing on his deafness, he contrived to spin out the discussions for eight months. Finally, the treaty of Lausanne was signed on 24 July, establishing the frontiers of Turkey as they are today. The Straits were declared international, and the capitulations were abolished (which was seen by the French as a snub). The most regretted loss was – and is – the vilayet of Mosul, which the allies were determined to keep because of its oil wealth, while the Hatay (the region around Alexandretta – Iskenderun), which had been given to French-mandated Syria in October 1921, was handed back to Turkey.

British troops left Istanbul in October 1923. On 13 October the capital was moved to Ankara. On 29 October Turkey was declared a Republic: Kemal was its President, Inönü its prime minister.

Kemal Atatürk

By any standards the achievement of Kemal as head of state is an extraordinary one. Though Kemal, like Mussolini, who came to power a few weeks before him, and like Hitler a little later, introduced a nationalist, populist revolution supported by the army, his was not a regime that laid stress or reliance on the outward show of military power. This may have been because the Turkish army has always had a different social role from that of a western army. Under the sultans, where there was no hereditary aristocracy and the bourgeoisie consisted mainly of non-Muslims, no significant Ottoman class emerged between the peasantry and the sultan. His office-holders and the landowners were chosen and could be disposed of at will. Only the army, formally slave though it was, had a structure and cohesion to give it a separate identity. Thus the army took on some of the characteristics of classes in other societies. Army intervention in Turkish history since Atatürk has always had the aim of protecting constitutional government; and so it was with the Nationalists. Kemal ceased to be a soldier and became a politician and father figure to his people: in June 1934 he adopted the name *Atatürk*, Father Turk.

The new society with which he replaced, in a matter of a few years, the centuries-old Ottoman system, was based on populist and nationalist principles and was strongly influenced by the ideas of Gökalp. The state was highly interventionist and deliberately secularist: Kemal could not, like the Bolsheviks, abolish religion, but he assigned it a modest place in a wider pattern of life.

DRAMATIC REFORMS

Between 1923 and 1934 a dramatic programme of reforms included the introduction of the international calendar and clock (1925), the metric system (1931), the legalisation of alcohol, the introduction of street numbering, the replacing of Friday by Sunday as the day of rest, and, most dramatically, the Turkification of the flowery Ottoman language and the introduction of the Latin script: this was done by decree, on 1 November 1928, that the Latin script was to be in universal use by the New Year. Kemal himself travelled the country

Kemal Atatürk

teaching the new alphabet to groups in village schools and halls. He also took the important symbolic step of abolishing the fez, causing consternation by travelling through the country wearing a Panama hat. In 1934 every Turk was obliged to adopt a surname (his own being, of course, the unique Atatürk).

All these achievements were not made without some opposition. Kemal's old rival, Enver, had disappeared from the scene in an obscure military adventure in Russia in 1922; so had Cemal, while Talat had been murdered in Germany in the previous year. Kemal's position was strong but not unassailable. In February 1923 the deputy for Trabzon, Ali Şükrü, a devout and fanatical Muslim, attacked Kemal for his excessive drinking and accused him of planning to have himself proclaimed sultan. Soon after this, Şükrü's body was found in a shallow grave near Kemal's villa: his death was blamed on an over-enthusiastic bodyguard, but Kemal's reputation was shaken.

ONE-PARTY RULE

The constitution allowed for the formation of other parties besides Kemal's Republican People's Party. In 1924 some founder members of the Turkish National Movement — Ali Fuat, Kiazim Karabekir and Rauf — wished to slow the pace of reform and announced the formation of an opposition, the Progressive Republican Party. However, soon one opposition deputy was shot dead by a People's Party member. When in February 1925 a Kurdish revolt broke out, it offered an opportunity for Kemal to request emergency powers for the government. Then, in June 1925, the PRP was proscribed. The country returned to one-party rule.

In 1926 there was a plot to assassinate Kemal, in which Şükrü's friend Ziya Hursid, and Kemal's former friend Colonel Arif were implicated. During July a treason trial was held. Arif and twelve others were publicly hanged in Izmir. Others (including Rauf) were exiled or imprisoned. Still others were set free (including Ali Fuat and Kiazim Karabekir), but took no further part in politics. In August a second trial resulted in the hanging of four men for alleged anti-government activity; thirty-seven were, however, acquitted. The contrast is worth making with the far more extensive purges in contemporary Russia.

THE GREAT SPEECH

In 1927 Kemal made his 'Great Speech'. Weeks of round-the-clock labour were devoted to the composition of this epic account of what he wished remembered of the years since 'I landed at Samsun on May 19,1919'. The speech was delivered to the Congress of the People's

Party on 15 October 1927, and went on for six daily sessions of six hours: when printed in English the following year, it ran to 724 pages.

The hat and alphabet campaigns of the following year made Kemal a familiar and popular figure throughout the country, and he did not discourage the growing 'cult of personality'. The Islamic ban on human images was rescinded, so that statues of Kemal sprang up all around the country, annoying the faithful of Islam, while they testified to his unique status in the country.

A further experiment at two-party government in 1930 was even less successful than the earlier one. The Free Party founded by Fethi served only to attract crowds of Islamic fanatics waving green flags. It seemed safer to dissolve the party again. The Islamic undercurrent continued to flow, and culminated in the Kubilay affair of 23 December 1930. In Menemen a rabble-rousing sheikh led the crowds from the mosque to attack public symbols of Kemal's Turkey. They were confronted by a detachment of troops under Lieutenant Mustafa Kubilay. They seized the young officer and sawed his head off with a hacksaw before the riot was put down by further troops. The sheikh was tried and executed; but the event demonstrated the strength of feeling in some quarters against Kemal's reforms.

Statist intervention in agriculture was represented by land reform, the introduction of new crops and the composition of Five-Year Plans (again, the parallel is there with Communist Russia). The İş Bank and the Etibank (Hittite Bank) were founded to encourage industry and commerce, and the exploitation of mineral resources. Turkey's first labour code was introduced in 1936.

DEATH OF THE GREY WOLF

The sensational achievements of Atatürk were not crowned by length of years. His hard living and, in particular, his excessive drinking saw to that. On 8 November 1938, in the Dolmabahçe Palace in Istanbul, he died of cirrhosis of the liver at the age of fifty-nine. The time was five past nine in the morning. All the palace clocks were stopped at that hour in tribute to his passing. For nine days the *gazi* (hero), as he had called himself, lay in state, before his removal to Ankara for his interment.

A Turkish legend speaks of the Grey Wolf which led the Turkish people out of the Central Asian steppes to its present home. Kemal had seen himself as that Grey Wolf: it was part of his Turkish consciousness. He had fulfilled the task of the wolf in giving his people a home in the modern world.

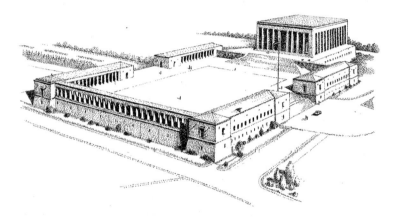

The Mausoleum of Atatürk

CHAPTER TWELVE

Modern Turkey,
1939–present

There was no dispute about who was to succeed Atatürk as President of Turkey; the prime minister, Ismet Inönü (1884–1973), succeeded naturally to the role. It was a difficult time on the international scene: the shadow of the Second World War was already falling across Europe, and Turkey, which had seen some economic improvement in the thirties, could not afford to become involved in another war. In the end the country remained neutral, signing a pact with Britain and France in October 1939, and a non-aggression pact with Germany in January 1941. War was only declared on Germany in 1945, when the allies had already won. However, the country did mobilise in readiness. The inflationary effect of the crisis prompted Inönü to introduce the famous Captain Levy Tax (*Varlik Vergisi*), which was intended to penalise war profiteers, though it was only applied to non-Turks (Turks, it was assumed, were honest businessmen). Those who did not or could not pay – many of them Armenian – were sent to labour camps where they lived, and in some cases died, in conditions of extreme hardship and misery. This policy reinforced the position of Turkey as a country for Turks alone, in which non-Turks must be assimilated or suppressed.

INTERNATIONAL ALIGNMENT

At the end of the war the question of Turkey's international alignment became important. In 1945 the USSR abrogated the non-aggression treaty it had signed with Turkey twenty years before, and renewed its claims to the Armenian cities of Kars and Ardahan. The Truman Doctrine of the USA however, introduced in 1947 to provide US aid to any state "threatened" by a communist power, ensured that Turkey received financial support under the Marshall Plan and, in the process, consolidated the partition of Armenia. Henceforth, there were officially no Armenians in Turkey, only eastern Turks.

Adnan Menderes

In 1946 a new party was founded in Turkey, the Democratic Party, with Adnan Menderes (1899-1961) as its dominant figure. Though the Democratic Party lost the1946 election, they won a huge victory in the 1950 election. Inönü was succeeded as president by Celal Bayar. The 1950s were the years of Menderes, who became prime minister. Turkey saw considerable economic growth – agricultural output doubled between 1950 and 1960, and gross national product grew four-and-a-half times – but the public debt tripled. The mass of the people applauded the democratic government, but the intellectuals – who tended to support the statist line of the RRP – became more vociferous in their opposition, and were strictly censored. The Democrats also introduced religious instruction in all schools, a step away from Kemalist secularism.

NATO

Turkey joined NATO in 1952, but also pursued an active diplomacy in the Middle East, where it antagonised some of its Arab neighbours by apparently regarding itself as NATO's representative in the Middle East. In 1955 Turkey and Iraq signed a mutual co-operation pact which became the nucleus of the Baghdad Pact, which soon included also Britain, Iran and Pakistan. This Pact, which stood for anti-communism, led in 1957 to extreme tension with Syria. When the Iraqi monarchy was overthrown in 1958, Turkey's eagerness to intervene was not well received by the western powers.

Crisis Coup

The crisis in Turkey's relations with the Middle East was compounded by increasing unrest at home. Inflation was rampant and the country was only saved from bankruptcy by a loan from the International Monetary Fund. Opposition to the Democrats became increasingly strident; the RRP staged a walkout in February 1960 and in April the Universities were closed because of violent demonstrations against the government. The crisis was diffused in 1960 by a bloodless coup which overthrew the Menderes government and installed a Committee of National Unity headed by General Cemal Gürsel who became President. A new constitution (Turkey's fifth) was introduced in 1961, and this was followed by the abolition of the Democratic Party, trials of 592 of its members and executions of fifteen of them, including Menderes.

The military coup acted in the way that was to become characteristic of Turkey, introducing martial law but at the same time acting as a guarantor of democracy. Elections in October 1961 returned Inönü as prime minister as the first in a series of coalition governments. The constitution contained more checks and balances than the earlier ones, and was considerably more liberal. It required a programme of land reform, tax reform and nationalisation, as well as improvements in social welfare (not all of which were carried out). The President was above party. In the 1960s the RRP emerged as a middle-class socialist party, while other parties emerged including the increasingly important Justice Party which from 1965 was headed by Süleyman Demirel. The sixties also saw the emergence of a number of leftist movements, including the Turkish Workers' party, and legal trade unions, including the left-wing DISK (1967).

This greater liberalism led to a wave of violent political activity. There was increasing agitation for land reform, and severe inflation. Rapid industrialisation also changed the complexion of politics. The growth of leftist ideas was associated with an increasing anti-Americanism. Americans in Turkey were subjected to petty displays of prejudice such as the refusal of barbers to cut their hair. In addition, Turkey's population of four million Kurds began to voice

Bülent Ecevit

their demands for a separate state; they became involved in the political violence, including a large demonstration in Erzurum in February 1970. Strikes of public employees added to the disorder.

By 1971 the inability of the government to control left-wing agitation led to the resignation of Demirel, and in March that year the military again took control, imposing martial law in eleven provinces and dissolving the Turkish Labour Party. Though the politicians outfaced the military and continued parliamentary rule, with a non-party government until 1975, Turkey was without a stable government for most of the 1970s. Political dominance fluctuated repeatedly between Süleyman Demirel and the reorganised Republican People's Party under Bülent Ecevit. The latter now emerged as a leftish representative of the technocratic and intellectual élite, but neither this nor the justice party proved able to deal with the increasing political violence and terrorist activity of the 1970s. Hijackings were carried out by Dev Genc (May 1972) and by the Turkish People's Liberation Army (October 1972), who also practiced kidnapping. All this was despite a brutal crackdown by the military authorities, leading in October 1972 to the first of numerous reports by Amnesty International condemning the practice of torture in Turkey.

Cyprus

In 1974 the Cyprus crisis added to the Political storm. During the 1960s President Makarios of Cyprus had expressed dissatisfaction with the power (especially the power of veto) of the minority Turkish population in Cyprus (some 20 per cent of the whole). In 1963 fighting erupted between the two communities and was only quelled by the installation of a United Nations peacekeeping force. None the less, tension continued, with extremist elements on the one side talking of complete union with Greece, and those on the other side about a partition of the island. In July 1974 an inept military coup by Nikos Sampson, supported by the ruling military junta in Greece, was followed in a few days by a Turkish invasion of the island. The failure of Sampson's coup precipitated the fall of the Greek junta and that country's return to democracy; but Cyprus was partitioned by the Turkish forces. The so-called Turkish Republic of Northern Cyprus was proclaimed in November 1983: to date this has been recognised by no country except Turkey. The crisis, coupled with disputes over rights to the Aegean continental shelf, brought Turkey close to war with Greece, and hostility and discontent still simmer, while the Greek churches of northern Cyprus, with their precious frescoes, fell into ruin. The need of a solution to the Cyprus problem became more urgent in the new millennium with Turkey's moves for admission to the EU (see below, p. 196–197). Cyprus was accepted as a candidate for membership, but how could Turkey be accepted if it did not recognise Cyprus as a whole? The absolute intransigence of the Turkish Cypriot leader, Rauf Denktash, came to be seen as a problem by all, and eventually the peoples of Cyprus took matters into their own hands and, in moves reminiscent of the fall of the Iron Curtain, began to move relatively unhindered across the 'green line'. In April 2004 a UN plan to reunite Cyprus as a single political entity was approved by the Turkish Cypriots, though Greek Cypriots were hostile. The problem remained not totally resolved at the end of 2004, but the confirmation of both Cyprus and Turkey as potential EU members meant that a solution must be found at least in practical terms.

Economic Instability

A balance of payments deficit was made more critical by the sudden rise in oil prices of 1974. Inflation in Turkey in 1975 was running at 30 per cent, a rate which continued for the next decade so that the lira slipped from TL19.25:$1 in 1977 to TL645:$1 in 1986. In 1975 unemployment reached two million (in a population of some 36 million). Terrorist activity continued, with the assassinations of Turkish diplomats by Armenians in 1975–7, and Kurdish disorders from 1978. In August 1978 it was estimated that there had been 2,000 political murders in Turkey since Ecevit's government came to power in February 1974, and such murders were running at a rate of some twenty per week.

The violence escalated through 1979, little helped by a restructuring of Turkey's debt and assistance from the International Monetary Fund. In November Ecevit resigned, and a month later was accusing Demirel of reforms which 'endangered democracy'. The violence became more intense in 1980, and a new element was added to the turmoil in the form of the fundamentalist Muslim National Salvation Party under Necmettin Erbakan, who demanded the overthrow of the government.

MARTIAL LAW

In September the military again carried out a coup under General

Kenan Evren who became President of the Republic. Martial law was introduced. Demirel, Ecevit and Erbakan were placed under house arrest (they were released a month later, though Erbakan was to stand trial for political agitation). Most western governments were pleased at the coup, and the people of Turkey breathed more easily as a result of the abrupt cessation of political violence. DISK was banned and many newspapers underwent short bans as a part of the suppression of leftist opposition. Civilian cabinet government however continued, and mid-1981 a National Consultative Council was appointed to draft a new constitution. When this was approved by referendum in July 1982 it gave much stronger powers to the President of the Republic, as Guardian of the State, including power to dismiss parliament if he saw fit. General Evren was appointed president for seven years. All previous political leaders were banned from political activity for ten years (a ban frequently flouted by Ecevit in the next years, resulting in several spells of imprisonment). The 1980 constitution banned political strikes and proscribed the radical parties, bringing to an end a twenty-year period of freedom for the left.

In November 1981 it was reported that there had been 43,140 arrests for political activity since September 1980. The film-maker Yilmaz Güney escaped from prison in October 1981 and was stripped of his citizenship in January 1983, thus drawing attention to the plight if the opponents of the regime, and the continuing ban on political discussions in the mass media.

Political parties were legalised again in May 1983, and elections in November 1983 saw victory for the newly formed Motherland Party under Turgut Özal, an economic expert who had been made deputy prime minister immediately after the coup. The economy was reformed on free market lines. Several banks and industrial companies were privatised. The lira was devalued and foreign exchange controls were scrapped. A slow economic recovery took place in the 1980s, though inflation continued to be high, rising to 74% in 1988, while job losses were severe. The new political stability of the country led to rapid growth in tourism, which accounted for $3 billion in receipts in 1987. Exports also increased, but the increase in GDP was attenuated by a very rapid growth in the population, from 44,736,957 to 51,428,944 in 1985. In 1987 Özal felt confident enough to pursue an application for membership of the European Union, an aim which he and his successors pursued doggedly ever after.

As part of the new look for Turkey the politicians executed in 1961 were rehabilitated, and amends were made to Menderes by naming Izmir's airport after him.

In October 1989 General Evren retired from the presidency and was replaced by Özal; the latter's sudden death in April 1993 led to the election of Süleyman Demirel, now prime minister, as President, and in June Mrs Tansu Ciller, a junior economics minister, became his successor as leader of the True Path (Dev Yol) party, which had been in government since 1991. She ruled in coalition with the Social Democratic People's Party (SHP). Her free-spending economic policies led to financial crisis. Responding with a cut in interest rates, she precipitated a flight of capital from the country and an increase in foreign debt. In 1994 the International Monetary Fund compelled Turkey to devalue as a condition of structured loans. Meanwhile, in that year, prices rose by 106%. Dissatisfaction with the economic situation led to the rise of the Welfare (Refah) Party under Necmettin Erbakan, the first Islamist party in the Turkish republic. In 1995 Erbakan became Prime Minister of a new coalition, with Ciller as his deputy, thus foreshadowing the most dramatic development in Turkey's politics which has dominated the new millennium.

Other issues that dominated the 1980s and 1990s included the continuing trials of large numbers of political activists. In November, 1988 Amnesty International reported 250,000 arrests in the preceding eight years. Despite General Evren's condemnation, torture continued to be practised in Turkish jails, and several prisoners have died as a result, though no executions were carried out after 1984 and the death penalty was abolished on 2 August 2002: this was but one of many reforms precipitated by the demands of the EU if they were to look with favour on Turkey's candidacy for membership. In 1992 Amnesty International condemned the continuation of political killings and torture in Turkey, and in 2002 they reported that torture was still rife despite genuine efforts to improve the situation. For several years hunger strikes have been taking place in prisons in protest at poor conditions and torture, and several prisoners have died.

Turkey's relations with its Aegean neighbour, Greece, remained uneasy, with Greece frequently objecting to alleged infringements of airspace and other misdemeanours. In 1996 the two countries nearly came to the point of war as a result of a dispute over two uninhabited islets off the Turkish coast, Imia (in Greek) or Kardak (in Turkish). To their use by a Greek to pasture a few goats, local Turks responded by planting a Turkish flag on one of the rocks. For several days the danger of war was real, until what seemed to many a comic-opera plot quietly played itself out. More serious was the alleged Greek support for Kurdish terrorism.

Kurdish Opposition

The fiercest political opposition into the 1990s came from the Kurds. Resentment had simmered among the Kurds since the provisions of the Treaty of Sèvres for an independent Kurdistan were ignored in the four countries involved: Iraq, Syria, Iran and Turkey. In the 1920s and 1930s many Kurds were wiped out in mass executions and in programmes to uproot their villages, ostensibly for irrigation. The Kurdish language was banned in 1924, on the familiar principle that to be part of Turksih society one must be a Turk. The Kurdish terrorist response was directed by Abdullah Öcalan from a base in Damascus, and consisted of targeted murders of, among others, teachers, mosque personnel, newspaper distributors and village guards. Some 250 schools and fifty health centres were destroyed. In 1988 the Kurds officially began their *intifada* (on the analogy of the Palestinian uprising against the Israelis), and in April 1990 a Kurd rising was quelled by mass executions accompanied by repeated atrocities. In 1993 it was estimated that 10,000 people had died in clashes between Kurds and the military since 1984. The Ciller government was not above showing a relaxed attitude to the activities of the Hizbollah death squads which repeatedly targeted Kurds.

In autumn 1990 a new political situation affected Turkey's relations with its Kurdish population, when Iraq invaded and annexed Kuwait. As soon as it became clear that the USA, urged by Kuwaiti and Saudi leaders as well as the near-universal condemnation of world opinion, would not accept the annexation, President Özal lent his support firmly to the American position. He supported western economic sanctions by closing the pipeline from Kirkuk in Iraq to Yumurtalik, and as the crisis escalated into war allowed bombing of Iraq by US planes from bases in Incirlik and Diyarbakir.

A corollary of this anti-Iraq stance was that Turkey liberalised its attitude towards the Kurds, since Iraqi Kurds were among the chief victims of Saddam Hussein's policies in Iraq. A number of restrictions were eased, so that the use of the Kurdish language was once again permitted. A distinction was made between the Kurdish people and the hard-line activists of the PKK, the Marxist Kurdistan Workers' Party.

After the conclusion of the Gulf War in summer 1991, when Iraq withdrew from Kuwait, there was a mass exodus of Iraqi Kurds fearing new attacks from the Iraqi government. Many of them found refuge in Turkey, but the PKK took advantage of the confused situation to mount guerrilla activities, against which Turkey retaliated fiercely with military activity including bombing. The heavy bombing of January 1992 was condemned by the EU, whom Özal angrily branded as 'supporters of terrorism', and was followed by the resignation of sixteen Kurdish deputies.

Action against the Kurdish opposition escalated with air raids on Kurdish bases in Northern Iraq in January–February 1994 and again in August, and with the burning of thirty Kurdish villages in south-eastern Turkey in October – an action described by the Minister for Human Rights as 'state terrorism'. In March 1996 the novelist Yasar Kemal was give a twenty-month suspended sentence for 'fomenting equality between peoples' because of his views on the Kurdish problem, but in October 1999 his voice was heard again, in concert with those of leading writers worldwide, calling for more rights for the Kurds.

Further offensives took place against the Kurds in October 1997, and in October 1998 relations took a new twist when Turkey accused Syria of supporting the Kurds: troops were mobilised and the two countries came to the brink of war until talks averted the crisis. Syria agreed as part of the agreement to expel Abdullah Öcalan, the leader of the PKK, which was behind the armed violence. Öcalan sought asylum in Italy while both Kurds and anti-Kurdish elements staged violent protests in major cities.

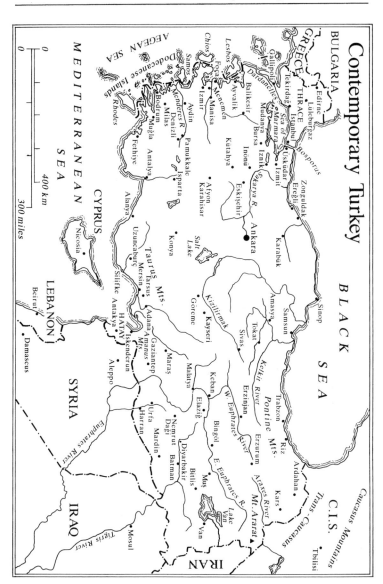

Contemporary Turkey

The drama of Öcalan continued for some years. Italy freed him from custody on the grounds that he was now in favour of an end to violence. He fled to Kenya where he was captured by Turkish forces on 15 February 1999; eight days later he was formally charged with treason and the responsibility for 30,000 deaths. A wave of bombings by Kurds in Istanbul in March and April did not deflect the course of the trial, which concluded in June with the imposition of the death sentence. Meanwhile, an amnesty was offered to any Kurds who surrendered. On 2 August Öcalan called for a ceasefire, and two days later the PKK officially ceased its operations. Öcalan now announced that he believed the armed struggle of the Kurds had been a 'historic mistake' and in January 2000 his death sentence was suspended, and finally cancelled in October 2002 in the wake of the abolition of the death penalty in Turkey. In 2005 Turkey agreed to a re-trial following a ruling by the European Court of Human Rights that his 1999 trial had been unfair.

Many of the Kurds' demands were slowly realised over the next few years, largely because of the demands of the EU for Turkey's candidacy. As early as November 2000 the head of the Turkish Intelligence Agency called for an end to the ban on Kurdish-language broadcasts, and soon the Kurdish language was allowed to be heard on the radio, in schools and in newspapers. Repeated programmes of human rights reforms over the next few years regularly included more recognition of the Kurdish population, and in April 2002 the PKK was dissolved and replaced by the more innocuous Kadek – the Kurdish Freedom and Democracy Congress. However, regular incursions against Kurdish forces in Iraq continue to take place, sometimes with the explicit support of the USA.'

A sore point for Turkey, as sensitive as the issue of the Kurds, has been the increasingly vocal demands of the Armenian community abroad that Turkey officially recognise the massacres of the Armenians at the beginning of the twentieth century as a 'genocide'. In May 1998 the French national assembly voted to recognise the killings as 'genocide'. Turkey responded with sanctions against French businesses in Turkey, which were maintained with vigour for a period, but then lapsed. A similar resolution by the US House of Representatives was abandoned in October 2000 because of the Turkish threat of reprisals in economic form as well as military support. In April 2000 the Israeli education minister caused a frisson by saying that the 'genocide' should feature in Israeli school textbooks. However, in 2004 the Turkish authorities permitted a showing of the film *Ararat* by the Canadian director Atom Egoyan, a sign perhaps that the country was more ready to discuss the issues than before. However, in 2005 the internationally famous novelist Orhan Pamuk was put on trial for insulting the Turkish state because he had mentioned the deaths of a million Armenians and 30,000 Kurds in an interview with a Swiss newspaper. After an international outcry the charges were dropped in January 2006; but the incident drew attention to the continuing sensitivity of the Turks on the matter. Then, in January 2007, Hrant Dink, the prominent editor of an Armenian newspaper, was assassinated as he left his office.

Islamic Fundamentalism

The 1980s and 1990s saw increasing agitation for a return to Islamic values in Turkey. In 1987 General Evren warned that Islamic fundamentalism posed as great a threat to Turkey as communism. The conflict was crystallised in the demand to allow the wearing of headscarves by women. Headgear being always important in Turkey, headscarves were banned in March 1989, but by December pressure had forced the rescinding of the ban. The issue has repeatedly reared its head, not least in the question of whether it was permissible to attend university while wearing one of these symbols of reaction and, in some views, anti-Turkism. In May 1999 one parliamentary deputy was prevented from being sworn in because she was wearing a headscarf. In July 2004 a law was mooted which would have made it a crime to ban university entrance to women wearing headscarves, but the law had to be abandoned.

The rise to power of Necmettin Erbakan and accession to the post of Prime Minister in 1995 led to many pro-Islamic moves and much rhetoric: though he claimed adherence to the dictum that 'Turkey is a democratic, secular and social state', his government fell under suspicion of promoting Islamist values by an increase in Islamic education and a purge of secular officials in the judiciary. Links were forged with the Turkic states of Central Asia, but a visit by Erbakan to Libya and other illiberal African Muslim states brought international condemnation. On February 28, 1997 the National Security Council presented Erbakan with a list of demands including the curtailment of religious education, and this led to what was known as the Process of 28 February, in which the military led a campaign to eradicate 'political Islam' from business and education. The army no longer bought its biscuits from Ülker because of the company's Islamic links. In May 2006 an Islamist lawyer, Alparaslan Arslan, opened fire on five judges in protest against the refusal of promotion to a female teacher who wore a headscarf to school. One of the victims died. The event led to a large demonstration re-emphasising the Turkish state's secularism.

Erbakan was forced to resign and a new government was formed under Mesut Yilmaz of the Motherland Party (ANAP). Nevertheless, educational reforms fell foul of Islamist opposition. In August 1997 the duration of compulsory schooling was extended from five to eight years. Islamists objected because it would raise the minimum age for enrolment in Islamic schools, and Erbakan called the move 'fascist secular thinking'. In January 1998 the Welfare Party was banned, and it was dissolved a month later, to be replaced in March by the Virtue Party. In April the Mayor of Istanbul, Recep Tayyip Erdogan, was sentenced to ten months imprisonment for 'inciting hatred' at an Islamist rally. He resigned in October. Erbakan was cleared of a similar charge in May, but continued under investigation for several years until he was sentenced to a year's imprisonment in March 2000 for a speech made in 1994 suggesting that Kurds should call themselves Kurds. A warrant was issued for his arrest in September 2000, and in December 2003 he was sentenced to more than two years in prison for misappropriating funds.

The eclipse of Erbakan facilitated the rise of Recep Tayyip Erdogan. When the Virtue Party was banned in June 2001, Erdogan founded the Justice and Development Party (AKP) on similar lines in August the same year. In a development that astonished observers, the AKP became the party of government the following year.

Governments had been shaky since 1998 when the Yilmaz government collapsed. Yalim Erez was invited to form a government but gave up the attempt, and was succeeded by the now elderly Bülent Ecevit, who headed a coalition government until early 2002, though becoming increasingly ill. An election was called in July and held in November, when the AKP gained an absolute majority. Erdogan was unable to head the government because of his pending prison sentence and his deputy Abdullah Gül became prime minister; however, in March 2003 Erdogan was permitted to stand in a by-election, which he won, and thus became Prime Minister (with Gül as foreign minister).

Erdogan's incumbency has surprised many by the rate of its activity and the many positive reforms that have been introduced. An austerity budget was introduced and many human rights reforms were effected. Many liberal Turks feared an avalanche of pro-Islamic measures, but with some exceptions these have not materialised. A proposed law to make adultery a crime was finally shelved in October 2004, to the relief of many. In 2008 a petition to the Constitutional Court threatened to close down the AKP, which had been re-elected in June 2007 with a decisive majority, on the grounds that it was attempting to undermine the separation of state and religion. The Court rejected the petition by a narrow majority, but a month later the AKP brought in the Protection of Youth bill which set out to make prayer facilities compulsory in all schools, and to require all buyers of pornography to register with the government. This again was received as an example of creeping Islamism.

A driving force of Erdogan's policies has been a determination to win recognition for Turkey's candidacy as a member of the European Union. This policy has supplanted the moves in the 1990s which seemed to bode Turkey's emergence as a leader in a pan-Turkic union to include the Turkic republics of the former Soviet Union – Kirghizstan, Kazakhstan, Uzbekistan and Turkmenistan, plus Azerbaijan – which held a summit meeting in Ankara in November 1992. There has been stiff resistance to Tutkey's candidacy in some European countries, notably Germany and France (where former President Giscard d'Estaing announced in November 2003 that Turkey should never be allowed to join the EU), but strong support in

Britain and also in the USA. In December Erdogan won from the EU a date for the opening of membership talks, and returned to a hero's welcome in Ankara on 19 December. Some compared him as a statesman with Atatürk himself. Many problems remain to be resolved, not least the status of Cyprus; but the increasing movement between the two halves of the partitioned island in the course of 2004 has reduced some of the tension here. Greece's hostility to Turkish membership of the EU has been considerably reduced as a result.

Earthquake Diplomacy

Another important solvent of Greek–Turkish animosity was a disastrous earthquake that took place in northwest Turkey on 17 August 1999. The epicentre was in Izmit, and Istanbul was very badly affected. 17,118 people died and 200,000 were made homeless. There were protests at the slow reaction of Ecevit's government and the authorities, but these were eclipsed by the very rapid assistance sent by many countries, among which Turkey's traditionally suspicious neighbour Greece was pre-eminent. As a result, Turkey was first on the scene when Athens was hit by an earthquake less than a month later, on 2 September. The Greeks agreed to substantial EU assistance to Turkey, and in addition to customs union between the EU and Turkey, which Greece had hitherto blocked. This was the first step on the path to discussions of Turkish membership.

On its eastern front, Turkey has entered accords over military and defence co-operation with Russia, and Russian tourism has increased. Turkey has extended its ties with its other neighbours, for example by linkage of its electricity supplies to those of Syria and Jordan as well as Armenia, and is playing a leading role in the Black Sea Economic Co-operation Organisation (BSECO), which may lead to some cleaning up of the most polluted sea on earth. The waters of the Tigris and especially the Euphrates are a bone of contention with Syria and Iraq. The Euphrates has no tributaries after it leaves Turkish borders, so that anything Turkey does materially affects the flow in its neighbour countries. The construction of a series of dams in Turkey to control water flow has met with protests from the countries affected.

Life in Modern Turkey

In 1994 Turkey's population was reckoned at 58.4 million, including up to twelve million Kurds. At the time of writing it is about 70 million. Inflation continued to gallop, and the lira which in 1961 had been TL9: $1 (US) was in 2004 TL1,250,000: $1. (Over 2 million to the pound sterling). A major economic crisis took place in May 2000, when the lira halved in value and numerous banks failed. An Economic Recovery Plan was devised by the Minister of State, Kemal Dervis, which involved restructuring of the banking sector, numerous privatisations, and a new set of agreements with the International Monetary Fund. These, like many Turkish policies in the 2000s, were tailored also to the requirements of the EU. Since 2001 economic stability has slowly returned (inflation in 2003 was down to 20 per cent), though at the price of high unemployment as well as much underemployment.

Until very recently Turkey remained a predominantly peasant society. In 1938, 90 per cent of its population were reckoned to be peasants. Traditional ways were paramount and have been well described by anthropologists (Paul Stirling, *Turkish Village*, 1965) and in occasional firsthand accounts (Mahmut Makal, *A Village in Anatolia*, 1954). An account of an urban bourgeois life can be found in Irfan Orga's *Portrait of a Turkish Family* (1950). Such accounts present an existence continued at close to subsistence level, with little use of cash and a preference for barter, as well as the continuance of colourful village customs and superstitions which are now dying out rapidly. Sixty years ago few villages contained shops, and necessities were acquired from travelling salesmen, while services, from tree-felling to musical entertainment, were provided by travelling craftsmen. A poem by Oktay Rifat, entitled 'Then and Now', concludes:

> Still in our peasants' hand a wooden plough
> Our people half starved
> Now
> As when it all began.

But the last sixty years have seen dramatic advances, with the establishment of agricultural banks to enable farmers to invest in modern equipment. At the same time international communications and trade have led to the rise of a provincial bourgeoisie and the growth of industry, much of it still small–scale, has led to a drain of population from countryside to town, with the rise of a small urban proletariat attended by the rise of trade unions and left–wing politics. By the 1970s Turkey was looking much like any less developed western country, and the advances in the thirty years following have been dramatic. The economic crisis of 2001 dented this progress, but the changed structures of Turkish society cannot be reversed.

Agriculture remains static and underdeveloped. Many Turks see the future for their country as increased industrialisation. Village factories have closed down all over Turkey, a situation that provided the theme for the award winning film by Nuri Bilge Ceylan, *Uzak* (Distant: 2004), which focuses on the problems of a man thrown out of work by factory closure and the tensions this imposes on the traditionally strong network of the Turkish family. The slogan 'Build us a factory!' is often heard. Even the educated classes are affected by unemployment and would welcome opportunities to work in the EU. The 'black economy' cushions the worst of the crisis for many though it dents state revenues. A symbol of hope in the fight against inflation was the creation of a new currency on 1 January 2005, the New Turkish Lira (YTL, Yeni Türk Lira) by removing six noughts from the existing currency. No longer do Turks and visitors have to spend time counting the noughts as they pull out the cash to pay for a coffee (let alone a carpet, or a house).

Seasonal labour is encouraged by the nature of the tourism industry, whose value grew from 3 billion dollars in 1987 to 7 billion dollars in 2001. Growth since then has been slower as a result of fears, especially among Americans, of Islamic terrorism in the wake of the attack on the World Trade Center in New York on 11 September 2001, the ensuing war in Iraq, and some terrorist activity in Turkey itself, notably a series of bombings in Istanbul and Ankara in November 2003 associated with the visit of US President George W. Bush to Turkey. It may be anticipated that EU membership will make a further dent in tourism as prices rise in line with EU levels.

Alongside these economic difficulties there have been substantial social reforms. Not least, the position of women has been steadily improved: they received equal rights in family and employment from November 2001.

The older social structure was not conducive to the flourishing of intellectual arts and accomplishments beyond the popular arts that had remained unchanged since the sixteenth century, such as folk-song and carpet-weaving. The former has perhaps become artificialised as a tourist attraction, but it also attracts enthusiasm as a popular art in Turkey. In 1997 a joint concert of the doyens of Greek and Turkish music respectively, Mikis Theodorakis and Zülfü Livaneli, spoke louder than words as a symbol of the cultural elements that unite two peoples so often at odds. Such rites as the performances of the Whirling Dervishes (the only dervish sect still permitted to exist in Turkey after Atatürk's abolition of the Muslim orders) not only bring in tourist audiences but are felt by the performers themselves as an expression of their religious devotion as well as their artistry. The carpet industry remains alive and traditional high standards, encouraged by such initiatives as the DOBAG project (Dogal Boya Aristirma ve Gelistirme – Research and Development of Natural Dyes), a co-operative enterprise to produce carpets to traditional standards in a village near Bergama. Few visitors will spend more than a few hours in Turkey before encountering the bewildering richness of this characteristic art, in which each region has its own distinctive patterns and colour ranges (tobacco colours for the tobacco-growing region of Milas, 'crab-claw' patterns, from Kars, rich red-and-blue mixtures from Bergama and floral patterns from Kayseri). Carpet-weaving is a woman's art and carried out on traditional looms with distinctive knots, different from the Persian knots: the test of quality of a Turkish rug is the smoothness and density of the knotting, which must be observed from the back.

HIGHER EDUCATION

Higher education was an insignificant feature of Turkish life until the 1960s. The Ottoman Imperial University was established in 1846, but though a building was erected, it was never opened for fear of revolutionary activities inspired by Europe's 1848 revolutions. Opened for the first time in 1869 but closed in 1871, re-opened from 1874–81, it was definitively inaugurated in 1900 and in 1933 became the University of Istanbul. Now there are a large number of universities in Turkey, many of them mainly technical, but including several private universities: Bilkent in Ankara, founded in the 1970s, was followed by Bilgi, Koc and Sabanci Universities in Istanbul. The former American institution, Robert College in Istanbul, became Bogazici University. In some of these the language of instruction is English. The universities were found in the 1970s to be breeding grounds for revolutionary and subversive – as well as anti-American – ideas, adding to the political instability of those years, but the government proved strong enough to survive without closing them. Their contribution to Turkey's prospects as an advanced country is naturally immense, and the government gives preference to such institutions against the demands of the likewise increasing religious schools.

ARCHAEOLOGY

Economic progress and a concern for the riches of Turkey's archaeological heritage sometimes go hand in hand, as with the Koç Foundation's support for many archaeological excavation and conservation projects: the restoration of the frescoes in the church of St Nicholas at Myra is but one example. (Vehbi Koç is the head of Turkey's foremost industrial dynasty). But sometimes they are at loggerheads. Two cases that caused considerable concern in the 2000s were the construction of the dams on the Euphrates at Birecik and Ilisu. The former resulted in the drowning, in 2000, of the Roman city of Zeugma. The international community was alerted rather late in the day to this crisis, and some fast work enabled rescue archaeology to be undertaken on the wonderful mosaics of the city, in which Turkish teams of archaeologists were centrally involved. But, as ever, not everything could be done, and much data as well as many beauties were lost to science, homes of course were also lost. An international outcry caused the postponement of the completion of the Ilisu dam in 2001, which would have resulted in the inundation of the medieval city of Hasankeyf and the resettlement of 30,000 inhabitants. Foreign teams have continued to work at many sites, for example at Çatal Höyük, the oldest city in the world, in Central Anatolia; but many Turkish universities are also heavily involved at individual sites, for example the University of Konya at Knidos (where the excavator's licence was suspended in 2008 following the collapse of some recently re-erected columns), the University of Ankara at Arykanda, and Ege University (with German collaboration) at Oenoanda. Increased awareness of the pillaging of the archaeological record is expressed in strict laws, strictly enforced, absolutely forbidding the removal of artefacts from any archaeological site. In March 2000, to take just one example, the USA returned 133 items found to have been looted from archaeological sites.

LITERATURE

The social changes since 1950 have also led to a huge growth in literature, which previously was the preserve of folk-poets or a few intellectuals of the ruling class. Those writers who have made most impact in the west are those who reflect the unsatisfactory condition of the lower classes in Turkey and their struggles for change: the poet Nazim Hikmet (1902–63), who was imprisoned in 1941 for subversive activities, and who went on to produce much of his best work in prison; and the novelist Yasar Kemal, who writes about the hard life of the peasantry in the wild landscape of the Çukurova in south-eastern Turkey. A similar case is that of the film-maker Yilmaz Güney, whose subject is again the miseries of rural life. But the film-maker Nuri Bilge Ceylan (see p. 198–199) makes his theme rather the impact of social change on urban dwellers. Post-modernism has also come to Turkish fiction in the work of Orhan Pamuk, suggesting that the social preoccupation has become less intense with economic advancement. Unfortunately little Turkish literature is translated into English.

Some things never change. Among these is the traditional quiet civility and hospitality of the ordinary Turks, their artistic sensitivity and the excellence of their cuisine. All these things make Turkey, for all its political tensions and problems, a rewarding and exhilarating destination for the traveller. They will become ever closer neighbours to the rest of Europe.

Chronology of Major Events

BC

ca 8000–4500	Neolithic Age
ca 7000	First settlement at Çatal Hüyük
ca 5400	First settlement at Hacılar
ca 4500–3000	Chalcolithic Age
ca 4500	Mersin fortress
ca 4500–3000	First settlements at Alaca Hüyük, Alışar, Canhasan and Beycesultan
ca 3000–2000	Early Bronze Age
ca 2300–2000	Alaca Hüyük; Troy II
ca 2000–1500	Middle Bronze Age
ca 2000	Arrival of Hittites in Anatolia
ca 1920–1740	Kültepe (Assyrian merchant colony)
ca 1700–1500	Hittite Old Kingdom
ca 1500–1200	Late Bronze Age
ca 1400–1200	Hittite Empire
ca 1286	Battle of Qadesh
ca 1275	End of Troy VI; early Vannic kingdoms
ca 1250	Fall of Troy VIIa
from ca 1220	Raids of the Sea Peoples
ca 1200	Mycenaean settlements in Anatolia
ca 1200–1180	Fall of Hattusa

Dark Ages ca 1180–875

ca 1000	First Greek colonies in Ionia
ca 835–25	Foundation of Urartu by Sarduri I
8th century	Ionian League: Phrygian kingdom
ca 756	Cyzicus founded by Milesian colonists

| ca 714 | Cimmerians sack Gordium |
| ca 700–600 | Greek colonies in northern Asia Minor |

Lydian Empire 685–547

6th century	Ionian Enlightenment
590	Urartu conquered by Medes
560–47	Croesus king of Lydia
550	Temple of Apollo at Didyma

Persian Empire

547	Medes conquer Lydian Empire and Ionia
500	Hecataeus of Miletus fl.
499	Ionian Revolt
498	Ionians burn Sardis
494	Battle of Lade; sack of Miletus
490	Battle of Marathon; Persians defeated
490–25	Travels of Herodotus
479	Battles of Mycale and of Plataea; Persians defeated
478	Foundation of Delian League
467	Battle of Eurymedon: Athenians defeat Persians
454	Delian League becomes Athenian Empire
432–404	Peloponnesian War
403–1	Expedition of the Ten Thousand under Cyrus and then Xenophon
400	Thibron of Sparta frees Greek cities of Asia
396	Agesilaus of Sparta in Asia
386	The King's Peace
377–34	Hecatomnid Dynasty in Caria
363	The Satraps' Revolt
353	Death of Maussollus
337	Kingdom of Pontus founded

Alexander the Great

334–23	Alexander the Great conquers Persian Empire
334	Battle of the Granicus
333	Battle of Issus

Successor Kingdoms

318–17	Antigonus controls Asia Minor
301	Battle of Ipsus: Lysimachus defeats Antigonus
300	Foundation of Antioch
295	Seleucus occupies Cilicia, Lysimachus Ionia
282	Asia Minor defects to Seleucus
282–133	Attalid kingdom of Pergamum
281	Battle of Corupedium: Seleucus I Nicator defeats Lysimachus
278	Gauls enter Anatolia
before 230	Attalus conquers Gauls
212	Jews settled in Asia Minor by Antiochus III
189	L. Manlius Vulso conquers Galatians
188	Treaty of Apamea; end of Seleucid rule in Asia Minor
after 188	Kingdom of Armenia founded
162	Kingdom of Commagene founded
133	Attalus III bequeaths kingdom to Rome
130	Roman province of Asia created
88	Mithridates VI Eupator overruns Asia Minor
84	Lycia incorporated in province of Asia
81	Rome annexes Pontus
74	Rome annexes Bithynia
69–34	Antiochus of Commagene; sanctuary of Nemrut Dağı
66	Bithynia becomes Roman vassal
63	Final settlement of the east by Pompey
40	Antony and Cleopatra married at Antioch
31 BC–AD 14	Reign of Augustus

Roman Empire

30	Roman Empire established

AD

40–56	St Paul in Asia Minor
43	Lycia becomes an imperial province
from 52	Arsacid kingdom of Armenia
72	Rome annexes Commagene
111	Pliny the Younger governor of Bithynia
123–31	Hadrian tours Asia Minor
165	Plague in Asia Minor
176	Marcus Aurelius tours Asia Minor

176–213	Abgar VIII of Edessa: first Christian king
3rd century	Barbarian invasions
306–37	Reign of Constantine
310	Conversion of Armenia to Christianity
324	Constantinople becomes capital of Roman Empire

Byzantine Empire

325	Council of Nicaea
329–79	St Basil the Great: monastic foundations
392	Christianity made state religion by Theodosius I
395	Separation of eastern and western empires
431	Council of Ephesus
527–65	Reign of Justinian I
532	Nika Riots; Building of Haghia Sophia; Justinian's treaty with Persia
533–62	Career of Belisarius
626	Avars and Slavs besiege Constantinople
627	Conquest of Persians by Heraclius
674	First Arab siege of Constantinople
717–87	Iconoclast period
718	Arabs decisively repelled from Constantinople
806–1022	Bagratid and Artsruni kingdoms of Armenia
809	Bulgar invasion
814–94	Peace with Bulgars
831–43	Second Iconoclast period
912–22	Bulgar wars
923	Bulgars take Adrianople and besiege Constantinople
1014	Bulgars decisively defeated by Basil the Bulgar-Slayer
1016	Selcuk Turks arrive in Anatolia
1054	Schism of Orthodox and Catholic churches

Selcuk Period

1022	Byzantium annexes Armenia
1071	Battle of Manzikert; Byzantine defeat by Selcuks
1078	Selcuks establish capital at Nicaea (Iznik)
1080–1292	Cilician Kingdom of Armenia
1097	First Crusade; Battle of Dorylaeum
1098	Principality of Antioch established

1147	Second Crusade
1176	Battle of Myriokephalon: Byzantine defeat by Selcuks
1187	Third Crusade
1204	Fourth Crusade: Sack of Constantinople
1204–61	Empire of Nicaea
1204–1461	Empire of Trebizond
1241–2	Mongol invasions destroy Selcuk power
1261	Michael VIII reconquers Constantinople
1280	Ottoman dynasty founded

Ottoman Period

1315–21	Building of Kahriye Camii
1326	Bursa becomes Ottoman capital
1329	Ottoman Turks take Nicaea
1365	Ottoman capital established at Edirne
1389	Battle of Kosovo (the Blackbird Field): Ottomans defeat Serbs
1395	Bayezit's siege of Constantinople
1396	Bayezit defeats Crusader army at Nicopolis
1397	Bayezit builds Anadolu Hisar
1397–1402	Siege of Constantinople
1402	Bayezit defeated by Tamerlane near Ankara
1439	Council of Florence attempts union of churches
1452	Mehmet II builds Rumeli Hisar
1453	Ottoman conquest of Constantinople
1461	Ottoman conquest of Trebizond

Ottoman Empire

1472	Defeat of Akkoyunlu
1491–1588	Career of Sinan
1521	Conquest of Belgrade
1522	Siege of Rhodes
1529	Siege of Vienna
c. 1530–46	Career of Haireddin Barbarossa
1535	Capitulations established with France
1570	Conquest of Cyprus
1571	Battle of Lepanto
1575–90	Wars with Persia

1578–1666	'Sultanate of the Women'
1581	Levant Company established in Smyrna
1593–1606	Wars with Hapsburgs
1611–84	Career of Evliya Celebi
1624	Capture of Baghdad
1645–69	War for Crete
1664	Turkish defeat at St Gotthart
1683	Turks repulsed from Vienna
1697	Turkish defeat at Zenta
1699	Treaty of Karlowitz
1703–54	The Tulip Period
1718	Treaty of Passarowitz
1727	First printing press established
1770	Catherine the Great invades Greece
1774	Treaty of Küçük Kaynarca
1821–9	Greek War of Independence
1826	Abolition of Janissaries (the 'Auspicious Event')
1826–c. 1876	The Tanzimat Period
1827	Battle of Navarino
1829	Treaty of Adrianople
1839	Rescript of Gülhane: the first Ottoman 'constitution'
1854–6	Crimean War
1858–1875	Risings in Bosnia-Hercegovina and Montenegro
1860	Massacres in Lebanon
1866–9	Cretan revolt
1876	Bulgarian atrocities; Constitution proclaimed
1876–1924	Career of Ziya Gökalp
1877	First Turkish parliament; Russian invasion
1878	Dissolution of parliament; Treaty of San Stefano (March); Cyprus Convention (June); Treaty of Berlin (July)
1881	Decree of Muharrem: financial restructuring
1885	Armenakan party formed in Armenia
1894–6	Massacres of Armenians
1907	Young Turk congress in Paris
1908	Attempted coup by Young Turks; Parliament restored
1909	Şevket and Kemal depose the sultan

Republic of Turkey

1912–13	Balkan Wars
1914–18	First World War

1915	Gallipoli campaign
1915–16	Deportations and massacres of Armenians
1918	Armistice signed at Mudros (October); British occupy Istanbul (November)
1919	Kemal arrives in Samsun; war of Independence begins
1920	Treaty of Sèvres
1921	Constitution proclaimed
1921–2	War against Greece in western Asia Minor
1922	Burning of Smyrna (September); Sultanate abolished (November)
1923	Treaty of Lausanne establishes Turkish frontiers; Republic proclaimed; Ankara becomes capital of Turkey
1923–34	Reforms of Kemal Atatürk
1924	Caliphate abolished
1928	Latin script introduced
1934	Surnames introduced
1938	Death of Atatürk

Modern Turkey

1938	Ismet Inönü becomes prime minister
1939–45	Second World War: Turkey neutral
1946	Turkey enters United Nations; Adnan Menderes founds Democratic Party
1952	Turkey joins NATO
1955	Baghdad Pact
1960	Bloodless coup: Committee of National Unity
1961	Execution of Menderes and others; Coalition governments
1960s	Emergence of Republican People's Party, Justice Party (Süleyman Demirel)
1971	Military coup
1970s	Power fluctuates between Demirel and RPP under Bülent Ecevit; terrorist activity; inflation
1973	Bosphorus bridge completed
1974	Turkish invasion of Cyprus
1980	Military coup under General Kenan Evren (November)
1982	New Constition approved by referendum
1983	Turkish Republic of Northern Cyprus proclaimed; Motherland Party formed under Turgut Özal
1988	Kurdish *intifada* begins

1989	Headscarves banned (March); ban rescinded (December); Evren retires from presidency; Özal becomes president
1990	Mass Kurdish rising suppressed; Kurdish language legalised (autumn)
1991	Gulf War; Iraqi Kurds take refuge in Turkey
1992	Bombing of Kurds (January); Motherland Party elected to government (October)
1993	Turgut Özall dies (April). Tansu Ciller becomes Prime Minister (June)
1994	Air raids on Kurdish basis in Northern Iraq (January–February, August). Thirty Kurdish villages burned by army (October). Government austerity package and devaluation of 28% (April)
1995	Kurdish Parliament in exile established in Netherlands (April). Mrs Ciller resigns but is invited to form new government; resigns again October
1996	Customs union between Turkey and European Union begins (January); Coalition government of Motherland and True Path parties formed (March): Mesut Yilmaz (Motherland) becomes Prime Minister
	Following Yilmaz' withdrawal from the coalition, a new coalition of True Path and Welfare (the Islamic Party) was formed (May). Necmettin Erbakan (Welfare) became Prime Minister
1997	The National Security Council drew up a plan, accepted by Erbakan, to combat Islamic extremism and protect Turkey's constitution (February–March). Military pressure on Erbakan's government led to his resignation in June. Yilmaz formed a new government, without participation of Welfare or True Path. Compulsory primary education from 5 to 8 years; enrollment in Islamic schools forbidden after September 1997. Casinos banned.
1998	Virtue Party formed in May to succeed banned Welfare Party (both Islamic)
	PKK leader Abdullah Öcalan flees Syria for Italy
1999	Öcalan seized by Turkish forces in Kenya: tried for treason and sentenced to death (June)
	Violent earthquake in NW Turkey (August 17): 17118 killed, 200,000 homeless: 'earthquake diplomacy' as Greeks provide help.

	New coalition government under Bülent Ecevit; EU grants Turkey candidate status (December)
2000	PKK renounces armed struggle (February)
	President Ahmet Nezdet Secer succeeds Suleyman Demirel (May); Hunger strikes in prisons in protest at conditions and torture (continuing to present); Roman city of Zeugma sunk beneath Birecik dam
2001	Economic crisis (February). Lira halves in value. Economic Recovery Plan devised by Kemal Dervis. IMF loans of $15.7 billion. Constitutional reforms: women receive equal status. Kurdish language permitted (November). Ilisu dam completed
2002	PKK dissolved and reformed as Kadek (April). Death penalty abolished (August). General election (November); AKP (Islamic) forms government
2003	Recep Tayyip Erdogan (AKP) becomes prime minister; 4 suicide bombs in 5 days in Istanbul (November) to coincide with visit of George W. Bush. Synagogues targeted as well as British consulate; British consul Roger Short killed.
2004	Bombs in Ankara and Istanbul (June) welcome George W. Bush. Penal code reforms. Proposed law to make adultery a crime withdrawn after EU pressure. EU agrees to set date for accession talks for Turkey (December)
2005	Currency reform. New Turkish Lira (YTL) introduced, with six noughts fewer than the old TL; trial of Orhan Pamuk for 'insulting the Turkish state' begun but abandoned
2006	Assassination of editor of Armenian newspaper *Hrant Dink*. Oil begins to flow from the Caspian Sea through the Baku-Tblisi-Ceyhan pipeline; Orhan Pamuk wins the Nobel Prize for Literature
2007	Foreign Minister Abdullah Gul becomes Turkey's 11th President
2008	Constitutional Court hears case against AKP Party for alleged 'anti-secular' activities
2009	Turkey hosts the UEFA Cup Final

Major Battles

ANKARA 1402
Bayezit I defeated by Mongols under Tamerlane and, according to legend, imprisoned in a cage.

BELGRADE 1521
Belgrade fell to the Ottoman Turks under Süleyman the Magnificent.

CONSTANTINOPLE, Sack of 1204
Constantinople laid waste and captured by soldiers of the Fourth Crusade.

CONSTANTINOPLE, Siege of 1453
Fall of Constantinople to the Ottoman army of Mehmet II.

CORUPEDIUM 281 BC
Seleucus I Nicator defeats Lysimachus and becomes ruler of Asia Minor.

DORYLAEUM 1097
Selcuks defeated by army of First Crusade.

EURYMEDON, RIVER 467 BC
Persians defeated at sea by Athenian navy.

GALLIPOLI 1916
Bloody defeat of allied, especially ANZAC, forces by the Turkish army; the victory through which Kemal (Atatürk) made his reputation.

GRANICUS, RIVER 334 BC
Alexander the Great's first victory over the Persian army.

INÖNÜ 1921
Greek army routed on 7 April by Turkish Nationalists under Ismet, who later
took the name Inönü from his success here.

ISSUS 333 BC
Alexander the Great's second victory over the Persian army.

LADE 494 BC
Persians crushed Ionian Revolt and sacked Miletus.

LEPANTO 1571
Ottoman defeat by European force under Don John of Austria.

MANZIKERT 1071
Byzantine army defeated by Selcuk Turks, ending Byzantine control of the
whole of Anatolia.

MOHACS 1526
Hungary fell to the Ottoman Turks.

MYRIOKEPHALON 1176
Major Byzantine defeat by Selcuk Turks.

NAVARINO 1827
Turkish fleet defeated by allies (Britain, France and Russia), asssuring Greek
victory in their War of Independence.

QADESH 1286 BC
Hittites under Muwatalli II defeated an Egyptian army under Ramesses II.

SAKARYA, RIVER 1921
Greek army routed on 13 August by Nationalist Turkish forces under Ismet
(Inönü).

TROY
Troy VIIa possibly sacked by Achaean Greeks *c.* 1250 BC – according to
legend after a war lasting ten years.

VIENNA, Siege of 1683
Turks repulsed from Vienna by John Sobieski.

List of Native Rulers

(Persian and Roman emperors are not included)

The Hittites

(all dates are approximate and follow the 'Middle Chronology')

BC

FOUNDERS

Pithana: *early 18th century*
Anitta: *mid-18th century*

OLD KINGDOM

Labarna: *1680–1650*
Hattusili I: *1650–1620*
Mursili I: *1620–1590*
Hantili: *1590–1560*
Zidanta I: *1560–1550*
Ammuna: *1550–1530*
Huzziya I: *1530–1525*
Telipinu: *1525–1500*
Tahurwaili, Alluwamna, Hantili II,
Zidanta II, Huzziya II, Muwatalli I: *1500–1450*

MIDDLE KINGDOM

Tudhaliya II (there was probably no earlier Tudhaliya): *1450–1420*
Arnuwanda I: *1420–1400*
Tudhaliya III: *1400–1380*
Hattusili II: *1380?*

HITTITE EMPIRE

Šuppiluliuma I: *1380–1340*
Arnuwanda II: *1340–1339*
Mursili II: *1339–1306*
Muwatalli II: *1306–1282*
Mursili III (Urhi-Tešub): *1282–1275*
Hattusili III: *1275–1250*
Tudhaliya IV: *1250–1220*
Arnuwanda III: *1220–1215*
Šuppiluliuma II: *1215–1200*

Urartu

Aram: *858–844*
Sarduri I: *844–828*
Ishpuini the Establisher: *828–810*
Menua the Conqueror: *810–785*
Argishti I: *785–753*
Sarduri II: *753–735*
Rusa I: *735–714*
Argishti II: *714–680*
Rusa II: *680–639*
Sarduri III: *639–635*
Erimena, Rusa III, Sarduri IV, Rusa IV: *635–590*

Seleucid Kings of Syria and Asia Minor

Seleucus I Nicator: *321–281*
Antiochus I Soter: *280–261*
Antiochus II Theos: *261–246*
Seleucus II Callinicus: *246–226*
Seleucus III Soter: *226–223*
Antiochus III the Great: *223–187*
Seleucus IV Philopator: *187–175*
Antiochus IV Epiphanes: *175–164*
Antiochus V Eupator: *164–162*
Demetrius I Soter: *162–150*
Alexander Balas: *150–146*
Demetrius II Nicator: *146–140, 129–125*
Antiochus VI Epiphanes: *145–142*
Tryphon: *142–129*

Antiochus VII Sidetes: *139–129*
Seleucus V: *125*
Antiochus VIII Grypus: *121–96*
Antiochus IX Cyzicenus: *115–95*

The Attalids of Pergamum

Philetaerus: *282–263*
Eumenes I: *263–241*
Attalus I Soter: *241–197*
Eumenes II Soter: *197–160*
Attalus II: *160–138*
Attalus III: *138–133*

Kings of Pontus

Mithridates I: *302–266*
Ariobarzanes: *265–255*
Mithridates II: *255–220*
Mithridates III: *220–185*
Pharnaces I: *185–169*
Mithridates IV Philopator Philadelphus: *169–150*
Mithridates V Euergetes: *150–20*
Mithridates VI Eupator: *120–63*

Kings of Bithynia

Zipoetes: *297–279*
Nicomedes I: *279–255*
Ziaelas: *255–228*
Prusias I: *228–185*
Prusias II: *185–149*
Nicomedes II Epiphanes: *149–128*
Nicomedes III Euergetes: *128–94*
Nicomedes IV Philopator: *94–74*

Kings of Commagene

Ptolemaeus: *163/2–130*

Samus II Theosebes : *130–100*
Mithridates I: *100–70*
Antiochus I Philoromaios Philhellen: *70–35*
Mithridates II: *c. 31*
Antiochus II did not reign
Mithridates III: *c. 20*
Antiochus III: *? – AD 17*
Roman annexation
Antiochus IV: *38–72*
Roman annexation to province of Syria

Armenia

Artaxias I: *190–161*
Artavasdes I: *? –138 (or possibly –95)*
Tigranes I: *?–? (possibly)*
Tigranes II (or I), the Great: *95–55*
Artavasdes II: *55–34*
Artaxias II: *33–20*
Tigranes III, Tigranes IV and Erato: *20–6*
Artavasdes II, Tigranes IV and Erato: *6 BC – AD 1*
Non-native rulers: *AD 2–52*

AD
ARSACID DYNASTY

Tiridates I: *52–75*
Sanatruk: *75–110*
Axidares: *c. 110*
Parthamasiris: *c. 110–14*
Roman province: *114–116*
Vologaeses: *116–140*
Sohaemus of Emesa: *140–60, 164–185*
Pacorus: *160–163*
Tiridates II: *217–222*
Chosroes I: *222–250*
Tiridates III: *287–336*

BAGRATID DYNASTY

Smbat the Confessor: *836–885*

Ashot I: *856–890*
Smbat I: *890–914*
Ashot II: *915–928*
Abas: *928–951*
Ashot III: *951–977*
Smbat II: *977–989*
Gagik I: *989–1019*
Ashot IV: *1020–1040*
Gagik II: *1042–1045*

Armenian Kingdom of Cilicia

Ruben I: *1080–1095*
Constantine I, Leon I, Thoros I, Ruben II: *1095–1148*
Thoros II: *1148–1168*
Ruben III: *1175–1185*
Levon II the Magnificent: *1185–1219*
Hethum I the Great: *1226–1269*
Leon III: *1270–1289*
Hethum II: *1289–1305*
Leon IV: *1305–1307*
Oshin: *1307–1320*
Leon V: *1320–1342*
(Guy of Lusignan): *1342–1344*
Constantine IV: *1344–1369*
Constantine V: *1369–1373*
Leon VI: *1373–1375*

The Byzantine Empire

Constantine I the Great: *324–337*
Constantius: *337–361*
Julian the Philosopher: *361–363*
Jovian: *363–364*
Valens: *362–378*
Theodosius I the Great: *379–395*
Division of eastern and western empires
Arcadius: *395–408*
Theodosius II: *408–450*
Marcian: *450–457*
Leo I: *457–474*

Leo II: *474*
Zeno: *474–491*
Anastasius I: *491–518*
Justin I: *518–527*
Justinian I: *527–565*
Justin II: *565–578*
Tiberius II: *578–582*
Maurice: *582–602*
Phocas: *602–610*

HERACLIAN DYNASTY

Heraclius: *610–641*
Constantine II Heracleonas: *641*
Constantine III: *641–668*
Constantine IV: *668–685*
Justinian II: *685–695*
Leontius: *695–698*
Tiberius III: *698–705*
Justinian II (again): *705–711*
Philippicus Bardanes: *711–713*
Anastasius: *713–715*
Theodosius III: *715–717*

ISAURIAN DYNASTY

Leo III: *717–741*
Constantine V: *741–775*
Leo IV: *775–780*
Constantine VI: *780–797*
Irene: *797–802*
Nicephorus I: *802–811*
Stauracius: *811*
Michael I: *811–813*
Leo V: *813–820*

AMORIAN DYNASTY

Michael II: *820–829*
Theophilus: *829–842*
Michael III: *842–867*

MACEDONIAN DYNASTY

Basil I: *867–886*
Leo VI: *886–912*
Alexander: *912–913*
Constantine VII Porphyrogenitus: *913–959*
Romanus I Lecapenus: *919–944*
Romanus II: *959–963*
Nicephorus II Phocas: *963–969*
John Tzimisces: *969–976*
Basil II the Bulgar-Slayer: *976–1025*
Constantine VIII: *1025–1028*
Romanus III Argyrus: *1028–1034*
Michael IV: *1034–1041*
Theodora and Zoe: *1042*
Constantine IX: *1042–1055*
Theodora (again): *1055–1056*
Michael VI: *1056–1057*
Isaac Comnenus: *1057–1059*
Constantine X Ducas: *1059–1067*
Romanus IV Diogenes: *1067–1071*
Michael VII Ducas: *1071–1078*
Nicephorus III Botaniates: *1078–1081*

COMNENIAN DYNASTY

Alexius I Comnenus: *1081–1118*
John II Comnenus: *1118–1143*
Manuel I Comnenus: *1143–1180*
Alexius II Comnenus: *1180–1183*
Andronicus I Comnenus: *1183–1185*

ANGELI DYNASTY

Isaac II Angelus: *1185–1195*
Alexius III Angelus: *1195–1203*
Isaac II Angelus (again): *1203–1204*
Alexius IV Angelus: *1203–1204*
Alexius V Ducas (Murzuphlus): *1204*

LASCARID DYNASTY (RULED IN NICAEA)

Theodore I Lascaris: *1204–1222*

John III Ducas Vatatzes: *1222–1254*
Theodore II Lascaris: *1254–1258*
John IV Lascaris: *1258–1261*

PALAEOLOGAN DYNASTY

Michael VIII Palaeologus: *1261–1282*
Andronicus II Palaeologus: *1282–1328*
Andronicus III Palaeologus: *1328–1341*
John V Palaeologus: *1341–1391*
John VI Cantacuzenus: *1347–1354*
Andronicus IV Palaeologus: *1376–1379*
John VII Palaeologus: *1390*
Manuel II Palaeologus: *1391–1425*
John VIII Palaeologus: *1425–1448*
Constantine XI Dragases: *1449–1453*

Empire of Trebizond

Alexius I: *1204–1222*
Andronicus I: *1222–1235*
John I Axouchus: *1235–1238*
Manuel I: *1238–1263*
Andronicus II: *1263–1266*
George: *1266–1280*
John II: *1280–1285*
Theodora: *1285–1297*
Alexius II: *1297–1330*
Andronicus III: *1330–1332*
Manuel II: *1332*
Basil: *1332–1340*
Irene: *1340–1341*
Anna: *1341*
Michael: *1341–1342*
John III: *1342–1344*
Michael (again): *1344–1349*
Alexius III: *1349–1390*
Manuel III: *1390–1417*
Alexius IV: *1417–1429*
John IV: *1429–1458*
David: *1458–1461*

The Selcuks of Rum

Tuğrul: *1037–1063*
Alp Arslan: *1063–1072*
Süleyman Şah: *1077–1086*
Kılıcarslan I: *1092–1107*
Melik Šäh: *1107–1116*
Mesut I: *1116–1156*
Kılıcarslan II: *1156–1188*
Keyhusrev I: *1192–1210*
Kılıcarslan III: *1204–?*
Keykavus I: *1210–1219*
Keykobad I: *1219–1236*
Keyhusrev II: *1236–1246*
Izzeddin: *1246–1283*
Kılıcarslan IV: *1246–1264*
Keyhusrev III: *1264–1283*
Keykobad III: *1283–1302*
Mesut II: *1283–1298*
Mesut III: *1298–1302*
Giyaseddin: *1302–?*

The Ottoman Empire

Osman Gazi (not sultan): *1288–1324*
Orhan Gazi: *1324–1359*
Murat I: *1360–1389*
Bayezit I the Thunderbolt: *1389–1403*
Interregnum: *1403–1413*
Mehmet I: *1413–1421*
Murat II: *1421–1451*
Mehmet II the Conqueror: *1451–1481*
Bayezit II: *1481–1512*
Selim I: *1512–1520*
Süleyman I the Magnificent: *1520–1566*
Selim II the Sot: *1566–1574*
Murat III: *1574–1595*
Mehmet III: *1595–1603*
Ahmet I: *1603–1617*
Mustafa I: *1617–1618*
Osman II: *1618–1622*
Mustafa I (again): *1622–1623*

Murat IV: *1623–1640*
Ibrahim the Mad: *1640–1648*
Mehmet IV: *1648–1687*
Süleyman II: *1687–1691*
Ahmet II: *1691–1695*
Mustafa II: *1695–1703*
Ahmet III: *1703–1730*
Mahmut I: *1730–1754*
Osman III: *1754–1757*
Mustafa III: *1757–1774*
Abdulhamit I: *1774–1789*
Selim III: *1789–1807*
Mustafa IV: *1807–1808*
Mahmut II: *1808–1839*
Abdulmecit I: *1839–1861*
Abdulaziz: *1861–1876*
Murat V: *1876*
Abdulhamit II: *1876–1909*
Mehmet V: *1909–1918*
Mehmet VI: *1918–1922*
Abdulmecit II: *1922–1924*

Presidents of the Turkish Republic

Kemal Atatürk: *1923–1938*
Ismet Inönü: *1938–1950*
Celal Bayar: *1950–1959*
General Cemal Gürsel: *1959–1966*
General Cevdet Sunay: *1966–1973*
Fahi Korutürk: *1973–1980*
General Kenan Evren: *1980–1989*
Turgut Özal: *1989–1993*
Süleyman Demirel: *1993–2000*
Ahmet Necdet Sezer: *2000–2007*
Abdullah Gül: *2007–*

Further Reading

General

DAVISON, RODERIC H. *Turkey: a Short History,* second edition (Huntingdon, Eothen Press 1991)

MARSHALL LANG, DAVID *Armenia, Cradle of Civilization* (London, Allen and Unwin 1970)

LLOYD, SETON *Ancient Turkey. A Traveller's History of Anatolia* (London, British Museum Publications 1989)

STONEMAN, RICHARD *Across the Hellespont: Travellers in Turkey from Herodotus to Freya Stark* (London, Hutchinson 1987)

1. Prehistoric Anatolia

BRYCE, T.R. *The Lycians* (Copenhagen, Museum Tusculanum 1986)

GURNEY, O.R. *The Hittites,* revised edition (Harmondsworth, Penguin 1990)

MACQUEEN, J.G. *The Hittites and their Contemporaries in Asia Minor,* second edition (London, Thames and Hudson 1986)

PIOTROVSKY, B.B. *Urartu* (London, Evelyn Adams and Mackay 1967)

SANDARS, N.K. *The Sea Peoples* (London, Thames and Hudson 1985)

2. The Persian Period

COOK, J.M. *The Persian Empire* (London, Weidenfeld and Nicolson 1983)

OLMSTEAD, A.T. *History of the Persian Empire* (Chicago, University of Chicago Press 1948)

3. The Greek and Roman Periods

BURY, J.B. *The Later Roman Empire* (two volumes; New York, Dover 1958)

GREEN, PETER *From Alexander to Actium* (London, Thames and Hudson 1991)

HERODOTUS *The Histories* (translated by Aubrey de Selincourt; Harmondsworth, Penguin 1954)

HUXLEY, G.L. *The Early Ionians* (London, Faber and Faber 1966; revised edition 1972)

KOROMILA, MARIANNE *The Greeks in the Black Sea from the Bronze Age to the early Twentieth Century* (Athens, Panorama 1991)

LANE FOX, ROBIN *Alexander the Great* (London, Allen Lane 1973)

MACDONALD, WILLIAM L. *The Architecture of the Roman Empire*, Volume 2 (New Haven, Yale University Press 1986)

MAGIE, D.L. *Roman Rule in Asia Minor* (Princeton, Princeton University Press 1950)

SHERWIN-WHITE, A.N. *Roman Foreign Policy in the East* (London, Duckworth 1984)

WALBANK, F.W. *The Hellenistic World* (London, Fontana 1981)

XENOPHON *The Persian Expedition* (translated by Rex Warner; Harmondsworth, Penguin 1949, 1972)

4. The Byzantine Period

ANGOLD, MICHAEL *The Byzantine Empire 1025–1204* (London, Longman 1984)

BROWNING, ROBERT *The Byzantine Empire* (London, Weidenfeld and Nicolson 1980)

CHAHIN, M. *The Kingdom of Armenia* (Beckenham, Croom Helm 1987)

HARVEY, ALAN D. *Economic Expansion in the Byzantine Empire 900– 1200* (Cambridge, Cambridge University Press 1989)

MANGO, CYRIL *Byzantium, the Empire of New Rome* (London, Weidenfeld and Nicolson 1980)

MILLER, WILLIAM *Trebizond: the last Greek Empire* (London, 1926)

NICOL, DONALD M. *The End of the Byzantine Empire* (London, Edward Arnold 1979)

RUNCIMAN, STEVEN *Byzantine Style and Civilization* (Harmondsworth, Penguin 1975)

RUNCIMAN, STEVEN *The Fall of Constantinople* (Cambridge, Cambridge University Press 1965)

VRYONIS, SPEROS *The Decline of Medieval Hellenism in Asia Minor and the Process of Islamization from the Eleventh through the Fifteenth Century* (Berkeley, University of California Press 1971)

5. The Ottoman Empire

ANDERSON, M.S. *The Eastern Question* (London, Macmillan 1966)
KINROSS, LORD *The Ottoman Centuries* (New York, Morrow Quill 1977)
SHAW, STANFORD J. AND SHAW, EZEL KURAL *A History of the Ottoman Empire and Modern Turkey* (Cambridge, Cambridge University Press 1976 and 1977)
STILES, ANDRINA *The Ottoman Empire 1450–1700* (London, Hodder and Stoughton 1989)

6. Modern Turkey

AHMAD, FIROZ *The Making of Modern Turkey* (London, Routledge 1993)
DOBKIN, MARJORIE HOUSEPIAN *Smyrna 1922: the Destruction of a City* (Kent, Ohio, Kent State University Press 1988)
DODD, C.H. *The Crisis of Turkish Democracy*, second edition (Huntingdon, Eothen Press 1990)
FROMKIN, DAVID *A Peace to end all Peace: the Fall of the Ottoman Empire and the Creation of the Modern Middle East* (New York, Avon 1989)
KINROSS, LORD *Atatürk: the rebirth of a Nation* (London, Weidenfeld 1964; reprinted Nicosia, Rustem 1981)
PALMER, ALAN *Kemal Atatürk* (London, Sphere 1991)
ROBINS, PHILIP *Turkey and the Middle East* (London, Pinter 1991)
WALKER, CHRISTOPHER J. *Armenia: Survival of a Nation*, second edition (London, Routledge 1990)

Historical Gazetteer

Numbers in bold refer to the main text and the number of the map on which the site appears is indicated thus [2]

Aezani, Aizanoi The site of the best-preserved Roman temple in Asia Minor, completed in the reign of Hadrian *c.* AD 125. [2]

Afyonkarahisar The centre of cultivation of the opium poppy in Turkey.[6] **50**

Aghtamar Palace and church on an island in Lake Van, built by Gagik II Artsruni (908–31). The reliefs are unique and include both Biblical and historical scenes. [4] **107**

Alaca Hüyük Major early Bronze Age site near Boğazköy (*c.* 2300 BC, contemporary with Troy II). A cemetery with thirteen tombs contained numerous weapons and treasures, including the curious 'standards' of abstract or animal form, probably finials for the bier.[1] **5, 6, 27**

Alanya On the site of ancient Coracesium. The Red Tower (1226) was constructed by the Selcuk Sultan Keykobad.[6]

Alexandria Troas Founded in 300 BC by Antigonus the One-eyed as Antigoneia; renamed Alexandria Troas by Lysimachus after his victory over Antigonus. The ruins are of Roman date, but in early modern times were commonly mistaken for those of Troy. [2] **17, 64, 67**

Alinda A Hellenistic city near the village of Karpuzlu, it was the country seat of Queen Ada of Caria who entertained Alexander the Great lavishly on his visit in 334 BC. The monuments cover a considerable extent and include a stoa of shops, defence towers and an aqueduct.[2] **57–8**

Anadolu Hisar Ottoman castle on the Asiatic side of the Bosphorus, built by Bayezit the Thunderbolt in 1397. **128**

Ani Capital of the Bagratid kingdom of Armenia: its cathedral is one of the finest specimens of Armenian ecclesiastical architecture. On the border with the former Soviet Union, it is hard of access and photography is forbidden.[4]

Ankara Ancient Ancyra, in the Middle Ages Angora, home of unusually fine goats' fleeces. The Emperor Augustus erected in his temple here a copy of his *Res Gestae*, his own account of his achievements. In 1401 Tamerlane defeated Bayezit I here and, according to legend, imprisoned the sultan in an iron cage which he took with him wherever he

231

went. In 1923 Ankara was made the capital of Turkey.[2,4,6] **175, 177, 181**

Antakya Ancient Antioch, founded 300 BC. Antioch was the major city of the eastern Roman Empire and was a cosmopolitan and comfortable city. From the 6th to the 10th centuries AD it was in Arab hands, and then returned to Byzantine control. In 1098 it was captured by the Crusaders and Bohemond became Prince of Antioch. In 1268 it was razed by the Mameluke Sultan Baybars. It is the centre of the Hatay, a district originally awarded to Syria at the end of the First World War but then returned to Turkey. Syria claims it as its own.[2,4,6] **62, 67, 91, 98, 119, 120**

Antalya The major resort on Turkey's southern coast. Founded in the 2nd century BC as Attaleia by Attalus II of Pergamum, it contains remains from every period of Turkish history and a good museum.[2,6] **120**

Aphrodisias City of Aphrodite, a Hellenistic foundation which flourished under the Roman Empire. It was home to a spectacular school of sculpture whose products include the magnificent series of imperial reliefs glorifying Augustus and his successors, as well as portrait statues of the first to third centuries AD. In Christian times it was renamed Stauropolis (City of the Cross), and then declined into the village of Geyre (=Caria). Excavations, chiefly since 1961, have revealed one of the most magnificent Roman cities in Turkey, and the best-preserved stadium anywhere.[2] **81–83**

Aspendus A Roman city with a notable theatre.[2] **49, 59, 82**

Assos/Behramkale An important Hellenistic city in a beautiful situation. Its ruler Hermeias was host to Aristotle and his successor Theophrastus for some years in the 4th century.[2] **69**

Ayas Major port of the Armenian kingdom of Cilicia. Visited in 1271 by Marco Polo, who knew it as Lajazzo.[4] **119**

Ayvalık A fishing village and holiday resort which was formerly an important Greek town (before 1922). On the island of Alibey adası is a now ruined Orthodox church. The nearby Şeytansofrası (Devil's table) is a noted beauty spot.[6]

Bergama Ancient Pergamum. In 282 the governor Philetaerus revolted from Lysimachus to Seleucus. Eumenes I established an independent kingdom which rapidly became a cultural centre and one of the finest cities of Hellenistic Asia. In 133 Attalus III left his kingdom to Rome, and there is also some Roman building. The world-famous library was removed by Mark Antony as a wedding present for Cleopatra.[2,4,6] **51, 64, 67, 68–70, 81–2, 85, 123**

Bin Tepe Burial mounds of the kings of Lydia (7th century BC).[2] **29**

Bodrum Ancient Halicarnassus. One of the foremost resorts on the Aegean coast, Halicarnassus was the capital of ancient Caria and site of the Mausoleum, the magnificent tomb built for himself by the dynast Maussollus and completed after his death by his wife.

The Mausoleum was one of the Seven Wonders of the World. In the 15th century it was demolished by the Knights of St John to build their castle of St Peter. Many fragments were recovered in the 19th century by Sir Charles Newton and brought to the British Museum. The castle is now a museum.[2,6] **42, 53, 57**

Boğazköy Ancient Hattusa, capital of the Hittite Empire, discovered by Charles Texier in 1834.[1] **5, 6, 15, 27**

Bursa Ancient Prusa, home of the orator Dio Chrysostom. In 1326 Bursa was captured by Orhan Gazi and became the capital of the Ottoman Empire. It contains a number of major Islamic monuments including the tomb of Bayezit, the Green Mosque and the Great Mosque.[2,4,6] **145**

Byzantium **46, 52, 87** *See* Istanbul.

Canhasan Neolithic site near Karaman: settlements from the end of the 6th millennium BC.[1]

Carrhae *See* Harran.

Çatal Hüyük Neolithic settlement, *c.* 6000 BC, near Konya: the earliest evidence for agriculture in Asia Minor. The houses, entered through the roof, are adorned with wall paintings including the world's first landscape.[1] **3—4**

Claros An oracular temple of Apollo with intriguing underground passages and a chamber below the feet of the colossal statue of the god. It flourished in the 4th century BC, and in Roman times.[2]

Colophon There are few remains to be seen of this important city of the Greek period, home of the philosopher Xenophanes (*c.* 565—500 BC).[2]

Constantinople **91—133** **passim** *See* Istanbul.

Cyzicus (near Erdek) The earliest Milesian colony in northern Asia Minor, *c.* 756 BC. In legend it was visited by Jason and the Argonauts. A temple, regarded as one of the wonders of the ancient world, was begun by Hadrian and completed by Marcus Aurelius (AD 167). It was severely damaged by earthquake in the 6th century, but much of the temple was still visible in 1431.[2] **26**

Didyma An oracular temple of Apollo, administered from Miletus, first founded in the 6th century BC. The present temple dates from the 4th century BC.[2] **38**

Dorylaeum (modern Eskişehir) Site of battle in 1097 at which a Crusader army defeated the Selcuks.[4]

Edessa **87, 98, 119, 120** *See* Urfa

Edirne Ancient Adrianople. Capital of the Ottoman Empire in the 15th century, and always the Ottoman's most important foothold in Europe. It was briefly lost to Bulgaria during the Balkan Wars (1912—13), and to Greece from 1920—22, but confirmed as part of Turkey after the First World War.[6] **121, 154—5**

Ephesus One of the earliest Greek colonies in Ionia and site of the famous temple of Artemis. The early temple received contributions from the Lydian king Croesus. It was burnt down on the night Alexander the Great was born by a madman named Herostratus; the Ephesians declined

Alexander's offer to build them another and did it themselves. For many years the site of the temple was lost, until it was rediscovered by J.T. Wood in the 1860s. In Roman times the city was one of the most important in Asia. It was a major port (river silt has now moved the coastline a mile further west) and many magnificent buildings were erected. In legend it became the home of the Virgin Mary and John the beloved disciple after the death of Jesus. The legend of the Seven Sleepers is set in Ephesus. The finds from the site are in nearby Selçuk Museum.[2] **29, 56, 58, 85, 99**

Erzurum (Byzantine Theodosiopolis) In Armenian tradition, the earthly paradise was located at Erzurum. The city has changed since then. It is the gateway to the northeast and the major city of eastern Turkey. It is a palimpsest of passing civilisations, with some fine Selcuk architecture. The climate is bleak.[4,6] **123, 165, 185**

Eyüp Shrine of the Muslim saint Eyüp (Job) on the Golden Horn: the third holiest site in Islam after Mecca and Jerusalem.

Fethiye Ancient Telmessus. A modern resort; the most noted ancient remains are the 4th century BC Lycian rock tombs.[2,6]

Foça Ancient Phocaea. When besieged by the Persian general Harpagus in 540 BC, the Greek inhabitants asked for one day to consider terms; overnight they left by sea, swearing never to return until iron they threw into the water should float. They settled on Cor-

sica.[2,6] **35**

Gallipoli Greek Kallipolis, Turkish Gelibolu. The scene of the allied landings in 1916 in which thousands, mainly Anzac troops, were slain and Kemal Atatürk made his military reputation.[6] **172–3**

Gordium Capital of ancient Phrygia. Here Alexander the Great loosed the 'Gordian knot', a knot securing a chariot to its pole, of which it was said that anyone able to undo it would become master of Asia. Alexander cut it through.[2] **27, 59, 71**

Göreme The rock-hewn churches and monasteries of the Cappadocian Fathers who followed the rule of St Basil (AD 329–79) are carved into volcanic pinnacles which are known locally as 'fairies' chimneys'. They contain impressive quantities of contemporary wall paintings.[6] **93**

Halicarnassus See Bodrum.

Harran Ancient Carrhae, the site of a battle in which Marcus Crassus was defeated by the Parthians in 53 BC; his head was used as a 'prop' in an impromptu Parthian performance of Euripides' *Bacchae*.[2,6] **77**

Issus Near modern Dörtyol. Scene of the decisive defeat of the Persian king Darius by Alexander the Great, 333 BC.[2] **59**

Istanbul Founded as Byzantium, in legend by one Byzas, as a colony of Megara (640–25 BC). In 323 it was adopted by Constantine the Great as the new capital of the Roman Empire. He named it New Rome, but it rapidly became known as Constantinople. For over a thousand years it was the seat of the Byzantine Empire (except from 1204–61 when

Franks ruled in Constantinople). Constantine brought artistic treasures from all over the empire to adorn his capital: these were housed in the Imperial Palace and the Baths of Zeuxippus, which occupied the site where the later buildings of Haghia Sophia and the Blue Mosque now stand. The centre of Constantinople was the Hippodrome where the racing factions, Blues and Greens, competed in their chariots. It was a riot fomented by these factions which led in 532 to the burning of much of the city and gave Justinian the opportunity to build the miraculous church of *Haghia Sophia* which still stands.

Theodosius II (408–50) was responsible for the building of the land walls which kept invaders at bay throughout that time. The major church dating from the 5th century is that of *St John of Studion* (Imrahor Camii); in the 6th century were built the well preserved church of *SS Sergius and Bacchus* and the *Church of St Irene*.

The city was frequently besieged by enemies: the Persians were finally repulsed by the Emperor Heraclius in AD 628, only to be rapidly replaced by the Arabs. The Arabs first besieged the city in 674 and were only repulsed by the use of the newly invented Greek Fire. Their last siege took place in 718; driven back at this time, they did not attack the city again. But in the north the Bulgars became a constant threat from the mid-8th century until their final defeat by Basil the Bulgar-Slayer in 1014. In 1071 the Selcuk Turks defeated the Byzantine army at Manzikert, but despite many attempts they never managed to capture Constantinople.

Twelfth-century (Comnenian) Constantinople saw considerable artistic activity: the *Church of the Pammakaristos* and the *Pantocrator Monastery* date from this period.

In 1204 the army of the Fourth Crusade under Venetian leadership entered Constantinople and ransacked and pillaged its treasures. They put to death the emperor and established a Latin ruler, Count Baldwin of Flanders, in his stead. Frankish rule continued until 1261 when Michael VIII Palaeologus, the last of a line of emperors-in-exile at Nicaea, recaptured the city.

The Palaeologan period saw a resurgence of artistic and intellectual activity of which the most splendid relic is the church of *St John in Chora* (Kahriye Camii).

In 1453 the city was captured by the Ottoman Sultan Mehmet II, finally breaching the land walls with the largest cannon the world had ever seen. Constantinople became the Ottoman capital and acquired the name Istanbul (from a corruption of the Greek *eis tin polin*, 'to the city'). The sultans lived in the *Topkapı Sarayi*, a huge complex of buildings which incorporated the harem, the quarters of the Janissaries and the Bab-i Ali, the seat of government, known to the west as the Sublime Porte. Mehmet built a number of mosques in the city, but the major change in its appearance was wrought by the architect Sinan, who worked under Süleyman the Magnificent, and constructed numerous mosques and other buildings in Istanbul, including the *Süleymaniye Mosque*, the *Şehzade Camii*, and *Kılıç Ali Paşa Camii*, in all of which Sinan can be seen wrestling with the forms and traditions of Haghia Sophia. The most famous of Istanbul's mosques, the *Blue Mosque*, was built by a pupil of Sinan for Sultan Ahmet (1609–16).

Istanbul was the capital and major commercial city throughout the Ottoman Empire, until 1923 when the capital of the republic of Turkey was relocated at Ankara.[2,4,6] **133, 152, 160, 163, 167**

Izmir Ancient Smyrna, a Greek foundation. In 1581 the Levant Company was established here by a group of English merchants, and this became an important diplomatic as well as trading link between Britain and Turkey. The population was mixed and included many Greeks and Armenians. All these were driven out in 1922 when Smyrna was fired as a culmination of the victorious march of Atatürk's army against the irredentist Greek army. Many perished in the flames or through atrocities.[2,6] **64, 85, 86, 142, 176–7**

Iznik Ancient Nicaea, founded in 316 BC by Antigonus the One-eyed. It was the capital of the Roman province of Bithynia. It changed hands many times through the centuries. Its Hellenistic grid is still recognisable, and it contains both churches and Selcuk monuments.[4,6] **90–91, 111, 123**

Kayseri Ancient Caesarea, named

after the Emperor Tiberius when Cappadocia became part of the empire in AD 17. It was much beautified in the Selcuk period, with numerous mosques and tombs.[2,4] **99, 109**

Konya Ancient Iconium; allegedly the first town to surface after the Flood. Earlier remains were overlaid when in the 12th century AD Konya became capital of the Selcuk Sultanate of Rum. It contains several mosques and the Convent of the Whirling Dervishes with the tomb of their founder Mevlana.[2,4,6] **3, 7, 109, 113, 127**

Kültepe Ancient Kanesh, an Assyrian merchant colony in the 2nd millennium BC, specialising in metalwork.[1] **7, 10**

Kuşadası Popular coastal resort with a fine 16th-century caravanserai, now taken over by Club Mediterranée.[6]

Kütahya Ceramic and tile-making centre of Turkey.[6]

Labranda Sanctuary of Zeus, with buildings sponsored by the 4th century BC dynast of Caria, Idrieus.[2]

Lüleburgaz The town contains a fine complex of buildings by the master Ottoman architect, Sinan.[6]

Manisa Ancient Magnesia ad Sipylum. A natural rock above the town is identified with the legendary Niobe, weeping eternally for her children until she turned to stone. The town itself is a pleasant one with a good mosque. The museum houses finds from Sardis.[6]

Manzikert Site of the epochal defeat of the Byzantine, by the Selcuks in 1071.[4] **109, 118, 121**

Midas Şehri 'Midas' Town', also known as Yazılıkaya; near Eskişehir. A rock face is carved into a pedimented tomb-front, known as the Tomb of Midas.[2] **27**

Milas Ancient Mylasa, the capital of Caria before Maussollus relocated to Halicarnassus. The town has a few Roman remains and is a centre for carpet-making with the distinctive Milas designs reflecting the colours of the tobacco grown in the region.[2,6] **52**

Miletus An early Greek colony and home of the first Greek philosopher, Thales: the early philosophers are therefore sometimes known as the Milesians. Miletus played a major part in the Ionian Revolt (499 BC) and was razed by Persia in 494 BC. In Roman times it was an important and prosperous town, with one of the largest theatres in the empire. The silting up of its harbour and the rise in the water-table led to its gradual decay, and its ruins are now often under water.[2] **18, 26, 32–3, 37–8, 42, 56, 69**

Myriokephalon Site of battle in 1176 at which the Byzantines were defeated by the Selcuks.[4] **121**

Nemrut Dağı A mountain in Commagene on which Antiochus I (62–32 BC) erected a vast monument incorporating colossal statues of Zeus, Mithras, himself, and other gods. Tours visit it, timing arrival for sunrise.[2,6] **78**

Oenoanda A remote Lycian city in which, in the 2nd century AD, a citizen named Antonius Diogenes erected an inscription, about 100 metres long, comprising a summary of the philosophy of Epicurus. Substantial fragments remain.[2]

Pamukkale/Hierapolis The Turkish name means 'Cotton castle' an allusion to the dazzling white deposits of minerals left by the thermal springs on the hillside. The Romans,

The monument of Antiochus I of Commagene at Nemrut Dağı

great lovers of baths, established a city by these healing if scummy waters after their annexation of Asia in 129 BC. Like its neighbours Laodicea and Colossae, Hierapolis early adopted Christianity: Paul's reference to the inhabitants of Laodicea who are 'neither hot nor cold' may be a reference to the luke-warm waters of Hierapolis. A tourist attraction even in antiquity was the Plutonium, a cave from which noxious gases emerged, allegedly a way to the Underworld. It became customary to test the effect of the gas by inserting small animals to see if they died. Among the more unusual monuments of Hierapolis is an extensive necropolis and the octagonal Martyrium of the Apostle Philip.[2,6]

Perge A Greek foundation of the colonising period. Its theatre and walls are Hellenistic, and there are also extensive Roman remains.[2]

Phaselis Extensive ruins of a Roman city.[2]

Priene A good example of the grid-planning style of city design introduced in the 4th century BC by Hippodamus of Miletus. **50, 58, 64, 80**

Rumeli Hisar A castle on the European side of the Bosphorus built in 1452 by Mehmet II as a preliminary to his attack on Constantinople. **128**

Samsun Ancient Amisus. It was at Samsun that Kemal Atatürk landed on 19 May 1919 to begin the campaign which was to lead to the establishment of the Republic of Turkey.[6] **175, 180**

Sardis Capital of the Lydian Empire (685–547) and later seat of the satrap of Ionia. The river Pactolus which runs through it was gold-bearing in antiquity, and the first coins were minted at Sardis. A large temple of Artemis was begun around 300 BC but not completed until after AD 150. The Roman civic buildings are exceptionally fine. In Roman times the city had a substantial Jewish population, whose synagogue has been excavated. It was one of the 'Seven Churches of Asia' mentioned in the Book of Revelation.[2] **22, 28, 31, 43, 58, 68, 83, 85**

Sassoun The heartland of Armenia, around which the legends of the Armenian heroes or 'daredevils' are located.[4] **107, 164, 172**

Side An important Roman city, built on the site of a town of an Anatolian people whose language has not been deciphered.[2]

Silifke Ancient Seleuceia, founded by Seleucus I (321–280 BC). In 1189 the Emperor Frederick Barbarossa was drowned here while leading the Third Crusade. For a while the city was in the hands of the Cilician Armenians before passing to the Selcuks and then the Ottomans (1471).[4,6] **119, 121**

Sivas Ancient Sebasteia. The town has some good Selcuk architecture. In September 1919 the first National Congress of the Nationalist movement took place at Sivas.[2,6]

Soli A Cilician city whose inhabitants, because of their inability to speak Greek grammatically, have given us the term 'solecism'.[2]

Sumela A monastery built in a spectacular gorge near Trebizond by

Emperor Alexius III in AD 1375.[4]
131

Tarsus Remains are slight, but there is an important museum, in this town where Alexander the Great in 333 BC caught a chill in the River Cydnus; where Antony and Cleopatra in 41 BC sailed up the river in a majestic barge; and where St Paul was born *c*. AD 5.[2,4,6] **84**

Telmessus *See* Fethiye.

Teos/Sığacık The remains of the 2nd-century BC Temple of Dionysus and the acropolis lie close to the village of Sığacık, rapidly being developed with housing projects. In the 3rd century BC the town was home of a group of travelling players, the Artists of Dionysus.[2] **33, 35, 66, 69**

Termessus The best-preserved Roman city in southern Turkey: most of the remains are of the 2nd century AD.[2]

Tlos An impressive Lycian site with 4th-century rock tombs, including the 'Bellerophon tomb', and numerous Roman buildings.[2]

Toprakkale A Byzantine castle modelled on Krak des Chevaliers in Syria; occupied by Armenians from 1151 to 1337, with Crusader interruptions, and then abandoned after surrendering to the Mamelukes.[4] **24**

Trabzon (Trebizond) Founded in the 8th century BC as Trapezus, a colony of Sinope, the city became, as Trebizond, the seat of one of three Greek empires which sprang up after the fall of Constantinople to the Crusaders in 1204. Its prosperity at this period is reflected in a number of fine Byzantine churches, with wall-paintings, in its well-preserved walls, and in the citadel which was the site of the Golden Palace of the Comneni. The city fell to the Turks in 1461.[2,4,6] **49, 111, 115, 123–4, 130–3, 135, 165**

Tralles Near Aydın. A Greek city founded by colonists from Argos and barbarians called Tralleis from Thrace. A prosperous city, it is mainly remembered as the birthplace of the architect Anthemius who collaborated with Isidore of Miletus on the building of the church of Haghia Sophia in Constantinople.[4]

Troy The scene of the legendary Trojan War, Troy is one of the most complicated archaeological sites in Turkey. Excavation has always been spurred by the hope of finding evidence to corroborate Homer's tale of the Greek sack of Troy, but the existence of that war is the object of increasing scepticism among scholars. It was first excavated in the 1870s by Heinrich Schliemann, who thought he had identified Homer's Troy in the rich stratum of Troy II. Modern opinion tends to locate the Troy of legend in one of the two continuous occupation levels Troy VI or Troy VIIa. A modern reconstruction of the Wooden Horse of legend lends atmosphere to a site which, despite its importance, often disappoints the visitor.[1,2] **5, 7, 11–12, 16–20, 22, 40, 43**

Trysa (Gölbaşı) Site of Lycian hero-tomb whose occupant is unidentified. The sanctuary was discovered in the 1880s and the relief sculptures removed to Vienna.[2]

Urfa Ancient Edessa. A Seleucid foundation, and capital of Osrhoene, it become a kingdom (132 BC) under eight kings called Abgar, of whom the eighth (*c.* 180) was the first Christian king. It fell to the Arabs in 638. It became an independent principality under the Crusaders. Capital of modern Urfa province.[2,6] **165**

Uzuncaburç Ancient Olba/Diocaesarea in Cilicia, an important Hellenistic city with extensive remains of tombs, Roman theatre, baths and temples.[6]

Van A city reputedly founded by Semiramis of Babylon. As capital of Urartu from the 9th century BC, Tušpa (Van)was besieged by Tiglath-Pileser III of Assyria (745–27). Urartian inscriptions on the Rock of Van were discovered in 1827 and first deciphered in 1882.[6] **23, 24, 76, 102, 171**

Xanthus The chief city of ancient Lycia and the seat of a dynasty under Persian control after 540 BC. The indigenous Termilae were gradually assimilated to Greek settlers. The 4th-century monuments show strong Greek influence. Their setting is spectacular. The best of them were removed to the British Museum by Charles Fellows in the 1840s.[2] **40–41**

Yazılıkaya A Hittite rock sanctuary close to the capital Hattusa (Boğazköy). A long open gallery is carved with more than sixty figures of gods and mythical beings.[1] **9, 13, 15**

Zonguldak The Anatolian equivalent of Port Talbot.[6]

Index

Note: this index is arranged according to the Turkish alphabet, in which accented letters (ö, ı, ç) follow unaccented letters (o, i, c).

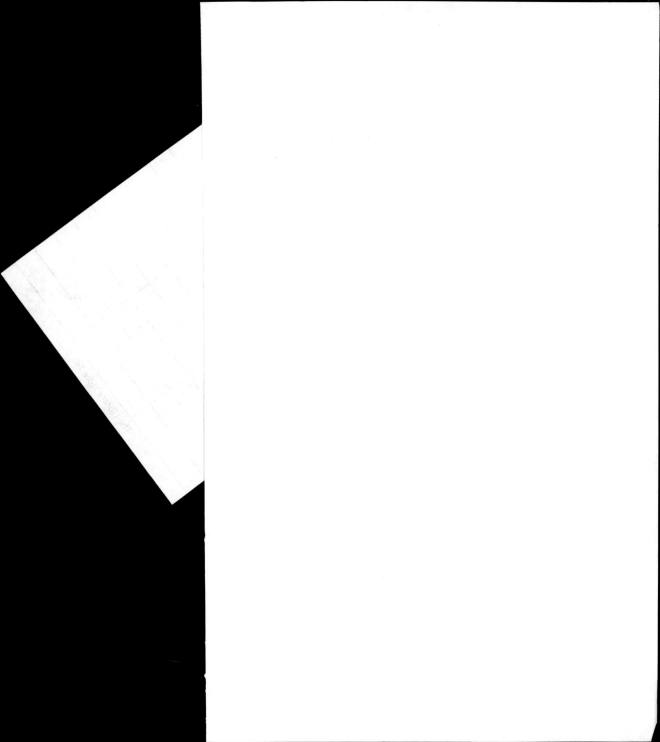

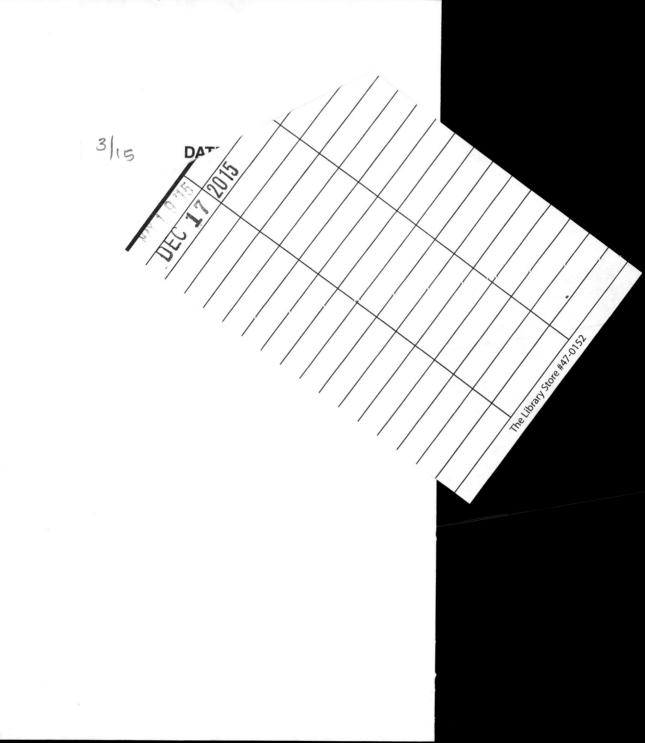